Beyond SUFFERING

A CHRISTIAN VIEW ON DISABILITY MINISTRY

STUDY GUIDE

CONTRIBUTING AUTHORS

CHUCK COLSON
BILL GAVENTA
JOHN MACARTHUR
KATHY MCREYNOLDS
JEFF MCNAIR

JONI EARECKSON TADA & STEVE BUNDY

WITH PAT VERBAL

CHRISTIAN INSTITUTE ON DISABILITY · JONI AND FRIENDS INTERNATIONAL DISABILITY CENTER

Senior Editor Pat Verbal · Associate Editor Chonda Ralston
Assistant Editors Rebecca Olson and Rachel Olstad

Cover: Hyatt Moore is an international artist who has written and designed a number of books,
including *In Search of the Source* and *In the Image of God*. He has been executive director of
Wycliffe Bible Translation USA and has also served in Guatemala, Papua New Guinea, and Canada.
Moore & Moore Art, Dana Point, California, www.hyattmoore.com.

Acknowledgements
We owe a deep debt of gratitude to a gifted group of experienced men and women who
contributed outstanding professional papers in their various fields of expertise.
Their wise counsel and support have made this course possible
and this book a reality. Thank you!

To order additional copies of this resource contact:
The Christian Institute on Disability
Joni and Friends International Disability Center
P.O. Box 3333, Agoura Hills, California 91376-3333
Email: cid@joniandfriends.org
Phone: 818-707-5664
Online: www.joniandfriends.org/BYS

Table of Contents

Module 1

Module 2

Module 3

Module 4

Appendix

INTERNATIONAL DISABILITY CENTER

Dear *Beyond Suffering* Student,

I'm so grateful to God that you are taking our premiere certificate course, *Beyond Suffering:* A *Christian View on Disability Ministry.* You are part of a rapidly growing, global movement that is reaching people with disabilities and their families with the love of Christ—a movement that is transforming hearts, families, communities and, yes, nations in the name of Jesus Christ.

Every movement needs a foundation that serves as an anchor for its ideas and worldviews. This is why we created *Beyond Suffering.* The leadership at the Joni and Friends International Disability Center and our Christian Institute on Disability has hammered out a comprehensive, college-level course that gives an overview to the theological and practical underpinnings of this movement.

There are many worldviews about disability that compete for our attention. However, none are as compassionate or as infused with life value and human dignity as the biblical worldview. It is my prayer that this important course will equip you with the skills necessary to think critically and compassionately about today's complex issues which impact people with disabilities and their families.

Thank you for seeking God in prayer as you study. Thank you for embracing new and different concepts that at first might be strange to your thinking. Most of all, thank you for taking what you learn and helping to give shape to the church in your community and its outreach to those with disabilities. May God's favor and grace rest on you, friend... we're so glad you're a part of this movement!

Yours in His care,

Joni Eareckson Tada

Foreword

The founder of a highly successful company was asked what it took to succeed. "The same thing it took to get started," he replied, "a sense of urgency about getting things done."

When I consider this quote, my mind immediately goes to Jesus' command in Luke 14:21,23 that we are to go out "quickly" and "compel" people affected by disability to fill the house of God. At Joni and Friends we seek to fulfill this urgent mandate throughout our ministry.

One of the ways Joni and Friends fulfills this mission is through the Christian Institute on Disability (CID). Since the CID opened in 2007, we have sensed the need for a comprehensive course that could shatter the Church's apathy toward disability ministry. To accomplish this, we prayed for like-minded, Christian professionals who could make significant contributions to such a study. These pastors, teachers, scientists, counselors, and disability leaders responded with well-researched, inspirational and very practical papers that form the text for this course. Thus, I am honored to present to you *Beyond Suffering: A Christian View on Disability Ministry*.

The most recent report from the World Health Organization (WHO) and the World Bank indicates that there are 1 billion people affected by disability in the world. "Disability is part of the human condition," says Margaret Chan, director-general of the WHO. "Almost every one of us will be permanently or temporarily disabled at some point in life. We must do more to break the barriers which segregate people with disabilities, in many cases forcing them to the margins of society."[1]

Those of us who know the forgiveness and grace of a loving God through the life, death and resurrection of his Son, Jesus Christ, must lead the way in reaching people with disabilities and including them in our communities of faith. Our sense of urgency comes from him and must be lived out through his Body, the Church. As you complete this course, you receive this commission and take your place in the ranks of disability ministry servants. If you do, we can change the way people think about God's plan for disability and suffering, and in doing so, God will be glorified and his family will be a beacon of hope.

Rev. Steve Bundy,
Vice President of Joni and Friends

OUR VISION

To accelerate Christian ministry to the disability community.

OUR MISSION

To communicate the Gospel and equip Christ-honoring churches worldwide to evangelize and disciple people affected by disabilities.

Introduction

Beyond Suffering: A Christian View on Disability Ministry is a ground-breaking course of study created to transform the way Christians view God's plan for disability and suffering. The textbook is the Word of God accompanied by a comprehensive collection of professional articles written by more than 35 experts in ministry, education, sciences and disability advocacy. This study guide contains 16 lessons, which are supported by video case studies and organized into four thought-provoking modules:

- An Overview of Disability Ministry
- The Theology of Suffering and Disability
- The Church and Disability Ministry
- An Introduction to Bioethics

Each module is designed to give Christians a solid understanding of the main issues involved in various aspects of disability ministry. In addition, the course encourages participants to reflect on their own personal journeys through suffering as they come to understand two essential points: 1) human brokenness reveals humanity's need for universal grace, and 2) the disability community challenges our understanding of the human condition.

Students who embrace this study will gain a sense of confidence in knowing that they are part of a movement that God is orchestrating to fulfill his command in Luke 14:21: "Go out quickly into the streets and alleys of the town and bring in the poor, the crippled, the blind, and the lame."

How Does the *Beyond Suffering* Program Work?

Beyond Suffering is the foundational training program of the Christian Institute on Disability (CID) at the Joni and Friends International Disability Center in Agoura Hills, California. Joni and Friends is a non-denominational, parachurch ministry that works with churches to accelerate disability ministry and to evangelize people with disabilities.

Beyond Suffering is a Christian education course designed to help believers understand God's heart for people with disabilities and to discover how believers around the world can play an active role in carrying out the Luke 14 Mandate. The courses are offered by Joni and Friends regional offices as well as other ministries with the support of the Christian Institute on Disability.

Led by master teachers, leaders and volunteers who have been personally impacted by *Beyond Suffering* and have a desire to reach out to their local churches and communities, this course has been held in churches and other venues around the world. *Beyond Suffering* is not owned by any particular denomination or church and may be offered in cooperation with various ministry organizations.

The Course Formats

Beyond Suffering can be taught in several different formats. The 16 lessons could be offered:

1) once a week for about 3 hours per session,
2) over several weekends, or
3) as a one-week intensive program.

The *Beyond Suffering Leader's Guide* includes further options to implement this dynamic course.

What Is Covered in Each Class Period?

Experienced educators, pastors and leaders will teach the course and present examples from their areas of expertise and involvement.

While lessons are uniform in structure, various teaching methodologies will be used. Many of the lessons are supported by a DVD case study taken from Joni and Friends TV Episodes, which greatly enhances the learning process. Students consider real-life situations related to disability and then have an opportunity to reflect on how to apply what they learned from that particular situation.

Course Materials

The *Beyond Suffering Leader's Guide* includes instructions for teaching the course, such as selecting the best format, recruiting guest speakers, preparing and leading a lesson, teaching methodologies, using videos, and much more. The text for the leader's guide comes on a CD-ROM that also contains PowerPoint presentations for each lesson. Also included in the Leader's Guide package are two DVDs with a promotional video, video introductions to the four course modules, and the video case studies used throughout the course.

The *Beyond Suffering Study Guide* includes 16 lessons, reflection questions, assignments for students seeking credit or a Certificate of Completion and a CD-ROM of the professional readings to be read with each lesson.

Enrollment Options

There are three enrollment options for this course:

1. **Certificate of Completion:** This option will enhance students' understanding of God's purpose in suffering and disability, and challenge their vision for serving in a local or global ministry. The certificate is earned through participation in lectures, discussions, DVD case studies, and selected readings. Students will also finish three assignments in order to apply for the Certificate of Completion.

2. **Enrichment:** Some students will want to work through these materials for personal enrichment rather than for a Certificate of Completion or academic credit. These students are encouraged to work through all of the lessons and read all of the papers. Although they are not required to do any of the assignments associated with the lessons, there is much to be gained spiritually and practically from the lessons and readings alone.

3. **Credit:** Students may earn undergraduate or graduate level credits for completing the Beyond Suffering Certificate Program. Please note that the accrediting institution may require additional reading and written assignments. For additional information about For-Credit options, please contact Joni and Friends. (cid@joniandfriends.org)

4. **Online:** Students can choose from three classes offered online through Joni and Friends.

- **A 16-week Certificate Course** includes video lectures and participation in weekly online group discussions. Assignments are submitted online and must be completed in the 16 weeks to earn the Certificate of Completion.
- **An Independent Study Program** allows students to work at their own pace, submitting assignments online, with six months to earn a Certificate of Completion.
- **The Leadership Training Seminar** is a five-day online training for students who completed the Certificate Course, and seek to become Certified Leaders of the *Beyond Suffering* Course. Potential leaders must submit an application and be approved before taking this course.

For a current schedule or additional information about any of the enrollment options, please visit www.joniandfriends.org/BYS.

Overview of the Four Modules

Beyond Suffering is a dynamic course in which a serious student can discover what God is doing in the midst of suffering around the world, as well as his ultimate redemption plan for us and for our world. The four modules will give the student a well-rounded introduction to the various aspects of disability ministry. Each module highlights a different facet of God's global purpose for welcoming people with disabilities into the church.

Module 1, An Overview of Disability Ministry, will help the student to identify some of the most prominent physical and intellectual disabilities. It will also enable the student to understand some cultural and personal perceptions about disabilities.

Module 2, The Theology of Suffering and Disability, will encourage students to consider some of life's most pressing questions. Not everyone with a disability considers himself or herself to be suffering and, conversely, there are many who do not have a disability yet still endure much anguish. Nevertheless, people often assume that a person with a disability must be suffering. This module explores the relationship between suffering and disability and explains some of the biblical passages addressing the problem of evil, suffering, and the sovereignty of God.

Module 3, The Church and Disability Ministry, presents some of the most practical aspects of mission and ministry and shows how the Church is to implement the biblical truths expounded upon in the first two modules. Students will come to understand some of the major biblical teachings addressing the Church's responsibility to reach the most vulnerable in every community around the globe.

Module 4, An Introduction to Bioethics, addresses an area that is extremely important to every person and family affected by disability: ethical issues in medicine. Individuals with disabilities and their families interact with the medical community more than the average population. They often need guidance concerning what would be the most beneficial and yet morally acceptable modes of treatment. This final module will explain why believers must become a reliable source of information and guidance on these issues in order to share our Christian views on life, meaning, suffering, and death.

Lesson Summaries

MODULE 1:

An Overview of *Disability Ministry*

Lesson 1	**Why Minister to People with Disabilities?** This lesson describes what individuals and families experience when disability first strikes. It also discusses hurtful stereotypes and labels attached to disabilities. One of the goals of this lesson is to encourage students to include people with disabilities as friends rather than simply observing them from a distance or viewing them only as the beneficiaries of charity.
Lesson 2	**What Defines a Disability?** This lesson covers simple definitions of the various disabilities and describes the differences between disabilities, impairments and handicaps. One of the primary aims of this lesson is to emphasize the use of disability-friendly language. Another important objective is to explain how family members and life cycles are impacted by disabilities.
Lesson 3	**A Historical Perspective on Disability** This lesson describes the historical perspectives of society toward people with disabilities and identifies the social roles that have worked against the disability community. It also gives credit to several advocates who have worked to bring about positive change for the disability community.
Lesson 4	**The Global Reach of Disability** The purpose of this lesson is to help the student understand the cultural perceptions and attitudes that impact the disability community. This in turn will show why international declarations supporting people with disabilities are important. This lesson will also highlight some of the advances in medicine, education, care and services for persons with disabilities.

Lesson Summaries

MODULE 2:

The Theology of *Suffering & Disability*

Lesson 5	**God's Sovereignty and Human Freedom: A Scriptural Perspective** Using Scripture as its basis, this lesson explains the sovereignty of God over all things, including disability. It highlights some views on God's sovereignty and human freedom throughout church history and also deals with the difficult issue of how God is sovereign and yet not responsible for sin.
Lesson 6	**The Problem of Evil and Suffering in Our World** This thought-provoking lesson covers the problem of evil and suffering, providing both a biblical perspective and a secular viewpoint, and reflecting on this problem in light of God's sovereignty. Students also consider the purpose of Christ's sacrificial death, as well as the purposes of his suffering from a biblical perspective. Finally, students will come to appreciate some biblical and modern examples of suffering.
Lesson 7	**Hope: A Proper View of Healing** This lesson covers the purpose of healing from a biblical perspective and discusses why some people are healed while others are not. Students will understand the role of prayer with respect to healing and reflect on the role of medicine in the Christian life.
Lesson 8	**The Gospel of Luke: A Framework for a Theology of Suffering & Disability** This lesson focuses on the Gospel of Luke and its significance in presenting Jesus' ministry to the poor, outcast and sinners. It explains that Luke's central section (chapters 9-18) is unique and may even be structured to highlight what was most important to Jesus while he was living under the shadow of the cross. The student will come to understand the implications of Luke's Gospel for understanding the rest of the New Testament's teachings on suffering and disability.

Lesson Summaries

MODULE 3:

The Church and *Disability Ministry*

Lesson 9	**Major Challenges of the Church on the Path to Maturity** Based on Scripture that discusses ecclesiology and the doctrine of the Church, this lesson highlights the importance of the Church's theological framework. It describes the images used in Scripture to define the nature of the Church and explains the six functions of the Church. This lesson will help the student understand the Church as a broken body, a suffering body, and how brokenness and suffering is a pathway to maturity. Students will get a sense of the seven movements of disability ministry.
Lesson 10	**How to Start a Disability Ministry in the Church** This lesson focuses on the nuts and bolts of starting a disability ministry in a church by first dispelling the myths about disability ministry. It shows how to enlist pastors and leaders in disability ministry and explains the steps to becoming a disability-friendly church. It also gives several effective ministry models.
Lesson 11	**Ministering to Children and Teens with Special Needs** There are many challenges facing children and teens with special needs. This lesson helps students understand some of these challenges by discussing the spiritual needs of this population, by showing how to adapt programs and curriculum to meet their unique needs, and by giving practical advice for typical children to welcome children and teens with special needs into their churches.
Lesson 12	**Ministering to Adults and the Elderly with Special Needs** This lesson focuses on adults with special needs by highlighting the life stages of spiritual formation for adults affected by disability. It describes effective teaching methods for this population and explains the benefits of building friendships with adults with special needs inside and outside of the church.

Lesson Summaries

MODULE 3 CONTINUED:

The Church and *Disability Ministry*

Lesson 13	**Outreach and Evangelism to Families Affected by Disability** Rarely do we think of families affected by disability in light of the Great Commission. The reason for this is that we do not understand the relationship between the Great Mission Statement, the Great Commission, and the Great Mandate. This lesson sheds light on this relationship and also provides reasons why people with disabilities may reject the Gospel. It describes how to present the Gospel to people with disabilities and offers some practical models for outreach.
Lesson 14	**Networking with Disability Ministries & Organizations** People in the disability community endure many obstacles as they make their way in this often inhospitable world. This lesson will help students appreciate some of these obstacles and will also explain how Christian and secular organizations can work together to relieve some of the burden. It provides practical ways to locate and network with government and private agencies, to work for social and ethical justice, and to understand Joni and Friends' worldwide initiatives.

Lesson Summaries

MODULE 4:

An Introduction to *Bioethics*

Lesson 15	**What Is Bio-Medical Ethics?** This lesson provides a basic definition of bio-medical ethics and explains why Christians should care about this very important issue. Students will examine the relevant history of bio-medical ethics and its importance to the recent developments of ethical theories.
Lesson 16	**Ethical Issues at the Edges of Life** Most ethical dilemmas take place at the beginning of life and at the end of life. This final lesson focuses on some of the dilemmas faced at these two "edges," such as abortion, prenatal testing, genetics, withholding and/or withdrawing treatment, end of life issues, and physician-assisted suicide.

Certificate of Completion Assignments

Assignment 1: The Exegetical Project (Inductive Bible Study)

The Scriptures are God's instrument to equip his people for every work of ministry to which he calls them (2 Tim. 3:16-17). This includes disability ministry. In order to complete the requirements for a CID Certificate of Completion, you will select a passage and use it to do an inductive Bible study. In this paper, you will discuss a topic from one of the four modules as it relates to the text you chose. This assignment highlights Scripture's ability to impact your life and ministry in powerful ways.

The purpose of this task is to give you an opportunity to do a detailed study of a major passage of Scripture and to understand the text in its original context. It is important that you learn how to exegete (explain, interpret) Scripture for yourself and for others.

This is a Bible study project, and, in order to do exegesis, you must be committed to understand the meaning of the passage in its own setting. Once you know what it means, you can then draw out principles that apply to all of us, and then relate those principles to life. The following simple three-step process can guide you in this personal study of the Bible passage:

Step 1. What was God saying to the people in the text's original situation?

Step 2. What principle(s) does the text teach that is true for all people everywhere, including here and now?

Step 3. What is the Holy Spirit asking me to do with this principle here, today, in my life and ministry?

Sample Outline for Exegetical Project and Paper Criteria

1. Write down what you believe is the main idea of your selected text.

2. Summarize the meaning of the passage. You may do this in two or three paragraphs or by writing a verse-by-verse commentary.

3. List one to three key principles or insights this text provides concerning some aspect of suffering and/or disability and/or disability ministry and/or God's character.

4. Tell how one or more of the principles may relate to one or more of the following:

   A. Your personal walk with Christ.
   B. Your life and ministry in your church.
   C. Situations or challenges related to suffering and/or disability.

As a reference, please feel free to read commentaries or Bible dictionaries and integrate insights from them into your work. Make sure that you give credit to whom credit is due if you borrow or build upon someone else's insights. Use references, footnotes, or endnotes. Be consistent with whatever form of citation you use.

Your exegetical paper should be three to four typed pages long and be turned in on time to your course leader according to the due date he or she sets for you. The paper should follow the outline given above and show how the passage relates to disability ministry. This paper is designed to show that you studied the passage, summarized its meaning, drew out a few key principles from it, and related those principles to your own life and disability ministry.

Selected Scriptural Passage:

_____

Study References Consulted:

_____

Key Principles for Suffering and Disability:

_____

_____

Assignment Due Date:

_____

Assignment 2: The Ministry Project

Certificate eligibility requires that you gain hands-on experience by participating in some aspect of disability ministry and reporting on it to your leader. This Ministry Project assignment calls for you to spend at least four hours gaining practical experience. You can create your own ministry opportunity or select one of the following:

1. Visit, observe and interact with a church disability ministry.
2. Evaluate and assess your church's interest in beginning a disability ministry or their needs for improving an existing ministry.
3. Interview an individual who works in the field of disability ministry.
4. Interview an individual with a disability or a family who has a member with a disability. Seek to gracefully listen and learn from their perspective regarding life with a disability.
5. Visit, observe and interact with a disability-related support group.
6. Shadow a home health RN, physical therapist, or occupational therapist.

Write a three-page paper describing the type of ministry or group you observed, detailing your experience and the lessons you learned. Be sure to include perceptions regarding strengths and weaknesses as well as thoughts and ideas for improvement and growth.

Selected Ministry Project:

_____

Ministry Project Contacts:

_____

Project Location and Date:

_____

_____

Assignment Due Date:

_____

Assignment 3: Lesson Reflection Questions

Certificate eligibility requires you to answer the reflection questions at the end of each lesson. These questions are intended to help you reflect on the main themes of the lesson, as well as the arguments and thoughts of the particular reading assignments. In your responses to the questions, you should be able to analyze the text—to read it, understand its thesis (main point), articulate its argument in a charitable way (whether you agree with the author or not), and then respond as to why you agree or disagree with the author. Reflection questions are located at the end of each of the 16 lessons.

Due Dates for Reflection Questions

_____ Module 1 An Overview of Disability Ministry
Questions for Lessons 1-4

_____ Module 2 The Theology of Suffering and Disability
Questions for Lessons 5-8

_____ Module 3 The Church and Disability Ministry
Questions for Lessons 9-14

_____ Module 4 An Introduction to Bioethics
Questions for Lessons 15-16

How to Use This Study Guide

Focus on and Review the Lesson Objectives

The lesson objectives are located in a sidebar on the first page of each lesson and summarize the main points. Use them as an interpretive guide to help you to understand, appreciate and remember what you are to learn in a particular lesson.

Study the Readings

In each lesson you will be prompted to read the professional papers located on the CD-ROM inside this study guide. Each selection applies to a particular section of the lesson. The lessons integrate the readings, which may be read before you begin a lesson or alongside the materials to be covered. Students will also be directed to read Scripture passages throughout *Beyond Suffering*. Unless otherwise noted, scriptural texts are from the *New International Version* of the Bible.

For those students enrolled for academic credit or for the Certificate of Completion, the papers are intended to provide the necessary background information to complete assignments.

Sections Per Lesson

For continuity, each lesson is divided into a similar number of sections, though some lessons may have a few more points depending on the particular topic. This uniformity is meant to help students focus and streamline study time. It also allows for flexibility in working through an entire lesson with a classmate or friend.

Pay Attention to the Key Word

The "key word" at the beginning of each lesson is designed to pique your interest and signal an important aspect of the lesson. It is not intended to be a one-word summary of the content of the lesson.

Watch Recommended Videos

As class time permits, leaders will show segments from the DVDs provided in the *Beyond Suffering Leader's Guide* and apply them to the lesson topics. These inspirational videos offer real-life examples of the principles being discussed. Students can also view most of the videos listed in the study guide at www.joniandfriends.org/ television.

Take Time to Ponder

Beyond Suffering deals with some very difficult issues that we cannot escape because they are indicative of the human condition. Therefore, we invite you to stop and contemplate an idea or a case study. Take the time to consider the relevance of an illustration or to examine pertinent Scripture that will deepen your grasp of the topics.

Become a Change Agent

May you put into practice the things you learn in this course. May you seek God's guidance to become his change agent in this global disability movement where people's hearts and minds are being transformed by the love and grace of our Savior, Jesus Christ.

MODULE 1

An Overview of
Disability Ministry

An Overview of Disability Ministry

Have you ever considered how attitudes impact our views of people experiencing disabilities?

As we begin this course we look at what defines disabilities, as well as the myths about their causes, which must be confronted. We will also seek to understand the life experiences of people with disabilities and their families. A critical aspect in this process involves the social consequences of a disability, which at times may be more difficult than the disability itself. Social consequences involve things like cultural perceptions and attitudes. An expert in this field whose work I admire is Dr. Wolf Wolfensberger. His writings on the "Eighteen Wounds of Disability" provide a solid framework for understanding the effects of the social consequences of disabilities.

Part three of this module presents a historical perspective on disability including the prevalent and hurtful behaviors, stereotypes or labels as seen everywhere from Hollywood movies to the historical narratives of places like Nazi Germany. These past influences greatly impact how people with disabilities are thought of today. I am excited for you to read a sermon by Catholic Bishop Von Galen who bravely stood up to the Nazi government. He defended individuals who were referred to at that time as "useless eaters" or "life unworthy of life." As a result of his bold advocacy, things changed for many individuals with disabilities. In light of this, Bishop Von Galen offers a challenge to us to be bold in our advocacy as well.

This module concludes with a discussion on the global reach of disability. Many experiences of individuals with disabilities are similar in different parts of the world. Others are impacted by cultural nuances related to traditions, economics, medicine and education.

This first module sets the stage for what is to come, because if you truly want to minister to people with disabilities, you must first identify with their life experiences. I invite you to dive into these lessons with an open heart and mind. May God bless you in your study.

Dr. Jeff McNair

Why Minister to *People* with Disabilities?

OBJECTIVES

Studying this lesson will help you:

✔ Understand the cultural perceptions and attitudes that impact the disability community.

✔ Describe what individuals and families experience at the onset of a disability.

✔ Identify hurtful stereotypes and labels attached to disabilities.

✔ Examine your past experiences with the disability community.

✔ Decide to include people with disabilities as friends rather than simply observing them from a distance.

✔ Consider your future participation in disability ministry.

If someone you love has a disability, the title of this lesson probably sounds like a rhetorical question. Shouldn't it be obvious? People are people, and they *all* need God in their lives, right? While we would be hard-pressed to find a Christian who doesn't agree, we can't ignore the fact that Christ's message is not reaching a great majority of people with disabilities who don't regularly attend church. Thus, we must consider that the question of why minister to persons with disabilities has more to do with believers than it does with those in the disability community.

In this lesson, we'll suggest some real-life reasons why Christians seem to be missing the mark—reasons that span centuries of ignorance and social injustices reaching around the globe. However, we'll also propose that the winds of change are blowing across colleges, universities and even some churches. Young adults who themselves have experienced broken homes, personal reverses and emotional pain are hungry to become authentic Christians. Religiosity repulses them. They have a growing desire to come alongside those who suffer. Thousands of them are seeking out the God Mike Yaconelli describes in his book *Dangerous Wonder*:

"The grace of God is dangerous. It's lavish, excessive, outrageous, and scandalous. God's grace is ridiculously inclusive. Apparently God doesn't care who He loves. He is not very careful about the people He calls His friends or the people He calls His church."[1]

In this course, you'll be challenged to join this emerging disability movement which is poised to storm the doors of the church with such radical inclusion that every man, woman and child with special needs will come to know and serve Jesus Christ in a Bible-believing church.

Awareness

Our conversations often center on people groups such as athletes, politicians, actors, coworkers or even criminals. But we rarely talk about people with disabilities unless they're family members. Why? Could it be because we tend to ignore what we fear? In this "me" generation, it takes courage to face weaknesses that we all share. But when we do, God shows up!

I. **When Disability Strikes**

Renee Bondi was a successful music teacher, singer and soon-to-be bride when she was thrust head first into the world of disability from a simple fall out of bed–and her world changed forever. In the months following Renee's diagnosis of quadriplegia, she faced many new challenges.

A. **Entering a Unique Cultural Group** – Renee went from being referred to as teacher, vocalist, and fiancée to patient, quadriplegic, wheelchair user and paralyzed lady. Occasionally, hurtful stereotypical labels were whispered about her in public. But through it all, Renee retained the title of Christ-follower.

B. **Learning a New Language** – Disabilities come with their own set of vocabulary words, medical terms and labels. Doctors attempt to explain tests and conditions with strange names. Fortunately, Renee had a supportive family and fiancé to help her through the maze of words and treatment decisions.

C. **Coping with Fears, Doubts and Depression** – Christians with disabilities experience the same steps to grief recovery as non-believers. Their fears and doubts are part of the human condition. We'll address this process in Lesson 2.

D. **Finding a New Normal** – The changing demands of a disability are stressful and ongoing for the individual, as well as family members. But with time and the proper support, Renee settled into a new lifestyle that focused on her true character and God-given abilities.

 **READ:** "When Disability Strikes" by Renee Bondi

> **Read 1 Samuel 16:7** and **2 Corinthians 4:18.**
> Examine your heart for evidence of assumptions
> you've made about people with disabilities. Confess
> your desire to see them through God's eyes.

II. **Social Constructions Impacting the Disability Community**

The social constructions of any society are made up of ideas that may appear to be natural and obvious to those who accept them, but in reality are entirely created by the culture. Typically, social constructs are choices made by people rather than laws of God or nature, and can include interpretation of any aspects of reality. Sadly, many of today's societal understandings are set by the media, where people with disabilities have never fared well.

> **Read Mark 7:5-13.** In Jesus' answer to the Pharisees' question about eating with unclean hands, he challenged their social structures. Did you catch it? Circle the words "tradition" and "commands." How are they used in contrast here? How are we like the Pharisees in these verses?

A. **Media Myths about Disability**

1. Myth of Pervasive Savants – Movies like *Rain Man,* portraying a man with high-functioning autism and a prodigious memory, raise more questions about disabilities than they answer. People with Autism Spectrum Disorders display a wide variety of behaviors and abilities; only a small percentage of them are savants.

2. Myth of the "Useless Eater" – This term was popularized in Nazi Germany as an excuse for genocide. It propagates the lie that people with mental or physical imperfections have no earthly value, except as research specimens, and should be put to death.

3. Myth of the Perpetual Victim – People using white canes or wheelchairs often appear on popular television programs as victims of crime or homeless informants. This myth suggests they're powerless to be heroes in our social stories.

4. Myth of Perpetual Tragedy – While the movie *Forrest Gump* lauded Forrest's many accomplishments, it managed to leave viewers feeling pity for this man of low mental abilities, but masked it in humor.

5. Myth of Perpetually Bitter Invalids – Because people with disabilities must continuously fight for their legal rights, they can falsely be seen as argumentative warriors with big chips on their shoulders. This is rarely the case.

B. **The 18 Wounds of Disability Ministry**

A disability can occur in a moment of crisis such as an accident, or result from a toxic environment or birth defect. Disorders can also emerge over time following such diagnoses as visual impairment leading to blindness, multiple sclerosis, Alzheimer's and conditions associated with aging. Disabilities are no respecter of persons, occurring in every age group, class, race and culture. But whatever the disability, people often experience a profound sense of devaluation and wounding that can be reinforced by societal attitudes.

In Dr. Wolf Wolfensberger's writings on social wounding he describes strategies that address the low status and poor treatment of certain individuals and classes of people. He suggests there is a collective unconsciousness about these assigned values that is undeclared, unacknowledged and even denied. Thus, most of us are totally unaware of how we act out these strategies in our social policies and daily lives.

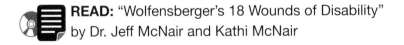 **READ:** "Wolfensberger's 18 Wounds of Disability" by Dr. Jeff McNair and Kathi McNair

Throughout this course we will examine ways to help prevent this devaluation and wounding through the power of the gospel of Jesus Christ. The book of Leviticus is God's religious training manual for the children of Israel. Leviticus 19:14 (*NKJV*) says, "You shall not curse a deaf man, nor place a stumbling block before the blind, but you shall revere your God; I am the Lord." This is God's command for us, as well as a picture of his heart for those with disabilities.

C. Religious Myths about Disabilities

It's clear from Scripture that God cares about people with disabilities. He constantly reminds us to be kind and merciful to everyone in need. Thus, well-meaning Christians have incorrectly deduced that children and adults with special needs are "special angels," whom God would automatically save due to their inability to care for themselves. They have been called "holy innocents," meaning they may even be incapable of sin or the results of sin. We reason that their disability must be punishment enough for their sins, which leads us to believe that they were put on earth to make us count our own blessings and to provide opportunities for our selfless service to others. This erroneous thinking disrespects and devalues people with disabilities as objects to be used for our personal edification.

These underlying myths are part of the social constructions of our culture that determine patterns of how we relate to the millions of people in our world with disabilities. We carry these hurtful ideas into our jobs, friendships and places of worship. As a result, we may unknowingly create obstacles for people not based on their functional limitations, but rather based on society's response to them. The best way to avoid these obstacles is by learning to identify with people who are disabled. Friendships tear down walls.

III. Identifying with the Disability Community

Before we can truly minister to the disability community, we must learn to identify with them. Too often there is an "us versus them" mentality or the idea of a great division between us, as though we had a huge boulder to climb over to get to the other side. The humor in this picture is that once we get to know people, their abilities, or lack of abilities, become moot points.

We may come to like them or dislike them based on their personalities or common interests, but our opinion usually grows beyond face value. This is why Jesus always stopped to

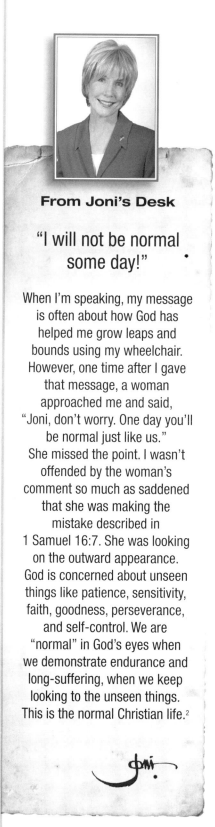

From Joni's Desk

"I will not be normal some day!"

When I'm speaking, my message is often about how God has helped me grow leaps and bounds using my wheelchair. However, one time after I gave that message, a woman approached me and said, "Joni, don't worry. One day you'll be normal just like us." She missed the point. I wasn't offended by the woman's comment so much as saddened that she was making the mistake described in 1 Samuel 16:7. She was looking on the outward appearance. God is concerned about unseen things like patience, sensitivity, faith, goodness, perseverance, and self-control. We are "normal" in God's eyes when we demonstrate endurance and long-suffering, when we keep looking to the unseen things. This is the normal Christian life.[2]

speak to people in need, because he saw into their hearts. With Jesus as our role model, how can we as Christians do any less?

What prompted you to enroll in this study? Was it because you know of someone with a disability who caused you to want to understand more about God's plan for suffering? God called you! His desire is that you come to consider "disability as a normal part of life in a broken world."[3]

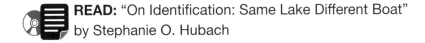 **READ:** "On Identification: Same Lake Different Boat" by Stephanie O. Hubach

Like many well-intentioned people, Stephanie Hubach once volunteered at a personal care home and struggled to identify with people she met there who were outside of her comfort zone—until she later looked into the face of disability in her own child. She began to understand that many of us think of relating with others by focusing on what we have in common, and some connect with others by focusing on how their group differs from another group, but God's identification with us is not based on either commonality or exclusivity. Instead, it is an identification of *intentionality*. While the expression "we're all in the same boat" reflects a view of commonality, and "we're in different lakes entirely" mirrors the idea of exclusiveness, "same lake, different boat" reflects the biblical reality that as human beings we are all *essentially* the same, but *experientially* different. We share a common story as people created in God's image and yet our life experiences may vary dramatically. Stephanie suggests that God—in a variety of ways—models for us the very intentional identification with others that he calls us to live out.

A. **Why minister to people with disabilities?**
   Christians are called to:

   1. Share the Gospel of Jesus Christ with *all* people. In Lesson 4 we'll discuss the Great Commission and how to evangelize individuals and families affected by disability. (Matt. 28:19-20)

   2. Work to alleviate suffering. (2 Cor. 1:3-5, Gal. 6:2)

   3. Mediate structures to change groups/organizations. (1 Cor. 12:7)

4. Stand up for social justice. (Ps. 82:3-4, Prov. 22:22-23)

5. Facilitate growth in the individual. (Phil. 1:6, Heb. 10:24-25)

6. Change society. (Prov. 31:8-9, Luke 10:36-37)

7. Love for love's sake. (Prov. 3:3, 1 John 4:8,19)

B. **What are your personal impressions of the disability community?**

1. Do you personally know someone with a disability?

2. Have you spent time with an individual or family affected by a disability?

3. Have you ever considered that one day you might have a disability?

4. How prepared would you be to accept a family member with a disability?

 READ: "A True Friend Identifies" by Joni Eareckson Tada

 GROUP DISCUSSION

Consider how you can build new friendships with people who have disabilities. Where could you meet them?

What interests might you have in common? Discuss your plan of action with your small group.

Reflections on Lesson 1

Why Minister to People with Disabilities?

1. Explain some of the challenges people face at the onset of a disability.

2. What is "social construction" and what role did it play in Jesus' response to the Pharisees in Mark 7:5-13?

3. Identify three myths about disability that are portrayed in the media and three myths drawn from religious thought.

4. Reflecting on McNair's description of Wolfensberger's 18 wounds, describe your church's response to people with disabilities.

5. Explain what Hubach means by the phrase "same lake, different boat."

6. Who are the people with whom you most closely identify? Why? In what ways do you feel "out of your comfort zone" when it comes to relating to people who have disabilities? Why?

7. List five reasons we should minister to and alongside people with disabilities.

8. Consider ways you could intentionally spend time with someone with a disability in the next few weeks. Write an action plan.

What Defines a *Disability?*

Some people with disabilities say the challenges that come with being disabled are not so much physical, but rather the negative attitudes they grapple with from society. Mark, a 25-year-old wheelchair user, admits that he envisions a planet or special country exclusively for persons with disabilities where issues of "normalcy" don't exist. Then he would not be disabled, because there would be no basis for comparison since everyone would appear the same. Mark would not be singled out to face limited opportunity in education, employment and social activities. Sadly, he can only dream of such freedom.

Our friends with disabilities didn't plan to have handicaps. Given a choice, most would choose a life without impairments. While they need to understand that God created them for his purposes, they also have a right to ask questions such as: What if the world could change? What if every person on earth was educated about disabilities until all fears and prejudices melted into genuine empathy for one another? This new reality could relieve suffering, heal lives and reveal God's love and mercy.

Whether you're trained in working with disabilities or new to the field, the extensive list of characteristics and terminologies can easily overwhelm. In this lesson, we'll discuss the basic kinds of disabilities and their causes, as well as their life-long impact on individuals and their families.

OBJECTIVES

Studying this lesson will help you:

✔ Define the difference between impairments, disabilities and handicaps.

✔ Describe the various causes of disabilities.

✔ Identify characteristics of physical, emotional, intellectual and developmental disabilities.

✔ Understand the broad scope of Autism Spectrum Disorder.

✔ Use disability-friendly language.

✔ Explain how family members and life cycles are impacted by disabilities.

♀ *Empathy*

Sympathy—sorrow in the face of another's suffering—is all too familiar to people affected by disabilities. While intended to offer comfort, sympathy can embitter one's soul when expressed as pity. Empathy, on the other hand, looks through eyes of common experience. Where were you the last time you truly felt empathy with another person? If you can't recall, humility is the road to get there.

Jesus said, "I am the way, the truth and the life."

JOHN 14:6

I. Moving Beyond Disability Labels

We sometimes hear people say things like, "I'm computer challenged," or "My golf handicap is embarrassing." We smile, knowing such weaknesses don't define them. It's helpful to keep this in mind as we define disabilities because there's a difference between the truths and the facts. For example, a new report prepared jointly by the World Health Organization and the World Bank was released in June 2011 stating that 15 percent of the world's population—some 785 million people—has a significant physical or intellectual disability.[1] It's a *fact* that if every American with a disability came together, they would equal the population of California and Florida combined.[2] Yet, the *truth* is they live in your community, attend local schools and shop at your supermarkets. While the statistical facts inform our understanding, they do little to define the outstanding individuals they represent.

A. Defining a Disability

According to the Americans with Disability Act (ADA), the term "disability" means, with respect to an individual: 1) a physical or mental impairment that substantially limits one or more of the major life activities of such individual; 2) a record of such an impairment; or 3) being regarded as having such impairment.[3] This definition involves some terms which are commonly confused since a person may struggle with one, two or all three.

1. An ***impairment*** is any loss or abnormality of psychological, physiological or anatomical structure or function; i.e. mental or physical constitution.

2. A *disability* is any restriction or lack of (resulting from an impairment) ability to perform an activity in the manner or within the range considered normal for a human being.

3. A *handicap* is a disadvantage for a given individual, resulting from impairment or a disability which limits or prevents the fulfillment of a role that is normal for that individual (depending on age, sex and social or cultural factors). Handicaps are often viewed in relationship to a person with a disability and their environment and can affect their participation in community life on an equal level with others.

READ: "The Fact Sheet on Persons with Disabilities"
(Appendix A)

While Robin Hiser would be counted in the statistics for Down syndrome, the label doesn't begin to describe the active lifestyle of this joyful Christian woman. At 53 years old, Robin is one of the most faithful Short Term Missionaries at Joni and Friends Family Retreats. She's an active volunteer in her church and community. As you watch the video, *When Robin Prays*, consider these questions:

· In what ways does Robin show us that she is aware of how some people view her?

· What or who impacted Robin's self-image and freed her to be the person she is?

· In what ways has Robin influenced your view of people with disabilities?

 VIEW: When Robin Prays (Joni and Friends DVDTV05)

II. **A Glimpse into the World of Disability**
It would be impossible to define the many different kinds of disabilities in this study. Basically, they can be grouped into several categories: physical disabilities, developmental

disabilities, learning disabilities, visual and hearing impairments, emotional/behavioral disorders and mental illness. Individuals can also acquire multiple disabilities, which involve various combinations of symptoms and diagnoses.

Physical Disabilities

A. **Physical Disabilities Limit Mobility and Activities**
Some of the most common physical disabilities are listed in the table below.

Disability	Cause	Impacts	Variables
Spinal cord injury	Severed or injured spinal cord	Movement, use of limbs, bowel functioning, nervous sensation	May result in partial or full effects (sensation, paralysis, etc.); susceptibility to infection
Missing limbs	Birth defects, disease, injuries	Physical function depending upon limbs affected	Number of limbs impacted and to what degree
Muscular dystrophy	Inherited gene passed on following X linked or autosomal dominant patterns	Movement through the degeneration primarily of voluntary muscles	Rapid or slow onset and progress, may affect involuntary muscles
Multiple sclerosis	Autoimmune disease attacking the protective sheath that covers nerves	Nerves causing deterioration and affecting the ability to walk and talk	Symptoms vary and MS can be difficult to diagnose
Spina bifida	Neural tube which becomes the brain and spinal cord does not develop or close properly resulting in problems with spinal cord and bones of backbone	Motor functioning and sensation below the point evidencing lack of development	May also impact bowel and bladder control
Stroke	Blood supply to a portion of the brain is reduced or cut off, damaging brain cells	Brain functioning in affected areas evidenced by a loss of speech, paralysis or damage of other functions	Effects and recovery prognosis vary
Acquired brain injury	Injury at or after birth due to trauma, disease, aneurysms, tumors or strokes	Movement, memory, cognition, and language	When, where and how brain is affected will mitigate outcomes
Post-polio syndrome	Linked to Polio infection, but exact cause of degraded motor function is unknown	Movement causing limited mobility and paralysis	Common in developing countries
Blind or Visually-impaired	Trachoma-infectious disease, cataracts, macular degeneration, glaucoma, retinitis	Vision in that it is limited to absent	Gradual or sudden loss of vision; some may be reversed with optics or surgery
Deaf or Hearing-impaired	Genetics, premature birth, infections or disease	Hearing in that it is limited to absent	May affect speech and learning; may be considered a cultural difference not a disability

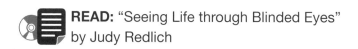

READ: "Seeing Life through Blinded Eyes"
by Judy Redlich

B. Developmental Disabilities Are Growing at Epidemic Proportions

Historically, some people within this classification were labeled "mentally retarded" and continue to be in many

Developmental
Disabilities

Disability	Cause	Impacts	Variables
Cerebral palsy	Neurological damage or abnormal brain development	Muscle strength, rigidity/flexibility, control, movement and balance, and speech	Spastic is most common form and in varying degrees, quadriplegia impacting all four limbs
Down syndrome	An extra copy of #21 chromosome, hence the name Trisomy 21	Intellectual function, muscle tone and social development	Effects range from mild to severe
Pervasive Developmental Disorder—PDD	Unknown	In various ways; PDD actually refers to the entire autism spectrum	Includes childhood autism, Asperger's and Rett syndrome, disintegrative disorder, and PDD not otherwise specified
Autism	Unknown	Communication and sensory integration resulting in difficulty interacting, learning leisure and play	Typically appears in first 3 years; effects range from mild to severe
Asperger's syndrome	Unknown	Similar to those with autism, particularly social interactions; often referred to as high-functioning autism	May include disabilities in speech and language
Childhood Disintegrative Disorder (CDD)	Unknown	Language, motor skills and social functioning	Typical development for 3-4 years followed by regression in motor functioning, language and social skills
Rett syndrome	Neurodevelopmental disorder almost exclusively affecting girls; characterized by normal early growth; followed by developmental delays	The purposeful use of the hands, brain and head growth, walking, with seizures and intellectual disability	Typical development followed by regression of development, at variable ages of onset
PDD-NOS (not otherwise specified)	Unknown spinal cord	Social functioning in a less severe manner than classic autism	Milder form of autism not evidencing all symptoms

countries. But today, developmental disabilities include a diverse group of chronic conditions that are due to mental and/or physical impairments. People with developmental disabilities may face challenges in fundamental life activities such as language, mobility, learning, self-help, and independent living. Developmental disabilities can begin anytime during a child's development up to 22 years of age and usually last throughout his or her lifetime.[4]

In 2010, disability advocates applauded the U.S. Congress for eliminating the negative term "mental retardation" from federal laws. "Changing how we talk about people with disabilities is a critical step in promoting and protecting their basic civil and human rights," said Peter Berns, CEO of The Arc, an organization promoting the human rights of people with intellectual and developmental disabilities.[5]

Researchers are eager to unlock the mysteries of developmental disorders, which are growing at epidemic proportions. See the table on the previous page for some common developmental disabilities.

C. **The Most Common Learning Disabilities**

1. **Attention Deficit and Hyperactivity Disorders** (ADD/ADHD)—Children have difficulty sitting still, controlling behavior, and paying attention. Hyperactivity and impulsivity cause fidgeting, excessive talking and impatience.

2. **Dyslexia**—Children demonstrate difficulty obtaining language skills at a level consistent with their intelligence. Despite average to above average intelligence, they struggle with reading and spelling.

III. **Autism Spectrum Disorder (ASD)**
We all get frustrated and anxious at times! Take a moment to recall a time when your stress level was so high that you almost shut down. Your head and stomach ached so badly that you couldn't think straight or remember what you said a moment ago. Now, imagine that you're only about a tenth of the way to empathizing with children who have severe autism.

This severe frustration is due to their inability to integrate sensory inputs at acceptable levels. Sights, sounds, touches and tastes can even be painful, so they may react aggressively by flapping their hands and hitting their heads. Or they may withdraw by not speaking or giving eye contact. They miss social cues and don't recognize other people's responses or interests. But there are some myths about autism that need to be dispelled.

The Autism Society

Since 1965, the Autism Society has been a leader in serving people with autism, their families and the professionals. They provide comprehensive on-line education, services and referrals at www.Autism-Society.org or call 1-800-3Autism to locate a chapter near you.

Myth 1—*We know the causes and cures for autism.* False! Medical research has yet to successfully identify the root cause of autism or offer a successful cure.

Myth 2—*All people with autism are not able to learn.* Not true! These friends learn differently, but they can all learn. Some have high IQs and excel in areas of interest.

Myth 3—*All people with autism behave the same.* False! People on the autism spectrum exhibit a wide range of behaviors and characteristics.

Myth 4—*Autism is caused by poor parenting.* This is utterly untrue since many parents of children with autism display exceptional tenacity and patience in rearing their children.

Dr. Laura Hendrickson left her practice as a medical doctor to raise her son, Eric, whose autism was diagnosed early. In her book, *Finding Your Child's Way on the Autism Spectrum,* she describes the challenges Eric faced growing up with high-functioning autism, such as difficulty handling change, inflexible thinking and learning difficulties. Henderson discovered that people with autism are capable of learning. Like the rest of us, they have innate strengths and weaknesses which make them unique. One of Eric's weaknesses was his sensitivity to sounds. However, in high school and college his sensitivity became a strength that helped him excel at foreign languages, which led to his vocation. In Lessons 12 and 13 we'll learn how to welcome and teach children and adults with autism at church, as well as view a video interview with Dr. Hendrickson.

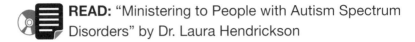 **READ:** "Ministering to People with Autism Spectrum Disorders" by Dr. Laura Hendrickson

IV. **Disability Friendly Language**

Language is powerful! Words can ignite passions or incite rage. Words compliment, discourage, persuade or prejudice us toward right or wrong attitudes, beliefs and actions. Language plays an important role in showing respect for persons with disabilities. As Christians, we want to avoid offensive language and show respect in ways that honor God. The Book of Proverbs tells us that "a kind word cheers" (12:25) and "a word aptly spoken is like apples of gold in settings of silver" (25:11).

A. **People First Language (PFL)**—People First Language recognizes that an individual is a person, a human being or a citizen first, and that the disability is a part, but not all of them. For example, rather than saying, "Paul is disabled," say, "Paul has a disability." Don't talk about the "autistic boy" or the "epileptic woman," but rather say "the boy with autism" or "the woman with epilepsy." An exception to PFL may be "deaf people" who prefer this term because they don't consider themselves disabled. They simply communicate using a different language.

B. **Avoid Hurtful Terms**—Don't use descriptions such as brain-damaged, slow learner or retarded. Rather, say "man with a brain injury" or "child with a learning difficulty." Avoid using "dwarf or midget." Dwarfism is an accepted medical term, but it should not be used as general terminology. Say persons of small (or short) stature; some prefer "little people." Nondisabled is the appropriate term for people without disabilities. Normal, healthy or whole are inappropriate.

C. **Language Guidelines**—The Life Span Institute at the University of Kansas has created a set of clear guidelines to help you make better choices in terms of language and portrayal. The *Guidelines* explain preferred terminology and offer suggestions for appropriate ways to describe people with disabilities. The *Guidelines* reflect input from over 100 national disability organizations and has been reviewed and endorsed by media and disability experts throughout the country. For a copy of the *Guidelines* visit: http://www.lsi.ku.edu/~lsi/aboutus/guidelines.shtml.

V. The Impact of Disability on Individual and Family Life Cycles

In Pastor Lon Solomon's book, *Brokenness*, he describes how his daughter's disability changed his family's life. Jill's seizures began in infancy, and after surviving more than 6,000 seizures, she is severely mentally and physically impaired. "The impact of Jill's sickness has been devastating for us," says Solomon. "There was physical and mental exhaustion ... then there was the grief—the grief of watching our dreams and plans for our little girl vanish ... All of our dreams for our own life would never be fulfilled either. Brenda and I will be serving Jill for the rest of our lives. [But] instead of considering it a burden, we consider it a privilege."[6] The Solomons are an example of a family who has found God's grace along the road of brokenness.

A. The Family Life Cycle

1. **Initial Diagnosis**—Families are entering a new world, coping with grief stages, informing family and friends, seeking government services and making ongoing medical decisions.

2. **Childhood and Siblings**—Families are adjusting expectations, helping siblings deal with stress, stretching their budgets, managing special education and various therapies.

3. **Transition to Adulthood**—Families are assessing levels of independence, seeking vocational and/or residential options and planning transitions.

4. **Adulthood**—Families are managing benefits, changing roles after the loss of parents, re-evaluating required services and facing additional diagnoses with age.

5. **End-of-Life**—Families are seeking moral and ethical guidance for end-of-life decisions, grieving the potentially long "goodbye" and considering life without their loved one.

B. **Why God Gave Us Emotions**

Our emotions are much like pain receptors for the body. Just as the searing pain of a hand placed on a hot stove forces a child to recoil from it, our emotions can be God-given indicators that something is awry. In Lesson 1, Renee Bondi shared the story of her devastating fall out of bed that resulted in a lifetime of coping with quadriplegia. With the love and support of her husband, Mike, and her family, Renee slowly waded through the grief process and grew stronger. But what happens when people try to push through without seeking support or acknowledging that their life has been forever changed by disability?

John, a successful businessman, seemed to quickly rebound from a car accident that left him confined to a wheelchair. He amazed his friends and colleagues by single-handedly resuming his regular business trips, maneuvering his wheelchair through airports and hotels with an uncanny determination to keep his upbeat personality. John ended up hitting an emotional wall that landed him in the hospital and eventually in counseling with Dr. Mark Baker.

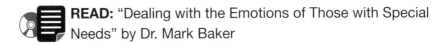 **READ:** "Dealing with the Emotions of Those with Special Needs" by Dr. Mark Baker

In order to minister to people with special needs, we must understand the importance of "grief work." We must learn to be good listeners, but also know when to refer someone to a professional counselor. We can assure those who are struggling with pain and grief that our emotions are an aspect of the image of God within us. Our feelings help us connect with God and others. In Mark 12:30 we read "Love the Lord your God with all your heart and with all your soul and with all your mind and with all your strength." As Christians who live by faith, we are led by our hearts more than we like to believe. Proverbs reminds us that our hearts guide our mouths (15:28), and we are to guard our hearts as the wellspring of our lives (4:23).

Steps to Grief Recovery

a. **Denial**—I can't believe this is happening to me!

b. **Anger**—I see what's happening, and I'm really mad about it!

c. **Bargaining**—I'll do anything I can to make it stop!

d. **Depression**—I'm very sad because I realize I can't change my situation.

e. **Acceptance**—I see that my life won't ever be the same, but maybe good will come from this.

Have you had a need in your life for grief work? Maybe you are currently in the middle of the process. If so, remember that you're not alone. There are Christian brothers and sisters who stand ready to walk with you, but even more importantly, there is a Savior, who has experienced it all before you (Heb. 4:15). Victory can be yours. *"But thanks be to God! He gives us the victory through our Lord Jesus Christ"* (1 Cor. 15:57).

Reflections on Lesson 2

What Defines a Disability?

1. Explain the differences between an impairment, a disability and a handicap.

2. Describe the causes and results of four types of physical disabilities.

3. In the video, *When Robin Prays*, what kinds of activities do people with disabilities enjoy doing?

4. Reflecting on Judy Redlich's paper on blindness, what are the challenges of being visually impaired?

5. Describe six common characteristics of people with developmental disabilities.

6. What are the common myths regarding autism?

7. What are some of Dr. Hendrickson's suggestions for relating to people with autism?

8. Why is it important to learn to use disability-friendly language?

9. How has your family's life cycle been impacted by the struggles they've faced?

10. Reflecting on Dr. Baker's paper, why did God give us emotions?

A *Historical Perspective* on Disability

OBJECTIVES

Studying this lesson will help you:

✔ Describe how history has viewed people with disabilities.

✔ Identify ideologies that have worked against the disability community.

✔ Understand the revolutionary issues which have surrounded disability.

✔ Appreciate leaders who have brought about positive change for people with disabilities.

✔ Consider historical legislation that has shaped perspectives on disability in our culture.

For better or worse, we're all curious about our heritage. The stories from previous generations help shape our self-worth and identity. In our present time of regulated accessibility, people with disabilities may be shocked by the "ugly" truths of the past. Who would want to identify themselves with centuries of loathing and deprivation?

European and American societies once viewed people with disabilities as "deviant in nature." They were seen as objects of dread and ridicule, sub-human and diseased organisms, even evil or possessed persons. Their neighbors misunderstood them and their origins, fearing their influence on society as well as their potential to "pollute" humankind.

Thankfully, we're living in the 21st century and times have changed, right? Decades of new discoveries in education, medicine and science have initiated great reforms in how our friends with disabilities participate in society . . . or have they?

Before we start patting ourselves on the back, we'll spend Lessons 3 and 4 looking at the slow progress of disability reform in advanced cultures and the minuscule changes in developing nations. We will glimpse the possibility of a different tomorrow—a tomorrow planted by Jesus Christ in the hearts of missional Christians.

🔑 *Apathy*

A wise man once said that the death of democracy will not be an assassination, but a slow extinction from apathy. Apathy shouts, "I am not responsible." This has been history's cry regarding people with disabilities. But Jesus Christ proved by example that there is no place in a Christian's life for apathy toward people with disabilities. Detect it! Confess it! Reject it!

I. **Disability Prior to the Rise of Institutions**

Throughout the ages people with disabilities have suffered a great deal of abuse and misunderstanding. In ancient Greece, the Spartans systematically destroyed their physically imperfect citizens, while the Athenians permitted their disabled to die of neglect. In Rome, a father was given the authority to destroy an imperfect child immediately after his or her birth. In the Orient, physically impaired infants were cast out into the wilderness to die by starvation or exposure. In India, physically defective babies were cast into rivers.[1]

Are you surprised to find a history lesson here, especially one with such depressing information? You may be tempted to skip over these horrendous abuses against people with disabilities and quickly move to modern solutions. Why is history so important in embracing life's challenges?

Read Deuteronomy 5:15; 8:2; 15:15; 24:22; 32:7.

Moses repeatedly told the Israelites to remember their suffering and to never forget God's deliverance. He used the word "remember" 16 times in the Book of Deuteronomy, adding the phrase "never forget" nine more times. Like Moses' followers, our generation must remember the mighty works of God in order to endure trials and stand up for our friends with disabilities.

II. The Birth of Institutions: From Hope to Horror

A. Hope for Persons Who Are Blind and/or Deaf

While those with visual or hearing impairments were pitied and abused by society, they were considered educable. In the late 1700s, institutions to teach children who were blind and deaf were founded in Europe by compassionate men who wanted to stop this harsh treatment. Pioneer Valentin Haüy (1745-1822) dedicated himself to creating special methods of teaching reading and writing. His way of embossing books was revolutionary and his success allowed him to raise enough money to open the Paris Institute for the Blind. One of his prized students was Louis Braille (1809-1852). Under Haüy's tutelage, Braille invented a raised point alphabet in 1829, which came to be known as the Braille system.[2] It was eventually introduced to America in 1860 and used at the St. Louis School for the Blind.[3]

The first permanent school in America for persons with deafness opened in Hartford in 1817. It was called the Connecticut Asylum for the Education and Instruction of Deaf and Dumb Persons. It originated in the heart of a father who was anxious about his beloved child's education. Dr. Mason F. Cogswell stated that there were probably 2,000 deaf and dumb persons in the United States and appealed to the General Association of Congregational Clergymen of Connecticut in 1812 for their prayers and support. Eventually, the school obtained public funding from the Congress of the United States and a permanent fund was provided.[4]

While the treatment and education of people with vision and hearing loss continued to improve, it was far less hopeful for persons with intellectual disabilities. Their path has been a treacherous road of peaks and valleys, with both godly innovators and evil tyrants along the way.

B. The First School for Idiots* 1851

1. **Edouard Seguin's** (1812-1880) faith brought great hope to *idiots* (his term) first in Europe and later in America. As a doctor and educator, Seguin was the first to create methods to deal with sensory and motor issues, age-appropriate activities and training for

employment. He also encouraged self-reliance and independence by giving people specific physical and intellectual tasks. Seguin made significant contributions to the humanity of persons with intellectual disabilities.[5]

   a. In 1840, Seguin founded the first private school in Paris for those with intellectual disabilities.

   b. He published the earliest systematic textbook used to deal with children with special needs in 1846.

   c. Seguin was the first president to the "Association of Medical Officers of American Institutions for Idiotic and Feebleminded Persons," which eventually became the American Association on Mental Retardation.

The growth of U.S. State Institutions for the Disabled was astronomical. In 1900 there were 12,000 people with intellectual disabilities living in institutions. As a result of new intellectual testing, that number grew to an estimated 400,000 by 1915.[6]

The following excerpt is from a speech Seguin gave in 1851 at the first U.S. school built exclusively for the "education of idiots:"

God has scattered among us—rare as the possessors of genius—the idiot, the blind, the deaf-mute, in order to bind the rich to the needy, the talented to the incapable, all men to each other, by a tie of indissoluble solidarity. The old bonds are dissolving; man is already unwilling to continue to contribute money or palaces for the support of the indolent nobility; but he is every day more ready to build palaces and give annuities for the indigent or infirm, the chosen friends of our Lord Jesus. See that corner-stone—the token of a new alliance between humanity and a class hitherto neglected—that, ladies and gentlemen, is your pride; it is the greatest joy of my life; for I, too, have labored for the poor idiot.[7]

2. **The Ugly "Idiot"**—Problems arose when these educational innovations failed to show the desired results. Schools were not designed to care for persons with

disabilities indefinitely, and only a small number of adults became productive members of society. Parents, who felt hopeless, wanted students to remain in schools, thus institutionalized care spread across America bringing a whole new set of predicaments.

III. The Age of Eugenics 1850-1950

A. The Eugenics Movement

The rise of institutionalized care turned a floodlight on the value and worth of persons with severe intellectual and physical disabilities. Test studies in human behavior began asking: Why can't Jane learn? Will her children be retarded too? Why is Johnny the way he is? What can he contribute to society? So began the birth of the Eugenics Movement. Eugenics, using applied and biosocial sciences, set out to genetically purify the human population. How? By sterilizing Jane and starving Johnny.

> "This remedy [sterilization] must, in the opinion of this committee, be the principal agent used by society in cutting off the supply of defectives."
> —from Eugenics section of the American Breeders Association, 1911

By 1926, twenty-three states had laws permitting sterilization of people with disabilities. Thankfully, religious groups protested, calling the laws a violation of human rights. But in a 1927 Supreme Court case that upheld the use of sterilization, Supreme Court Justice Oliver Wendell Holmes ruled, "It [sterilization] is better for the world, if instead of waiting to execute degenerate offspring for crime, or to let them starve for their imbecility, society can prevent those who are manifestly unfit for continuing their kind. . . . Three generations of imbeciles are enough."[8]

Eugenic practices fell out of favor when the movement became associated with the genocide in Nazi Germany. Mark P. Mostert suggests that the methods used for mass extermination in the Nazi death camps originated in the treatment of people with physical, emotional and intellectual disabilities. He identifies six key markers which allowed a highly sophisticated Western society to commit mass murder. While reading Mostert's paper, consider the lessons that can be carried forward into a world where disabilities are growing at epidemic proportions.

READ: "Useless Eaters: Disability as Genocidal Marker in Nazi Germany" by Dr. Mark Mostert. http://www.regent.edu/acad/schedu/uselesseaters/text/2743414051_1.pdf

---

VIEW: "Useless Eaters: Disability as Genocidal Marker in Nazi Germany" Regent University School of Education, http://www.regent.edu/acad/schedu/uselesseaters/

> *"There is no such thing as a life unworthy of living."*
>
> BISHOP CLEMENS AUGUST GRAF VON GALEN,
>
> OUTSPOKEN CRITIC OF THE NAZI REGIME

B. **The Voice of the Church**

Thankfully, multitudes of Christians cried out against the crimes of the Eugenics Movement and the Nazi regime. Many, no doubt, wept in agonizing prayer for the halt of such degrading atrocities. Sermons were preached by brave leaders hoping to stop the tide. One such pivotal message came from Bishop Clemens August von Galen (1878-1946) who attacked the Nazi practice of euthanasia and condemned the "mercy killings" taking place in his own diocese.

 **READ:** "The Third Sermon in Defiance of the Nazis" by Bishop von Galen

How does the Bishop describe the posture of Jesus in such tragic times?

What biblical evidence does the Bishop use to plead his case for Christian courage?

IV. **The Age of Reform 1950-1990**

Reform: to change into an improved form; to amend or improve by removing fault or abuse; beneficial reversion to repair, restore or correct.

A. **Thinking Differently**

By the end of World War II, the world had witnessed

enough human suffering and welcomed a new era of peace and compassion for all people. Disability reform began to move into the area of political reform.

1. **President Franklin D. Roosevelt (1882-1945)** served three successful terms as President of the United States from a wheelchair due to polio. Although Roosevelt did his best to hide his disability, his courageous leadership during the Depression and World War II changed expectations and gained respect for persons with physical disabilities.[9]

2. **President John F. Kennedy's (1917-1963) sister, Rosemary, had an intellectual disability.** He created the President's Panel on Mental Retardation in 1961 to study ways to include people with intellectual disabilities in everyday life in America. Following the Panel's report, "Combating Mental Retardation," new programs were introduced in education and hospital reform.[10] The Kennedys also helped launch the Special Olympics and a wide-range of initiatives for persons with disabilities.

3. **Burton Blatt (1927-1985)** was an educator, author and disability advocate. His 1966 book, *Christmas in Purgatory*, exposed the horrid conditions in institutions. In Lesson 4 you'll learn more about The Burton Blatt Institute, a world leader in disability civil rights issues.

4. **Wolf Wolfensberger (1934-2011)** developed the theory of Social Role Valorization (SRV), which was discussed in the Lesson 1 reading, "Wolfensberger's 18 Wounds of Disability." The major goal of SRV is to support socially valued roles for people in their society.

5. **Gunnar Dybwad (1909-2001)**, an International Disability Rights Advocate, played a vital role in persuading the Pennsylvania Association for Retarded Children (PARC) to file a lawsuit in Pennsylvania that established rights of children with disabilities to a free education in 1972.[11]

B. **"So how did we get to a place like Willowbrook?"**
This is the question then-rookie reporter **Geraldo Rivera**

asked after his film crew snuck into the Willowbrook State School on Staten Island in 1972. Rivera was inspired by Robert Kennedy's 1965 visit when he described what he saw as a "snake pit." Rivera's report exposed the inhumane and filthy conditions of the residents with disabilities and called for reform. His report stirred government action and won him the Peabody Award. The film *Unforgotten* documented Rivera's reports and is available for purchase on Amazon.com.

VIEW: Video (3 min.): Willowbrook: the Last Great Disgrace
http://www.youtube.com/watch?v=k_sYn8DnlH4

Reports like Kennedy's and Rivera's fired up disability advocates to push for greater reforms, including the following:

- 1972—The Normalization Principle sought to normalize the lives of people with disabilities by giving them a pattern of everyday life similar to that of other individuals in their society.

- 1973—Rehabilitation Act of 1973, particularly Section 504, which provided students with disabilities the same educational materials and curriculum as their peers.

- 1975—PL 94-142 Education of All Handicapped Children Act (EAHCA)

- Late 1980s—U.S. institutions began to be phased out in favor of community living.[12]

- 1990—EAHCA became the Individuals with Disabilities Education Act (IDEA) with minor amendments and was amended significantly in 1997 to expand the definition of disabled children to include developmentally delayed children between three and nine years of age.[13]

V. Democratization of Disabilities 1990-Present

In recent times, people with disabilities have made great strides in self-advocacy and independent living. Their stories have appeared on television, in feature films and print media. This media presence has placed pressure on governments to provide fair and equal opportunities.

A. Americans with Disabilities Act (ADA)

Upon the recommendation of the National Council on Disability, the Americans with Disabilities Act (ADA) was signed into law in 1990 by President George H.W. Bush. For a copy of the ADA, visit the U.S. Department of Justice's website at www.ada.gov/pubs/ada.htm. Joni Eareckson Tada served as a member of the council under President Ronald Reagan and President Bush.

From Joni's Desk

"I will never forget that day!"

After the signing ceremony on the South Lawn [of the White House], our council retired to a nearby hotel for a reception. As champagne got passed around, our council's executive director, Paul Hearne, said he wanted to make an announcement.

"The ADA will mean that there will be mechanical lifts on buses," he said, "and ramps into restaurants…open doors in places of employment." Paul then fell silent again. After a long moment, he continued, "But this law will not change the heart of the bus driver. It will not change the heart of the restaurant owner or the employer." After another long pause and with wet eyes, Paul Hearne lifted his glass in a toast: "Here's to changed hearts."[14]

> "Medically handicapped people are still hidden from history as they are from the rest of life. What history they do have is not so much theirs as the history of others either acting on their behalf or against them." Ryan and Thomas (1987)

B. Here's to Changed Hearts!

In this lesson's introduction, we contemplated if it was indeed time to "pat ourselves on the back" over the sweeping reforms for those in the disability community. However, it seems that each advocacy hero of this movement has led us further down the path into some new stumbling blocks. These issues will be more evident in Module 4: An Introduction to Bioethics.

Most families affected by disabilities are grateful to live in the 21st Century with greater opportunities for their loved ones than ever before in history. But families like the Boatrights, who have twin daughters with developmental disabilities, continue to face overwhelming challenges. Clay Boatright wrote about one of them in his editorial for the *Dallas Morning News* on November 14, 2008.

Laws and public policy reflect the heart of a country and the soul of a nation. God reminds us in Ezekiel 11:19-20, "I will remove from them their heart of stone and give them a heart of flesh. Then they will follow my decrees and be careful to keep my laws. They will be my people, and I will be their God." I don't want America to move into the future with a heart of stone.[15]

 READ: "Ignoring God's Children" by Clay Boatright

Does apathy still exist in society toward people with disabilities? In the church? In our own hearts?

Your Personal History with People with Disabilities
Create a timeline of the encounters you've had with people with disabilities from your earliest memories to the present. Consider how those experiences have shaped your attitudes and actions.

Reflections on Lesson 3

A Historical Perspective on Disability

1. Why is it important to understand the history of the disability community?

2. How were people with disabilities characterized prior to the rise of institutions?

3. What contribution did Edouard Seguin make to children with disabilities in the mid-1800s?

4. What led to the rapid growth of institutionalized care in the U.S.?

5. What fears fueled the Eugenics Movement?

6. From Mostert's paper, "Useless Eaters," identify the six key markers that allowed mass murders.

7. In Bishop Clemens August von Galen's sermon, what motto did he call for as their only hope for peace in the face of evil?

8. How were the media reports about Willowbrook State School instrumental in bringing about disability reform?

9. What does Joni's reflection on the National Council on Disability's reception say to us today?

10. Has this brief historical look on disability impacted your thinking? In what ways?

The *Global Reach* of Disability

OBJECTIVES

Studying this lesson will help you:

✔ Discuss the needs of people with disabilities in developing countries. [1]

✔ Understand the cultural perceptions and attitudes that impact the disability community.

✔ Appreciate the significance of international declarations supporting people with disabilities.

✔ Describe international opportunities in disability ministry and education.

✔ Understand how to get involved in the global disability community.

Teo grew up knowing his place in life. His family owned a coffee plantation in the tiny mountain village of Jesus De Otoro, Honduras. Teo would work the land, as his father had before him, build a house and provide for his children. But his dreams crumbled when the unthinkable happened. A farming accident took away the use of Teo's legs along with his livelihood, his future, and his freedom. Trapped in his house, this once hard-working young man slipped into despondency. Although Teo's life was turned upside down, he still had the love and support of his friends and family. In many countries people with disabilities are shunned and treated as cursed outcasts.

The United Nations estimates that 10 percent of the world's population lives with disabilities.[2] More than three-quarters of them live in developing countries, where poverty is the general rule. They're on the lowest end of the social and economic scale, surviving only on their humanity and courage to stay alive. Even in relatively rich countries in Europe and North America, many people with disabilities live in isolation and poverty. When a Joni and Friends Wheels for the World team visited Teo's village, they brought him a second chance in more ways than one.

"God's gift of a wheelchair has given me freedom," Teo says. "And spiritually, I have been given an even greater gift. Jesus changed my life and took me into a new future." Today, Teo has a beautiful wife and child. He works as a wheelchair mechanic at a Joni and Friends repair shop, using his mechanical skills to give others the same freedom he found. "To be useful and capable, to be able to work and support my family is a return to my manhood," Teo says. "Jesus restored all this to me and more, beginning the day he brought a wheelchair to my life."

Joni and Friends is only one of the dedicated Christian ministries and organizations that are reaching out to families affected by disability around the world, but many more willing hands are needed.

℞ *Community*

The absence of community breeds isolation. The price of isolation is splintered lives and damaged societies. People with disabilities, who live in every community, often experience this destruction firsthand. As the world contracts into a technological, global village, Christians must represent God's design of authentic kinship—the kind that mends broken lives and nurtures faith communities for all people.

I. Worldviews of People with Disability

- 15% of the world's population—some 785 million people—have a disability, according to the latest reports from a study by the World Health Organization and the World Bank.[3]

- 90% of children with disabilities in developing countries do not attend school, according to UNESCO.

- In some countries, 80% of people with disabilities are unemployed.

- For every child killed in warfare, three are injured and acquire a permanent disability.[4]

A. How Core Beliefs Become Worldviews

Our worldviews are shaped by our core beliefs, which have been molded by the values of our parents and communities. Whether we choose to admit it or not, our behaviors speak volumes about the things we value in life. Our collective actions only serve to raise the volume until they resound with a tune of acceptable norms which define social culture. And very few people march to their own drum.

B. Religious Attitudes Impact the Disability Community

In certain religions and social systems people with disabilities are shunned, viewed as cursed, treated as objects

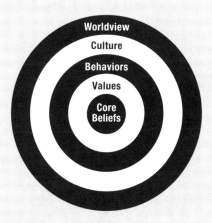

Core Beliefs are ideas that we hold to be true about the world and form our realities.

Values are ideals people or societies hold to be good or worthy based on our beliefs. Values affect our judgment of what actions can or cannot be compromised.

Behaviors are influenced by values. Every personal or societal behavior is simply a form of living out what one believes.

Culture results from common behaviors in families and in a society that become "Societal Norms." These norms guide our collective actions and define what is socially acceptable. These acceptable norms are another term for culture. This definition is an over-simplification, since there are many sub-cultures within each culture formed by other activities, such as arts and music. Nevertheless, even the most complex cultural phenomenon can be traced back to a set of basic, core beliefs.

Worldviews are the result of collective perspectives, through which people understand the world around them. They form the basis of how people live their lives; i.e. their "View of the World."

Our core beliefs—based on our backgrounds, religions and social systems—are the greatest influence on our worldviews. Unfortunately, most of our worldviews about persons with disabilities have developed with limited facts and inaccurate information. These limitations have lead to harmful attitudes and unwarranted fears. Worldviews have also distorted religious beliefs, leading to the greatest falsehoods.

of charity, shamed or dishonored. The United Kingdom's Department for International Development reports that the mortality rate for children with disabilities may be as high as 80 percent in poor countries, adding that in some cases it seems as if these children are being targeted and "weeded out." [5]

While most world religions have sacred writings that speak of love, mercy and benevolent service, many of them fail to apply these virtues to people with disabilities. This is due to their faulty worldview on suffering and disability, which we'll discuss in Module 2. The following descriptions are not intended to represent the formal religious views of disability by these religions, rather they are sketches of the realistic outcomes of religious views that are not biblically-based.

1. In Hinduism a person with disabilities is thought to have "bad karma" and is demoted to the lowest social class.

2. In Islam a person with disabilities is seen as an object of charity or a disgrace in a "shame and honor" culture. A disability is that person's fate.

3. Under Communism people with disabilities are identified as non-contributors in society, and therefore, they are of no use.

4. Buddhism tells a person with a disability to deny and ignore his or her plight. It simply does not exist.

5. In Spiritism people with disabilities are cursed.

6. Secular Humanists believe that people with disabilities are victims. They can only be integrated into society at a significant expense.

7. Under Fascism a person with disabilities is an economic drain on society.

8. For those who practice "religious legalism" people with disabilities are objects of charity. They are the focus of ministry projects, which highlight results rather

than relationships. The real needs of the disability community are the responsibility of the government, not the religious community.

9. In Christianity, people with disabilities are often seen as "problems" to be fixed or "burdens" to endure rather than "people" to be embraced. Christianity often sees people affected by disability as "victims" to be pitied and ministered "to" instead of ministered "with."

C. Social Stigmas, Taboos and Curses

- A social stigma is a mark of disgrace for a person (or family), bringing bad luck, or a punishment for sins he or she committed. As a result, those with disabilities are excluded from education, employment and community activities. Social stigmas leave people to beg for just enough to survive. Those without disabilities give alms, not out of compassion, but in order to obtain spiritual grace and forgiveness for themselves.

- Taboos are prohibitions imposed by social customs. The prohibition may be against touching or speaking to a person with a disability for fear of immediate harm from a supernatural force. In some cultures, a taboo is tribal law.

- A curse is a calamity or disaster pronounced on someone by another person, a higher being or a mythical deity. Curses are believed to cause bad or evil things to happen to the person who has been cursed and/or to their family. Some cultures believe people have become disabled as the result of a curse placed upon them. Therefore, they are marginalized in the community.

For over 10 years, Rev. James Rene, Director of Internships at the Christian Institute on Disability, has lead ministry teams to many developing countries and witnessed the abuses caused by these erroneous ideologies. Rev. Rene is passionate about teaching biblical truths that free people with disabilities from these chains. He works to empower national church leaders.

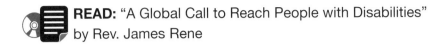

READ: "A Global Call to Reach People with Disabilities" by Rev. James Rene

Have you personally ever confronted any of the religious tenets or stigmas that Rev. Rene described? How did you respond?

II. **The 60ᵗʰ Anniversary of the Universal Declaration of Human Rights**

In the previous lesson, we discovered that attitudes toward the disability community changed after World War II. When the United Nations adopted the Universal Declaration of Human Rights in 1948, it was considered one of the most ground-breaking documents ever written and brought renewed hope for people with disabilities. However, it took several decades before discussions on the floor of the United Nations began to move from seeing disability through the lens of a welfare mentality to a dialogue on the true meaning of human rights.

READ: The Preamble of The Universal Declaration of Human Rights
http://www.un.org/en/documents/udhr/

While the Declaration has provided a framework for standards of civil societies, its success faltered due to the United Nations' lack of power to enforce its principles on the world stage. As a result, by the time the U.N. began planning the 60ᵗʰ Anniversary celebration of the Declaration in 2008, some groups were calling for governments to apologize for six decades of human rights failures and to recommit themselves to concrete improvements.[6]

The United Nations' efforts to bring dignity to the disability community have continued in endeavors such as:

- 1981—The International Year of Disabled Persons
- 1982—The World Programme of Action concerning Disabled Persons
- 1983-1992—The United Nations Decade of Disabled Persons
- 1994—The Standard Rules on the Equalization of Opportunities for Persons with Disabilities

- 2005—International Holocaust Remembrance Day (January 27)[7]
- 2006—The Convention on the Rights of Persons with Disabilities, the first major human rights instrument of the 21st century.[8]

Soon Christian denominations began to recognize the needs and organized to provide greater support for persons with disabilities:

- 1978—Pastoral Statement of U.S. Catholic Bishops on People with Disabilities was adopted by the United States Conference of Catholic Bishops. http://www.ncpd.org/views-news-policy/policy/church/bishops/pastoral
- 1982—The 67th General Convention of the Episcopal Church established a Task Force on Disabled and Handicapped Persons to encourage opportunities within the church. http://www.disability99.org/id41.html
- 1985—Jean Vanier founded the International Federation of L'Arche to serve men and women with intellectual disabilities. Today L'Arche is in 135 communities in 36 countries. http://www.larche.org
- 1998—The National Council of Churches published a Policy Statement, "Disabilities, the Body of Christ and the Wholeness of Society," and in 2000 created "The Accessible Congregations Campaign." http://www.ncccusa.org/news/00news86.html

---

READ: The Preamble of the Convention on
Rights of Persons with Disabilities
http://www.un.org/disabilities/convention/conventionfull.shtml

---

"We seek to be communities where people, whatever their race, religion, culture, abilities or disabilities, can find a place and reveal their gifts to the world."

JEAN VANIER

III. WE SPEAK TO NATIONS... BE FREE!

"Declare His glory among the nations, His marvelous deeds among all peoples."—Psalm 96:3

Joni Eareckson Tada's best-selling biography, *Joni*, catapulted her onto a national stage in 1979, and led her to launch Joni and Friends. Since then she has personally visited more than 45 countries. She is a highly sought-after conference speaker both in the U.S. and overseas. Joni's numerous articles and over 35 books have been translated into many languages. The Joni and Friends five-minute radio program is heard on over 1,000 broadcast outlets and has received the "Radio Program of the Year" award from the National Religious Broadcasters. In 2008, her ministry expanded through the "Joni and Friends Television Series," airing on television networks around the world.

As Joni reflected on her 31 years of ministry, she saw how God had expanded the territory of Joni and Friends in disability ministry to the far reaches of the world. That's why Joni chose "We Speak to Nations... Be Free!" as JAF's 2011 ministry theme. It's from Psalm 96:3, a verse very close to her heart. "I believe God wants to not only change the landscape of the American church, but of the worldwide church," Joni said.

Since its inception, Joni and Friends has been dedicated to extending the love and message of Christ to people who are affected by disability around the globe. They are committed to recruiting, training, and motivating new generations of people with disabilities to become leaders in their churches and communities. Joni's books have been translated into over 43 languages and read in houses, huts, chalets and shacks.

Today, the Joni and Friends International Disability Center serves as the administrative hub for an array of programs which provide outreach to the worldwide disability community. These include the Wheels for the World international wheelchair distribution ministry; Family Retreats, which provide respite for those with disabilities and their families; Field Services to provide church training along with educational and inspirational resources at a local level; and various worldwide partnerships with ministry associates and affiliates.

In 2007, Joni and Friends established a key department, The Christian Institute on Disability (CID). The Institute is aggressively promoting life, human dignity and the value of all individuals—despite their disabling condition—from a biblical perspective.

 VIEW: Wheels for the World (Joni and Friends DVDTV12)

IV. Join the Global Disability Movement

A. New Educational Opportunities
Rev. Steve Bundy, Vice President of Joni and Friends, is amazed by the number of requests he receives from

international colleges and seminaries. "Since 2000, Joni and Friends has been expanding our involvement in international ministry by affiliating with like-minded, Christ-centered ministries abroad," says Rev. Bundy. "These partners are committed to heightening disability awareness within their churches and communities, and to equipping and training leaders to serve people affected by disability. Because of the enormous opportunities for disability ministry and curriculum to be strategically placed in international ministries, our International Outreach Department is working with churches, Christian non-government organizations and institutes of higher learning in over 30 countries."

In 2010, a group of international teachers became students when 60 people, representing 27 countries, attended a disability ministry course through a partnership with Joni and Friends and The Master's Academy International. The 32-hour course served as the launching pad for what leaders from both organizations believe is the start of a fruitful partnership. Upon completion of the course, the teachers were challenged to use the training to equip pastors and leaders in their own countries.

New courses have also been well-received in U.S. colleges, according to Rev. Bundy. "When Biola University in Southern California offered its first-ever course on the theology of suffering and disability, registration filled up within one hour," Rev. Bundy said. "Through partnerships with the Joni and Friends Christian Institute on Disability, California Baptist University now offers a master's degree in disability studies—the first of its kind from a Christian institution—on campus and online."[9]

During the 2010 World Conference on Evangelism in Cape Town, South Africa, Rev. Bundy highlighted what he sees as a global awakening to disability ministry. "We are by no means the trailblazers in the disability movement. We follow in the footsteps of compassionate leaders like Jean Vanier, founder of L'Arche and Henri Nouwen, who lived out his faith by moving to a L'Arche community.[10] We join a historical and global faith community in educating and equipping tomorrow's ministry leaders," Bundy explained. The following paper is an excerpt from his presentation.

READ: "Hope for the Global Disability Community"
by Rev. Steve Bundy

Rev. Bundy claims there is a growing global disability ministry movement. Do you agree or disagree?

What signs have you observed that offer hope for the millions of people affected by disability in developing countries?

B. **International Networking Opportunities**

Mission-minded religious organizations are continuously seeking Christians "ready to roll their sleeves up" to serve in developing countries. Volunteers and short-term missionaries can be a voice for adults and children with disabilities. Many denominations offer missions opportunities. Global conferences such as Lausanne Committee on World Evangelization (www.lausanne.org), Through the Roof (www.throughtheroof.org), Christian Blind Mission (CBM) International (www.cbm.org), and the World Council of Churches (www.oikoumene.org) open many people's eyes to the needs of the disability community. Visionary leaders in the disability community have expressed the need for a global conference on disability ministry to exchange ideas and facilitate ministry in developing countries. In Module 3 we'll discuss additional networking opportunities with disability ministries and organizations.

The Annual International Day of Persons with Disabilities—December 3rd

This is a special day to take stock of the status of one of the world's largest and most neglected groups, who face colossal obstacles in their efforts to lead a meaningful life and benefit from the full range of human rights and development opportunities available to other members of their societies. For more information on how to get involved visit the United Nations Enable website at

http://www.un.org/disabilities/default.asp?id=109.

Then share what you've learned with your family and friends.

Reflections on Lesson 4
The Global Reach of Disability

1. What is a worldview? How does our worldview affect people with disabilities?

2. Give examples of a social stigma, taboo and curse.

3. According to Rev. Rene's paper, what does the Bible teach about cures for people with disabilities?

4. List some of the needs people with disabilities have in developing countries.

5. As you read the Preamble of the Universal Declaration on Human Rights, which points most stood out to you and why?

6. Have the human rights efforts of the United Nations succeeded or failed? Why?

7. Describe the characteristics of the members of the Wheels for the World Team in the video you watched.

8. If you could serve people with disabilities as an international intern or missionary, which country would you choose and why?

MODULE 2

The Theology of
Suffering and Disability

The Theology of Suffering and Disability

Historically, the church has often been slow to embrace individuals and families affected by disability. In this module, as we examine why this is true, we discover that one of the factors involves a somewhat faulty view of the sovereignty of God and his perspective of disability. Unfortunately, religion has often been a source of hurtful myth such as the idea that a lack of faith can prevent people from being healed and that people with disabilities are cursed. This kind of flawed thinking can disillusion people, sending them into a downward spiral of despair and hopelessness.

We also look at why Christian doctrine matters and how it shapes what we believe. A closer look at Scripture clearly presents an overview of disability from Genesis to Revelation. We'll look at the Luke 14 Mandate and the teachings of Jesus that challenged the religious and cultural views of his day, as well as our contemporary views. One of the most powerful mandates in the New Testament calls for the house of God to be filled with people affected by disabilities. Thus, our challenge must be to discover our individual roles in bringing them into the church and into the family of God.

In the study of these biblical truths, we'll hear about real people who have journeyed through disability, like my friend Nick Vujicic, who was born with no arms and no legs. But Nick found God's plan and purpose for his life through understanding the sovereignty of God. I know you will enjoy the readings, the lectures, and discussions in Module 2. My prayer is that you will be both challenged and inspired.

Rev. Steve Bundy

God's *Sovereignty* and Human Freedom:
A Scriptural Perspective

Most Christians would find it impossible to recall how many sermons they've heard in their lifetime. For some, the number would be in the thousands, on countless topics. But how many sermons have you heard on the virtues of pain? Dilemmas about suffering and disability raise difficult questions about the sovereignty of God. Whether it addresses a paralyzing accident that cuts short the life of an actor like Christopher Reeves, or a neighbor's child who is left profoundly disabled after nearly drowning, a three-point sermon outline cannot answer life's hardest questions. On the contrary, man's attempts to answer can sometimes lead to splintered views on the sovereignty of God in our world as well as in our personal lives as Christ-followers.

Some people believe that God stands back as an observer of the historical and current affairs of mankind, participating only when invited into the situation. Many are influenced by popular books such as *When Bad Things Happen to Good People* by Rabbi Harold S. Kushner. According to Kushner, God is a bystander who neither causes nor participates in any tragedy we might face. His only role is to come alongside us after the fact. If this were true, how can we call God the Supreme Ruler of the universe?

In the next four lessons, we'll discuss the evangelical Christian doctrines of God's sovereignty, our human calamities, Satan's role in suffering and our hope in Christ. You may hold different views than the ones presented here. If so, we encourage you to search God's Word and prayerfully take your questions to him. This is a struggle that impacts every person regardless of race or nationality, as represented by this statement from the Lausanne Committee on World Evangelization:

> *God may not initiate all our trials, including diseases, birth deformities and injuries, but by the time they reach us, they are his will for us for whatever time and purpose that he determines.*[1]

OBJECTIVES

Studying this lesson will help you:

✔ Explain from Scripture the sovereignty of God over all things, including disability.

✔ Describe some views on God's sovereignty and human freedom throughout church history.

✔ Explain how God is sovereign, but not responsible for sin.

✔ Understand the decrees of God's will as both directive and permissive.

✔ Recognize Christianity as a knowledge tradition, as well as a "seeking" faith.

Authority

We rebel against, blame and yet yearn for strong leadership. Ever since the Garden of Eden, man has struggled with obedience and submission to God's sovereignty. Our culture feeds this drive for autonomy and independence, while Scripture points to the potter and the clay. Can we truly be pliable in God's hands and trust him, even when things make no sense?

I. Has Doctrine Become a "Dirty" Word?

As we saw in Lesson 3, history has proven that churches have been incredibly slow to embrace families affected by disability. While leaders continue to offer excuses such as inadequate facilities, resources and volunteers, the core of the problem may be hiding in a faulty view of the sovereignty of God. How we view our relationship with God affects how we see the world, especially the world of disability. Dr. Dallas Willard, author and professor of philosophy at the University of Southern California, stresses the holistic quality that is required: "Christian spiritual formation is the process through which the embodied/reflective will takes on the character of Christ's will. It is the process through which (and you know Gal. 4:19) Christ is formed in you and me."[2] One father of three children with severe disabilities describes it this way: "In my observation, people who display a close walk with God are naturally drawn to my children, touching them and talking to them, even though my children are non-verbal. But others who admittedly struggle with their faith tend to walk on the other side of the hall at church, hardly noticing my children."

Without clear statements of belief, the church itself is in danger of becoming a "disabled body." Dr. Kathy McReynolds, Director of Academic Studies at the Christian Institute on Disability, is concerned. She has observed that when believers forsake Christian doctrine, they not only neglect their high calling to minister to and protect the most vulnerable, but they fail to make use of the divine tools God gave them to engage culture. As you read the following paper, consider Dr. McReynolds' emphasis on the importance of doctrine, calling it "energetic, dramatic, and utterly alive."

READ: "Why Christian Doctrine Matters"
by Dr. Kathy McReynolds

> *Do your best to present yourself to God as one*
> *approved, a workman who does not need to be ashamed*
> *and who correctly handles the word of truth.*
> 2 Timothy 2:15

II. The God of Scripture Is Steadfast, Not Stony

It is difficult to see news photos of starving children in Africa, elderly adults crippled by hurricanes in Haiti or soldiers blinded by landmines in war zones without questioning God's goodness and mercy. These realities make no sense to the human mind. Yet the Bible gives us clear insight that as tragic as life can be sometimes, we have a loving God, who in his sovereignty holds us in the palm of his hand (John 10:28-29).

As Christians, we may question the love of God during crises, especially if we do not have a biblical perspective on the sovereignty of God. The word *sovereignty* denotes that God is ultimately in control of all circumstances and situations in our lives, including suffering and disability—that is, whether by means of causing or allowing such events.

In his book *Suffering and the Sovereignty of God*, John Piper writes:

> God is absolute and eternal and infinite. Everything else and everybody else is dependent and finite and contingent. God himself is the great supreme value. Everything else that has any value has it by connection to God. God is supreme in all things. He has all authority, all power, all wisdom—and he is good "to those who wait for him, to the soul who seeks him" (Lam. 3:25)...And what I mean...when I say that God is sovereign is not merely that God has the power and right to govern all things, but that he does govern all things for his own wise and holy purposes.[3]

A Christian Evangelical Position on the Sovereignty of God

The theological position of Joni and Friends is that the sovereignty of God is in, over and through all circumstances. God is concerned about human suffering and calls his people to respond with com-

From Joni's Desk

"Does this mean that God wants disease and injury?"

Scripture indicates that not only is God sovereign to physical injuries or illness, but he is Lord over the changes and alterations that transpire within the womb (Ps. 139:13,15-17). The key here is how we use the word "want." God doesn't want disease to exist in the sense that he enjoys it. He hates it just as he hates all the other results of sin—death, guilt, sorrow and catastrophes. But God must want disease to exist in the sense that he wills or chooses for it to exist. If he didn't, he would wipe it out immediately. So God is neither frustrated nor hindered by Satan's schemes, but he permits suffering to serve his own ends and accomplish his own purposes.[4]

passion. Whether your position is that God *causes* or *allows* suffering, in any case, he permitted it to enter human history. He is involved in our pre-suffering and post-suffering, as well as present in all circumstances of our lives. All humanity experiences suffering.

III. The God of Scripture Acts with Power and Purpose

Is God really in control? This is a question Nick Vujicic hears a lot from the millions of people who come to hear him speak all over the world. Nick is a businessman with a college education, an author and an inspirational speaker. His website has received millions of hits, and he achieved all this before his twenty-eighth birthday. Yet Nick's greatest desire is to live a life that showcases the sovereignty of God, and he's quick to admit that it requires a daily surrender.

 VIEW: I've Got Questions (Joni and Friends DVDTV08)

When you saw that Nick has no arms and no legs, what were your first thoughts about him?

What questions did Nick ask God? Have you ever struggled with some of the same questions? Why was Nick able to accept his disability and surrender his life completely to God?

You can learn more about Nick's ministry, Life Without Limbs, at www.lifewithoutlimbs.org.

A. The Decrees of God

There comes a time in our lives when we, like Nick, must wrestle with the decrees of God, which have been established in eternity past, present and future. God's decrees declare his sovereign control over every realm and over all events. Ephesians 1:11 tells us that he "works out everything in conformity with the purpose of his will."

READ: Romans 9:11 and 11:33-36; Psalm 104:24; Proverbs 3:19

A decree is a single plan encompassing all things. A decree of God is a wise plan because God is wise, as well as omniscient, omnipresent and omnipotent. His plan is perfect because he is perfect.

A decree of God has two aspects:

1. In the *directive* will of God, we see there are some things of which God is the author, that is, he directly brings about the events: he creates (Isa. 45:18), he controls the universe (Dan. 4:35), he establishes kings and governments (Dan. 2:21).

> "The decrees of God are his eternal purpose, according to the counsel of his will, whereby, for his own glory, he had foreordained whatsoever comes to pass."
> **The Westminster Shorter Catechism of 1647, question 7**

2. In the *permissive* will of God, he may bring about his will through secondary causes. For example, God doesn't bring about sinful acts. Man is responsible for his own actions, but God often uses those sinful acts to fulfill his will and purpose (Gen. 50:19-20; Acts 2:23; 4:27-28).

B. **God's Decrees Over Crisis, Life and Death**

No trial, disease, illness, accident or injury reaches us apart from God's permission. Throughout the Scriptures we are confronted with this truth:

- Who can speak and have it happen if the Lord has not decreed it? Is it not from the mouth of the Most High that both calamities and good things come? Lamentations 3:37-38
- I form the light and create darkness, I bring prosperity and create disaster, I, the Lord, do all these things. Isaiah 45:7
- You know quite well that we were destined for [trials]. 1 Thessalonians 3:3
- [God] works out everything in conformity with the purpose of his will. Ephesians 1:11

Pastor and scholar John MacArthur says believers should not be surprised or resentful when they encounter difficulties because God has told us to expect them. In his book *The Power of Suffering: Strengthening Your Faith in the Refiner's Fire*, MacArthur writes:

> One primary reason many believers today have a hard time accepting the role of suffering in their

lives or in the lives of friends and loved ones is that they have failed to understand and accept the reality of divine sovereignty. Many also fail to see adversity from God's perspective.... The reality is the sovereignty of God, which, when rightly understood and properly embraced, serves as the foundational lens through which Christians may see all truth in Scripture more clearly. Knowing about God's sovereignty in all things does not mean we will have comprehensive understanding, but it gives us a proper hope in midst of the more difficult and less clear aspects of His working in our lives (Gen. 18:25; Isa. 55:9).[5]

IV. **The God of Scripture Is Sovereign over Disabilities: From Genesis to Revelation**

In biblical times, the treatment of people with disabilities ranged from cruel rejection to becoming objects of pagan worship. Among Israel's neighbors, babies with disabilities were left to die from exposure. If they survived, their miseries included being taken advantage of as beggars or prostitutes and facing a premature death. At the other extreme, an Egyptian king was thought to be supernatural and was worshiped because of his disfigurement. Mankind may shun those with disabilities or laud them, but what does the Bible say?

Disabilities: From Genesis to Revelation

A. **Genesis to Exodus: God Gave Us a Beginning Without Disabilities**

Ultimately, God is responsible for disabilities, as he himself points out in Exodus. However, in the beginning there were no disabilities. When sin entered the world through Adam and Eve, it brought pain, suffering, disability and even death with it (Gen. 3:1-24).

B. **Exodus to Deuteronomy: God's Gracious Law Makes Provision for Disability**

As Creator, God assumes responsibility for disabilities. When Moses questioned his own ability to speak for God, the Lord told him, "Who has made man's mouth? Who makes him mute, or deaf or blind? It is I, the Lord!" (Exodus 4:11). That is ownership!

C. **Isaiah to Malachi: God's Prophets Promise Future Hope for Disability**

God will establish people with disabilities (Micah 4:6-7) and will deliver them from oppressors (Zeph. 3:19).

D. **Matthew to Revelation: Jesus Offers Hope and a Way for Disability**

In his paper, "God's Story of Disability," Dr. David Deuel writes: "When Jesus came to earth, in addition to dying on the cross for sin, his mission was to repair the effects of the curse and fulfill what the law commanded. He revealed what wisdom prescribed and the prophets had predicted for persons with disabilities. As his commissioned agents, we continue the work he began. Yet, many are surprised to discover that part of God's plan for people with disabilities was to not only glorify Jesus, but also minister to others— not just in their disabilities, but because of them."

1. Jesus had compassion for people with disabilities (Matt. 20:34; Mark 1:42; John 9:1-3).

2. Jesus brought glory to God by healing people with disabilities (Matt. 15:30-31).

3. Jesus demonstrated that he is God by healing people with disabilities (Luke 7:22).

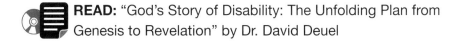 **READ:** "God's Story of Disability: The Unfolding Plan from Genesis to Revelation" by Dr. David Deuel

Reflecting on Dr. Deuel's paper, how do you think God himself views disabilities? How is his view different or similar to your own view of disabilities?

These are very important questions because, while this lesson highlights the scriptural truths concerning God's sovereignty over all things, there is room within the biblical and evangelical scope for varying views concerning the relationship between God's sovereignty and human freedom. This is evident in the various models of providence that have been developed in the history of Christian thought. In other words, models of providence can be divided into two broad categories: general sovereignty vs. specific sovereignty:

- Specific sovereignty holds that God decrees everything that happens, including disability, in advance. This is more or less the view that has been laid out in this lesson.
- General sovereignty holds that God intentionally limits the use of some of his power and allows certain things, like disability, to occur. The rationale for this view is that if humans fell into sin, God must have limited his abilities in order to allow for human freedom.

However, God is still at work in the world; he is not like the watchmaker who wound the clock and then stepped away from it. God is still all-powerful and he knows the future and allows certain things, like disability, to happen. He knows how we will respond, and he provides his grace and guidance in order to ultimately accomplish his purposes. The point is that there is some room within Christian orthodoxy to allow for variations on divine decrees, providence and free will. Our challenge is to search the Scriptures for ourselves as we seek to faithfully interpret and understand its multi-faceted truths. As has been stated, Christian doctrine matters precisely because it is true for all people for all time. [6]

V. Christianity's Great Fortress: True Knowledge

The scientific and medical discoveries of the 21st century, which are allowed according to the sovereignty of God, are being used to explain away the very existence of God. To the new atheists, who write some of today's best-selling books, science has made Christianity an old-fashioned, powerless dogma—a worthless credo. They say Christians have an imaginary God and claim that science proposes ways to create a better society by appealing to human intellect rather than some alleged, absolute *Truth*. And in response, many religious leaders teach that Christianity is essentially a profession of faith, rather than a body of knowledge. "Christian doctrines are not merely creeds to which we believers down through the ages have given a vote of approval," says Dr. Kathy McReynolds. "It is time for the church to take back what rightly belongs to her; that is the truth that Christianity is a knowledge tradition."

 **READ:** "Christianity: A Knowledge Tradition" by Dr. Kathy McReynolds

It is only human to grapple with God's *Truth* for each and every life situation. Christian pastors and counselors often sit across from hurting parents. What would you say to a parent whose child was born with a serious disability and faced years of pain and uncertainty?

Pastor Lon Solomon, whose daughter has multiple disabilities, confidently tells parents that Almighty God sent their child into their lives for his own divine purpose. It doesn't matter to him if you call it God's direct or permissive will. In his book, *Brokenness,* Solomon goes on to say:

> Now you may have a bigger problem with the idea of a God who personally afflicted a child with a disability and sent him into these parents' lives than with the idea that God simply allowed this to happen. May I suggest that there really is no difference between the two concepts? If God is truly the sovereign God of the universe as he claims, then what he allows is synonymous with what he sends...Regardless of the intermediate causes of any given affliction, we must realize that the sovereign controller of all things in the universe is making the final choices. Even Satan himself has no independent authority in this universe. God orchestrates every circumstance that touches every life to accomplish his perfect purpose. There are no accidents, coincidences or acts of fate in this world.[7]

In Lesson 6, we will continue to see how God's sovereignty triumphs over the evil Satan devises to bring us the redemptive work of Jesus Christ.

 GROUP DISCUSSION

What are some evidences of God's sovereignty in your lives?

Where is it easy to surrender to his reign and where is it most difficult? Share several ways you might better represent what you believe about God in your daily life.

Reflections on Lesson 5

God's Sovereignty and Human Freedom: A Scriptural Perspective

1. Why is a doctrinal position on God's sovereignty so vital to understanding suffering?

2. Consider a time you personally questioned God's authority in your life. What helped you find his purposes?

3. According to the Scriptures, what is God's role in suffering and disabilities?

4. Is God sovereign over man's sin? Why or why not?

5. How did the story of the man who was born blind in John 9:1-12 help Nick Vujicic understand the sovereignty of God?

6. Explain the difference between the *directive* will of God and the *permissive* will of God.

7. What defenses do we have against the powerful attacks on Christianity by the new atheists?

8. Describe how you would counsel an individual with a physical disability who was questioning their faith in God.

The Problem of *Evil & Suffering* in Our World

OBJECTIVES

Studying this lesson will help you:

✔ Explain the problem of evil and suffering from a biblical perspective.

✔ Understand some secular views on the problem of evil and suffering.

✔ Discuss the problem of evil in light of God's sovereignty.

✔ Describe some purposes of suffering from a biblical perspective.

✔ Appreciate redemption in light of the problem of evil and suffering.

In Lesson 6 we will discuss evil and suffering in the broader context as it relates to the Fall of Man recorded in Genesis 3. This is not to say that disabilities or people with disabilities are evil (or sinful) in any way, or that everyone with a disability is suffering. In fact, many in the disability community would say that they don't *suffer* nor consider themselves as "sufferers" any more than their friends without disabilities. Our purpose here is to contrast the fallen world we live in with the goodness of God's plan for our lives.

From Joni's Desk

"I need God in my suffering."

When we wonder why we must suffer, we're actually asking questions of someone. That someone is God. But why he created suffering doesn't really matter. The only thing that matters is how we respond. When we can't find the answers we're looking for, we can find peace in the only true answer: We need him! Affliction is the lowest common denominator for all of us.

In Philippians 1:29, the Bible tells us to expect suffering: "For it has been granted to you on behalf of Christ not only to believe on him, but also to suffer for him." No matter how strong our faith is, it's natural to ask why.

After many years of suffering, I've concluded that God allows one form of evil, suffering, to expose another form of evil, sin. It is as if God turns suffering on its head and helps us to feel the sting of sin when we suffer so that as we are headed for heaven we're reminded of how poisonous sin really is. So suffering is this jackhammer, a sand blasting machine that strips away the fear, anxiety, self-centeredness, complaining and "I don't care" attitude toward others who hurt. God allows

Continued
on next page

🔑 Surrender

Jesus willingly laid down his life; no man took it from him. Through surrendering to the evil that nailed him to the cross, Jesus found joy in his suffering. Thus, it's true for us, that only in our own total surrender can we discover God's purposes in life's most painful circumstances. And when we do, we join a fellowship of sufferers who continuously overcome evil by offering God their sacrifices of praise.

I. Suffering Creates Victims or Victors

One minute Jim and Janet Slaight were enjoying the first day of summer vacation with their four children and in the next they were being whisked away in separate ambulances, leaving behind the lifeless body of their four-year-old daughter. Their world was turned upside-down when an on-coming car hit their van traveling over 90 miles per hour. At the scene, Janet recalled gaining consciousness just long enough to hear her oldest daughter crying and to see emergency responders kneeling near the wreckage, weeping. All Janet could do was call out to God.

While some may say this family had become victims of Satan's evil plot to destroy their faith and witness, the Slaights consider themselves *victors* rather than *victims* of some cruel fate.

The scientific study of the relationship between victims and their offenders is called "victimology." It is most closely associated with the criminal justice system, but can also include human rights violations. Individuals who consider themselves victims often experience fear, anger, nervousness, guilt and shame. They have difficulty sleeping, feel negative about themselves and vulnerable in society.

It is important to note that *suffering* does not necessarily have the same connotation as "being a *victim*." Many people with disabilities do not consider themselves victims any more than the rest of humankind. While they acknowledge the real suffering that can result from disability, it is incorrect to generalize that all people with disabilities are victims. Unfortunately, more suffering comes ***not*** as the result of a disability, but as a consequence of the attitudes and actions of individuals and society.

A. **Suffering, The Great Equalizer**

At some time in life, everyone experiences one or all of the four main categories of suffering, whether they're disabled or not. However, the degree and duration of our suffering may be very different. Some people with disabilities may undergo deeper levels of suffering in most of these categories than those without disabilities. Their experiences may also be life-long, rather than a one-time "crisis" with a beginning and end.

Categories of Suffering

1. **Physical suffering** can include bodily pain and discomfort, as well as cognitive and mental health issues.

2. **Spiritual suffering** is a consequence of sin and separation from God.

3. **Emotional suffering** is brought on by circumstances of life such as heartbreak, divorce, loss of a loved one and other disappointments.

4. **Social and/or cultural suffering** involves socio-religious, socio-economic, and/or socio-political discrimination and segregation.

Causes of Suffering

1. **Circumstances**—Because we live in a fallen world, disability is often the result of tragedy, illness, disease or defect. James 1:2-4; Rom. 8:19-20

2. **Persecution**—Suffering in the name of Jesus is found throughout Scripture. Heb. 11:23-38; John 15:18-19; 2 Tim. 3:12; Philip. 3:10

3. **Discipline of God**—God's correction leads to repentance and growth, exemplified by a child learning from repercussions or a vine growing after being pruned. Heb. 12:5-11; John 15:2, Heb. 5:8

From Joni's Desk
Continued

affliction to rip all of that away so that we can see the world through the eyes of Christ.

God hates evil and suffering. He tells us in his Word to relieve suffering, and he relieves it every day. We can be sure if our hearts hurt for someone, God felt that pain first. He felt my pain first. Our souls are strengthened through suffering. To know God better, we must know our suffering better. And as we do, we become less "me" focused and more God focused.

Who shall separate us from the love of Christ? Shall trouble or hardship or persecution or famine or nakedness or danger or sword? No, in all these things we are more than conquerors through him who loved us.

ROMANS 8:35,37

B. **Satan, The Great Victimizer**

The Bible describes Satan as "the god of this age" (2 Cor. 4:4). He is at war with the kingdom of God and his battle plan is to destroy mankind. These demonic forces have the capacity to harass and torment humans, tempting them to do all kinds of evil. They can even afflict individuals with mental oppression and physical infirmity. There are instances in Scripture where a demonic spirit gained access to a person's soul (mind, will and emotions) or physical body. However, as we discussed in our lesson on global disability and history, it is a tragic error to assume that all disabilities are caused by Satan's evil plan. People around the globe have been greatly harmed by false deliverance sessions where demonic curses are thought to be broken.

The Book of Revelation assures us that Satan and his demonic entities have already been defeated by Christ's work on the cross. They will be eternally damned in the lake of fire, but until then they will try to take every human soul with them. [1]

C. **The Problem of Evil**

Some Christians become disillusioned in their faith and abandon hope because of their experiences with suffering and evil. They reason that if God is all-good and all-powerful, evil things would not happen. So, since evil does exist, God must either not be good or not be powerful enough to eliminate evil from our lives. The problem of evil is a complex issue that has inspired many books on *theodicy*, which is the study of God's goodness v. evil in the world. In this lesson, we will not take an exhaustive look at this subject, but encourage further study. [2] There are three traditional theodicies: 1) Free Will Defense, 2) Natural Order Defense, and 3) Greater Good Defense.

1. **Free Will Defense** says evil is not a thing; rather, it is the absence or loss of good. It is not coeternal with God, nor is it something God created. It was brought into the world by man's free choice. God allows evil because it gives man the ability to choose between what is good or perfect and what is evil or imperfect. For man to truly be in relation to God, he must choose to do so.

2. **Natural Order Defense** says suffering is a result of man's free choice or of natural events that occur as a result of The Fall. Since suffering is thereby not a moral issue, God doesn't interfere but simply allows events to run their course.

3. **Greater Good Defense** says God does not like evil, but allows it because of the greater good it brings mankind. This includes bringing glory to himself and drawing mankind to him. Ultimately, the good that comes from evil outweighs its negative impact in the world.

While Christians may not agree on a single view, our ministry with those who suffer must always be governed by love. In Dr. David Anderson's book, *Reaching Out and Bringing In*, he emphasizes pastoral care in the midst of these questions.

Even if the person is able to accept the logic in these defenses, they may bring little comfort. When counseling a person who is facing disability-related issues, it is helpful to distinguish between the *problem of evil* (an intellectual and academic concern) and the *problem of suffering* (an existential and practical issue). A proper pastoral response requires knowing which issue the person faces: The problem of evil is an intellectual question requiring an intellectual answer. The problem of suffering, however, is a practical question focusing on everyday matters of coping and resolution. We must discern which question is being asked and respond accordingly: Intellectual answers to practical questions may seem hollow; practical responses to intellectual questions may seem shallow.[3]

D. **Contrasting Religious Views on Suffering**

Christianity offers a unique perspective on our earthly existence and God's relationship with evil and suffering. This view is in sharp contrast with modern secular and postmodern thinking. Chuck Edwards, Director of Bible Study Curriculum at Summit Ministries, writes and speaks on the importance of understanding others' beliefs as a way of strengthening our own moral values and actions. "Every worldview has a certain assumption about nature and the existence of God," says Edwards. "They cannot be proven in the sense of scientific proof or a mathematical equation. This is not to say there are no reasons for holding certain presuppositions, or that some assumptions are therefore more rational than others. But whatever the case, there is a faith element that persists."[4]

In his paper, "Worldview Analysis of Suffering and Disability," Edwards uses three major headings to analyze today's worldviews and compare them with a biblical worldview:

- **Cosmic Humanism** is an umbrella term for the eastern religions of Buddhism and Hinduism. Western-style New Age Spirituality is derived from these two religions. Another, more general term that describes this over-arching worldview is transcendentalism. The Cosmic Worldview assumes that everything that exists is part of god; god is all and in all—The One. Humans are part of the god-force described as goodness, blissful peace and harmony. Suffering is either an illusion or the result of bad Karma from past lives.
- **Naturalism** is the second major heading under investigation. This is divided into two worldviews: Secular Humanism and Postmodernism. The naturalist believes that nature is the ultimate and only reality, and nature has no goal or purpose. The supernatural does not exist, so God, angels and the human soul are manifestations of human imagination, just like leprechauns and unicorns. Thus, human value is simply a choice of the collective society. A disabled person is unlucky and should try to "get out of it." A world without rules, controls or borders is Postmodernism.
- **Theism** includes the worldviews of Islam, Judaism, and Christianity. Theists believe that God is real, personal, all-powerful and all-knowing. For the Jew, suffering comes from sins that need to be repented of and we should work to earn favor with God.

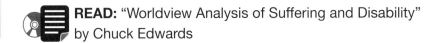 **READ:** "Worldview Analysis of Suffering and Disability" by Chuck Edwards

II. Job, The Victor Over Suffering

The Old Testament story of Job gives us great insight into the sovereignty of God over the temporary rule of Satan in the world.[5] Dr. Larry Waters, Associate Professor of Bible at Dallas Theological Seminary, has written and taught extensively on Job's life. He says, "The Book of Job is a mixture of divine and human wisdom which addresses a major life-issue: why righteous people suffer undeservedly. It shows that the sufferer can question and doubt, face hard questions of life with faith, maintain an unbroken relationship with God, and still come to a satisfactory resolution for personal and collective injustice and undeserved suffering."

 READ: "The Problem of Evil and Suffering" by Dr. Larry Waters

According to Dr. Waters, what are the three areas of Satan's attack of Job?

What impact did Job's friends have upon him and why?

III. Jesus, Our Model for Suffering

In the midst of our darkest hour when all brotherly comfort fails to touch the depth of our pain, Jesus stands with open arms as the ultimate expression of empathy. In his paper, "According to His Compassion," Dr. John MacArthur, Pastor and President of Master's College, says, "God's fullest self-expression came in the Person of Jesus Christ—God in human flesh. The incarnation itself was an expression of sympathy and identification with our weakness (Hebrews 4:15). In Christ we can see countless expressions of divine compassion translated into human idioms that we easily understand and identify with—including sadness, sympathy, and tears of sorrow. Though sinless himself, Jesus suffered all the *consequences* of sin in infinite measure—and in so suffering, he identifies with the misery of all who feel the pains of human anguish."

 READ: "According to His Compassion" by Dr. John MacArthur

Explain Dr. MacArthur's use of the term "divine impassibility."

What parallels does Dr. MacArthur draw between the account of David and Mephibosheth and the compassion of Christ toward society's outcasts?

He was despised and rejected by men, a man of sorrows, and familiar with suffering. Like one from whom men hide their faces he was despised, and we esteemed him not. Surely he took up our infirmities and carried our sorrows, yet we considered him stricken by God, smitten by him, and afflicted.

Isaiah 53:3-4

The **Power** of the **Incarnation**

Scripture reveals that Jesus, although he was fully God, shared in our humanity in every way (Hebrews 2:14-18). While on earth, he lived as a man, and like a man, he suffered. The prophet Isaiah revealed that Jesus "was despised and rejected by men, a man of sorrows, and familiar with suffering" (Isaiah 53:3). Let's consider some of the suffering that Jesus experienced, some of which is much like our own. [6]

Verses	SUFFERING JESUS EXPERIENCED
Matthew 2:13-15	Lived as a refugee in Egypt
Matthew 2:16-18	Knew that his coming had caused the deaths of many baby boys in and around Bethlehem
Matthew 4:1-11	Was tempted by Satan after forty days and nights of fasting—one day for every year the Israelites wandered in the wilderness
Matthew 12:14; John 11:45-53	Jewish religious leaders plotted to kill him.
John 7:12	Some people believed he was a deceiver.
Mark 6:1-4	The people of his hometown rejected him.
John 8:57-59; 10:31-39	At various times, people tried to stone him.
Matthew 23:37-38	Heart ached over Jerusalem's terrible future
Matthew 26:36-40	Was overwhelmed with sorrow and loneliness in Gethsemane
Matthew 26:47-56	Was abandoned by all his disciples when the crowd came to him in Gethsemane
Matthew 26:60	Was accused by false witnesses during his trial
Matthew 26:67-68; 27:30-31	Despite his innocence, was spit on, struck with fists, slapped, beaten, and mocked
Matthew 27:32-35	Was crucified by Roman soldiers
Matthew 27:45-46	Was separated from God the Father because of the sin of the world that he bore for our sake

IV. **God, The Great Redeemer**

Throughout this lesson there has been a sharp contrast between Satan's evil purposes, God's redemptive plan and man's response.

Satan's Purposes

Hates mankind; people mean nothing to him; loves evil; commands demonic forces; bold and effective; exhorts God's highest creatures to curse God

God's Plan

Loves mankind; hates suffering; administers justice; offers redemption; never withdraws; needs no defense

Man's Response

Expect suffering; follow Jesus' model; draw closer to God; show rewards of righteousness; join fellowship of sufferers; fear God; humility; love

A. **Why Does God Allow Suffering?**

1. **Suffering Leads Others to Christ**

   Joni Eareckson Tada, who has lived with quadriplegia for over 40 years, serves God from a wheelchair. She impacts millions of people for Christ. Joni believes that it is only in the context of a sovereign God that suffering has any purpose. Apart from a loving God, who uses suffering for his glory and purposes, our suffering is meaningless, but in his hands suffering can bring others to faith in Jesus Christ. In the manual, "Through the Roof" by Joni Eareckson Tada and Steve Jensen, Joni writes:

   > You see, we are to God the fragrance of Christ. The world can't see Jesus endure suffering with grace because he's not here on earth, but you and I are. And we can fill up in our flesh what is lacking in His afflictions (Col. 1:24) and in so doing become that sweet fragrance, that perfume, that aroma of Christ to God. What a blessing, a privilege, an honor! What elation!... We will shine His light. The way I see it, I've been given so much, I must pass on the blessing. We simply must, must pass on the hope to others.[7]

   A disability allows the life of Christ to be manifested to others through the flesh. God builds strength, virtue, compassion, faith and sacrificial love into his children *"to become conformed to the likeness of his Son"* (Rom. 8:29).

2. **Suffering Cultivates Brokenness and Dependence on God**

   Brokenness is a prerequisite for a follower of Christ. The cross is a symbol of suffering and death. In Luke 9:23 Jesus said, *"If anyone would come after me, he must deny himself and take up his cross daily and follow me."* Notice that our surrender is a "daily" rather than a one-time experience. Jesus is the ultimate example of brokenness because he denied himself the right to his godly nature and submitted to suffering and even death (Philip. 2:5-11).

In his book *Brokenness*, Pastor Lon Solomon confirms this point:

> The Bible tells us that broken followers of Christ become God's special friends. God takes delight in them. God reveals more of himself to them, not because he loves them more than other Christ-followers, but because he is able to communicate himself to them in deeper, more intimate ways. When we come to Christ, in some way or another, we come broken. At some point we see our sin and we realize we need him and we have a hunger and a thirst for him... The reason for this is rooted in the very nature and character of God.[8]

Suffering is often the tool that God uses to bring about brokenness. It is the chisel he uses to carve self-sufficiency and self-dependence out of our lives. Brokenness deepens our faith and leads to dependency upon the Savior.

But he said to me, "My grace is sufficient for you, for my power is made perfect in weakness." Therefore I will boast all the more gladly about my weaknesses, so that Christ's power may rest on me. 2 Corinthians 12:9

3. Suffering Transforms Us into Christ's Likeness

Jesus learned obedience by *"the things he suffered"* (Heb. 2:10; 5:8). As believers, our highest calling is to be transformed into the image of Christ. The Apostle Paul knew that nothing could eradicate his selfish desires and transform him into the image of Christ like suffering. In Philippians 3:10, Paul declared: *"I want to know Christ and the power of his resurrection, fellowshipping in his sufferings and being conformed to his likeness, even his death on the cross."* He underlined this for the Christian life in Romans 5:3-4: *"Not only so, but we also rejoice in our sufferings, because we know that suffering produces perseverance; perseverance, character; and character, hope."*

4. Suffering Teaches Us Compassion for Others

The Lausanne Committee for World Evangelization addressed disability in their 2004 Lausanne Occasional Paper entitled, "Hidden and Forgotten People— Including Those Who Are Disabled":

> A disability creates an intimate identification between a person and his Savior, empowering him to minister out of weakness and brokenness, as did Christ. In outreach and missions, God often uses vulnerability or weakness as a point of identification to initiate his work. Philippians 2:6-8 says that Jesus, *"being in the form of God, did not consider it robbery to be equal with God, but made himself of no reputation, taking the form of a bondservant and coming in the likeness of men... he humbled himself and became obedient to death, even death on the cross."* Jesus calls us to minister through our weakness to a world of broken cultures, failed economies and collapsed political systems. Identification is the model Jesus chooses to establish his kingdom.[9]

When people with disabilities trust God, he is revealed as a God of supreme and massive worth, who is important enough to love and obey despite pain. As suffering bonds Christians to the Man of Sorrows, they have something eternally precious in common with Christ—their affliction. Our scars, anguish, rejection and pain give us a small taste of what our Savior endured to purchase our redemption.

5. Suffering Gives Us an Eternal Perspective

Jesus told us in Matthew 6:24 that we cannot serve two masters; we will love the one and hate the other. Jesus was speaking of the impossibility of serving God while lusting after material gain. We cannot love God with all our heart while loving the things of the world. It was this eternal perspective that allowed Christ to humble himself through suffering, even to the point of death. Paul reminded us of this in 2 Corinthians 4:16-18, *NASB*: *"Therefore we do not lose heart, but though our outer man is decaying, yet our inner man is being renewed day by day. For momentary, light affliction is producing for us an eternal weight of glory far beyond all comparison, while we look not at the things which are seen, but at the things which are not seen; for the things which are seen are temporal, but the things which are not seen are eternal."*

B. **Celebrating God's Sovereignty Over Evil and Suffering**
With so much evidence of God's power to help us stand as victors, not victims, of human sufferings, shouldn't the church be a place of celebration? In the book, *Suffering and the Sovereignty of God*, John Piper suggests that the church is missing the mark.

The church has not been spending its energy to go deep with the unfathomable God of the Bible. Against the overwhelming weight and seriousness of the Bible, much of the church is choosing, at this very moment, to become more light and shallow and entertainment-oriented, and therefore successful in its irrelevance to massive suffering and evil. The popular God of fun-church is simply too small and too affable to hold a hurricane in his hand. The biblical categories of God's sovereignty lie like land mines in the pages of the Bible waiting for someone to seriously open the book. They don't kill, but they do explode trivial notions of the Almighty. [10]

V. **From Tragedy to Triumph**
Although the Slaight family's world was turned upside-down the day of their tragic car accident, they were never alone in the ensuing chaos. Their church family was ever-present during the long months of healing and restoration. Their faith in God became the foundation on which they slowly rebuilt their lives. Two of their children were paralyzed, never to walk

again. Hannah, who is a teenager, refused to let her paralysis keep her from a full life. Her determination was obvious when it came time to get her driver's license. Her mother watched for over two hours as Hannah practiced lifting and pulling her body from her wheelchair, maneuvering in and out of the driver's seat until she was ready for her driver's test. Hannah continues to be a strong witness for Christ in her school and church's youth ministry.

Janet and Jim Slaight have consistently prayed that God would use the tragedy that took their daughter to draw others closer to him. They are living testimonies of Romans 8:38-39:

> "For I am convinced that neither death nor life, neither angels nor demons, neither the present nor the future, nor any powers, neither height nor depth, nor anything else in all creation, will be able to separate us from the love of God that is in Christ Jesus our Lord."

Their story is documented in the Joni and Friends TV episode titled, *From Tragedy to Triumph*, which you can view at www.joniandfriends.org/television.

 GROUP DISCUSSION

According to Scripture, what do evil and suffering have to do with our spiritual formation?

Reflections on Lesson 6

The Problem of Evil and Suffering in Our World

1. Describe the four main categories of suffering. Share your personal experiences with one or more of them.

2. Why is Satan so effective at creating victims in our society and causing Christians to doubt their faith?

3. Name the three major secular views on suffering discussed in Chuck Edwards' paper. Compare one of them to your own biblical view of evil and suffering.

4. According to Dr. Waters, why did God put Job through so much suffering? Did Job solve the problem of evil and suffering?

5. What is God's redemptive plan in allowing suffering in the world?

6. What does Hebrews 4:14-16 tell us about Jesus' role in our suffering and our choice to live victoriously over evil?

Hope: A Proper View of *Healing*

OBJECTIVES

**Studying this lesson
will help you:**

✔ Understand sickness
and health in light
of Scripture.

✔ Describe the purpose
of healing from a
biblical perspective.

✔ Discuss why some
people are healed
and others are not.

✔ Describe methods
of healing in the
New Testament.

✔ Understand the
role of prayer in
incomplete and
complete healing.

✔ Appreciate the role
of medicine in
the Christian life.

The grand ballroom of the Sheraton Hotel in Denver, Colorado, was jammed with 2,000 church leaders anxious to see a gymnastics team called "Break the Barriers."[1] Right on cue, the stage exploded with the big band sounds of "This Is My Country," as strobe lights caught sparkling red, white and blue clad young people jumping, tumbling and high-flying through the air. Some carried American flags; others waved colorful streamers overhead. Marching in cadence, many sang out, while others used sign language. Their joy and passion for God and country inspired a cheering audience, which seemed to hardly notice the disabilities of the 35 gymnasts. One boy who was blind flipped through the air from a tall platform onto the shoulders of a boy with autism. A teenager with Down syndrome pushed the wheelchair of a child with cerebral palsy. Adult spotters kept watch as the kids constructed human pyramids. A couple of stronger boys even carried smiling kids in wheelchairs over their heads. The finale softened the mood as the team swayed arm-in-arm to the song "God Bless America." Standing to their feet, the audience locked arms and joined in the song.

Those leaders represented hundreds of churches without disability ministries, but many hearts were challenged that day. Challenged to see beyond physical or mental limitations, into the hearts of young people created in the image of God and ready to serve him and bring him glory. Those gymnasts became ministers in their own right, exemplifying the truth of Philippians 4:4, "Rejoice in the Lord always. I will say it again: Rejoice!" We will never know how many new disability ministries were born that day, but we know that barriers were broken.

Christians are people who offer hope to the hurting. In order to do that, we need a proper understanding of sickness and health in light of Scripture. Many people with disabilities are rarely sick and would say that they feel no need to be healed. Could this be true? Others undergo painful medical and surgical procedures in order to live a healthier life. In this lesson, we will discuss the difference and define true healing—body, mind and soul. We'll also look at why some people are healed, as they were in Jesus' day, and why others are not. We'll find that prayer is the key that connects us to the Great Physician who is the answer to all of our questions on healing.

🔑 *Glory*

A multi-billion dollar marketing industry promotes health and beauty aids that promise personal glory and achievement, but it fails to mention their temporal value. On the other hand, God is glorified when his children turn to him for healing during times of affliction because his health plan is eternal. True healing is the courage to live, the courage to suffer and the courage to die.

I. **What the Bible Says about Healing**

Have you ever known anyone who has been healed?

In today's culture, people don't automatically think about the God of the Bible when they hear this question. They ask questions like: What kind of healing—physical, emotional, or spiritual? Healed how—through medicine, experimental therapies or exorcism? Or maybe a religious pilgrimage, meditation or some new diet? An internet search for the word "healing" produces 71 million sites with 1.5 million of those referring to some kind of "divine healing."

As Christ's followers, we need only one source to believe in healing—the Holy Bible. In many recorded instances, Jesus healed men and women suffering from physical disabilities, including blindness, deafness, paralysis, a withered hand, and leprosy. In six cases, Jesus healed people who suffered from mental illness or ailments. There are even accounts of mass healings in the New Testament where Jesus healed many people. [2] He also dismissed the notion of sickness and disabilities resulting from punishment, curses, or demonization. [3]

disagree

Quaker and theologian George Fox summarized the biblical accounts of healing this way: "Many great and wonderful things were wrought by the heavenly power in those days:

for the Lord made bare his omnipotent arm, and manifested his power, to the astonishment of many, the healing virtue whereby many have been delivered from great infirmities."[4] Yet even in light of Scripture, Christians can have misconceptions about divine healing and disabilities.

A. **A Wrong View of Healing**

One of the most hurtful myths about healing is the notion that if people simply have enough faith, they will be healed. This idea is preached in many churches and it has bankrupted the faith of countless believers who have yet to be healed. This view reasons that sickness is the work of Satan, and Jesus came to destroy the works of evil.[5] Jesus healed people during his lifetime, and God never changes. Therefore, he is still healing today.[6] We have the promise that whatever we ask in Jesus' name we will have if we have faith.[7]

When this false view is embraced, believers often experience a downward spiral into despair. In her book, *A Step Further*, Joni Eareckson Tada shares her feelings following a prayer service in 1972 where she was prayed for and anointed for healing. As the weeks passed and there was no change in her condition, troublesome questions vexed her mind and heart.

- *I have prayed the prayer of faith—but have not experienced anything.*
- *Perhaps it is going to be a gradual healing—God can work like that.*
- *Is there sin in my life? Did I and others pray correctly, saying the right words?*
- *Do I not have enough faith? What is wrong with me that God's favor is not on me?*
- *I experience despair and discouragement because God's plan does not include me.*
- *I feel exclusion in some churches and groups.*[8]

This mental anguish sent Joni into a deeper search of the Scriptures where she discovered that healing is an inward journey that has more to do with the heart and soul than the physical body. During times when Joni feels the most broken, she has learned that God has the power to raise us out of despair, which heals our very souls.

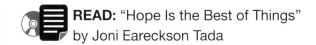

READ: "Hope Is the Best of Things"
by Joni Eareckson Tada

What does Joni mean when she says she takes up her cross daily?

In Joni's story of Ron and Beverly, what kind of healing did they receive?

A. **Where does healing fit into the world of disability?**
There are a number of words used in the New Testament for physical as well as spiritual healing. Although sometimes used for physical healing, *sozo* and *iaomai* typically carry the meaning of spiritual healing, which is the primary focus of New Testament healing. Spiritual healing is the salvation of the soul.

a. Matthew 9:22—Jesus spoke to the woman with the issue of blood, saying: *"Daughter, take courage; your faith has made you well* (sozo).*"*

b. Matthew 10:8—Jesus commissioned the 12 disciples for ministry, giving them the mandate to *"heal* (therapeuo) *the sick."*

c. Matthew 15:31—People were amazed when they saw *"the crippled restored* (hugiaino).*"*

d. Ephesians 2:8—*"For by grace you have been saved* (sozo)..." The context here refers not to physical healing, but to spiritual healing. The same is true for 1 Peter 2:24, *"by his stripes you were healed* (iaomai).*"*

1. **Finding Peace When There Is No Cure**

"Healings" and "cures" are terms often used synonymously, but healing has a much broader meaning than simply to cure someone. Cures may eliminate the symptoms, if not the disease or disability itself. The term healing describes well-being, peace, comfort or support, but may not imply a cure. This explanation sounds good on paper, but what about when you're face-to-face with parents asking, "With so many people praying for our daughter, why doesn't God simply heal her?"

Parents Steve and Melissa Bundy, whose son has autism and muscular dystrophy, have wrestled with this question and found the answer doesn't come overnight. It is a process of knowing God in a greater capacity and learning to appreciate their son as God's unique and perfect gift.

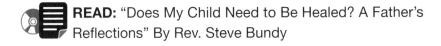 **READ:** "Does My Child Need to Be Healed? A Father's Reflections" By Rev. Steve Bundy

- When someone is "cured" from a disease or disability by a miracle, therapy or medicine, does this mean true "healing" has taken place? Why or why not?
- What was Jesus trying to say about healing when he quoted Isaiah 53:5, "The punishment that brought us peace was upon him and by his wounds we are healed"?
- According to Rev. Bundy's paper, what is the definition of spiritual healing?

2. **Scripture Emphasizes Spiritual Healing, not Physical Healing**

   a. The soul will live forever, the body will not. Although physical wellness is encouraged and should be sought, true biblical health and wholeness relate to the spirit, not the physical. For example, Paul's physical body was broken after years of beatings and poor treatment. He reminded the Corinthians that these bodies are like temporary tents—our new bodies will be in heaven (2 Cor. 5:1).

   There is a misconception that "wholeness" is the absence of any deficiencies in our bodies or lives. But everyone has deficiencies. Everyone Jesus healed eventually died. Wholeness is a matter of contentment based on one's perspective—a biblical perspective defines wholeness in terms of relationships, not physical or material conditions.

b. Spiritual healing includes a right relationship with God—i.e., salvation.

c. Spiritual healing includes a right relationship with people—i.e., community.

Christ's primary mission was to redeem man for eternal life and a right relationship with the Father (John 3:16). His second primary mission was to restore right relationship one to another (John. 17:20-21). In biblical times people with disease or disabilities were often excluded from community life and part of a person's "healing" involved restoring him or her to community.

When a "cure" was the means to accomplish this, then Jesus did so. Otherwise, his ministry was to the heart and soul of mankind. For example, in Luke 5:17-26, Jesus healed a man who had been lowered to him through the roof of a house. Here, Jesus initially healed the man by forgiving him of his sins, thereby restoring him to God. There was no need to provide a physical cure to restore him to community, because he was already in relationship with caring friends, as evidenced by the text. It is only when Jesus discerned the thoughts of the Pharisees that he cured the man's physical condition, saying *"so that you may know that the Son of Man has authority on earth to forgive sins..."* Even in curing the man Jesus' focus was on restoration to a right relationship with God—that is, true healing.

II. **Healing: Ultimately God's Decision**

Although Scripture clearly states that faith is at work during healing, there are many biblical examples which demonstrate that God ultimately decides who will be healed.

READ: 2 Kings 20:1-6

Isaiah's message from the Lord indicated that Hezekiah's illness would lead to his death and that he would not recover.

When Hezekiah cried out to the Lord, he responded, "I will heal you... I will add fifteen years to your life." The Lord decided to heal Hezekiah with the indication that he would die in 15 years. The decision was in the Lord's hands.

God revealed himself as Jehovah Rapha ("The Lord Our Healer") and he will heal sickness and disease according to his sovereign purposes. God may choose not to heal a person while on earth, for reasons we do not always understand.

It is a mystery why some receive healing and some do not. His ways are far above our ways! What we do understand clearly in God's Word is that his ultimate desire and priority is to heal the soul of man. This takes place when one becomes born again (receiving salvation) by accepting God's Son, Jesus Christ, and his work on the cross. This is the greatest miracle of all! God desires that all men would be saved and transformed into the image of his Son. Our "outward man" is perishing (aging, becoming increasingly weaker) and will eventually die, but our "inward man" will grow from glory to glory (2 Cor. 3:18; 5:1).

A. The Church Is a Healing Community

God calls the church community to minister to people affected by disability. He has not called us to "cure" every hurt, pain, sorrow or disability. Instead, he has called us to bring biblical "healing" to one another. Second Corinthians 1:3-4 tells us that he is "the Father of compassion and the God of all comfort, who comforts us in all our troubles, so that we can comfort those in any trouble with the comfort we ourselves have received from God." The church is also told to pray for those who need healing.

READ: Mark 6:13 and 16:18; James 5:14

The Bible clearly teaches us to pray for the sick and the suffering. Whether God heals a person physically while on earth or chooses to reveal his power through their weakness, this is up to him. He works out everything in conformity with his eternal will. Concerning our physical bodies, God has purposed that we will all receive a glorified body in heaven for eternity (1 Cor. 15:51-53).

Lord, teach us to pray.

Luke 11:1

The primary focus and priority of Christ's church should be spiritual healing and transformation of the soul by means of ministering the Gospel and teaching God's Word and ways. Pastor John Piper experienced this when he was diagnosed with cancer in 2006. He now warns believers not to waste their cancer (or any other kind of disability and illness), but to use it for the glory of God. In his book, *Suffering and the Sovereignty of God*, he writes, "I believe in God's power to heal—by miracle and by medicine. I believe it is right and good to pray for both kinds of healing. Cancer is not wasted when it is healed by God. He gets the glory and that is why cancer exists. So not to pray for healing may waste your cancer. But healing is not God's plan for everyone. And there are many other ways to waste your cancer...You will waste your cancer if you do not believe it is designed for you by God...What God permits he permits for a reason." [9]

III. **The Prayer of Faith**

Over the past nine years, David Lyons, vice president of The Navigators, and his sister, Linda Richardson, have taken God's graduate course in prayer. They both kept a prayer journal documenting their struggles as David's son, Ian, and Linda battled cancer. In their book, *Don't Waste the Pain: Learning to Grow Through Suffering*, they share their family's journey. David wrote the book's preface shortly after Ian went home to be with the Lord in April 2009 at the age of 12. Linda, who was diagnosed in 2000, continues to trust God for each new day in spite of the pain she suffers. Doctors have marveled at the way she has moved in and out of remission, which they can't explain. Linda and her many prayer partners know that God has miraculously kept her alive for his purposes. But Linda says it is not about her. She writes:

> You see, our prayers aren't just about healing for the sick. They're also used to bring the people praying into a more personal experience with God... A river runs along the bank as it courses down its path. Most of us will remember the river, but not so its banks.
>
> There might be places we notice, but it's the river that matters, the river that carries the power of the water, the river that runs to the sea, the river that

transports people and goods. It's the river that has the name. It's the river we remember.

I don't want to be the river. (I'm not the river.) I want to be the bank along the river of God. I hope he's using me to reveal himself to the world, to show his glory and power, but I myself am incidental. I know I'll change as he touches me, but that's between him and me... It's the river that ultimately determines its own course. The river has all the power. God has all the power. He uses us; we can't control or change him.

What He's done in my life is amazing. Then, again, it's not. It's what he does.[10]

The following paper reveals the lessons about prayer that God has taught Linda and David.

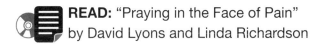

READ: "Praying in the Face of Pain"
by David Lyons and Linda Richardson

What does "going out on a limb" have to do with prayers for healing?

What do the Scriptures have to say about praying through our anxiety?

IV. **How to Pray for Healing**

It's been said that prayer is the hardest work a Christian will ever do. Sadly, this truth is reflected in the small number of people who show up at church for dedicated times of prayer. It's easier to say, "I'm praying for you" than to actually do it. In the following paper, Joni Eareckson Tada models the heart of a true prayer warrior as she visits with people who have come to understand the sustaining power of prayer.

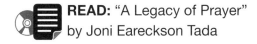

READ: "A Legacy of Prayer"
by Joni Eareckson Tada

Steps to Praying for Friends with Disabilities:

· **Be a good listener.** Listen to friends who share their concerns and fears. Listen to God as you ask him to show you how to pray for this person's specific need, which may be a simple request for a peaceful night's sleep.

San Francisco
Giants' Pitcher Loses
Arm to Cancer . . .

Dave and Jan Dravecky wrestled with God's plan after Dave lost his pitching arm to cancer, thereby ending his baseball career. Today, as the founders of Endurance, they encourage people who struggle with life's harsh realities.

- **After you've listened, politely ask** your friend if this is a good time to pray with them. Observe their body language as well as their words. Offer to come by at another time if you feel any hesitation on their part.
- **When a friend expresses their struggle** with prayer due to their pain, assure him that a loving God does not fault him for his inability to pray due to pain and suffering. God hears the faintest whisper. "Lord, all my desire is before you; and my sighing is not hidden from you" (Psalm 38:9, *NKJV*).
- **Pray specifically and boldly** for God to come with his healing power and touch. Martin Luther said this about praying for his sick friend, "I besought the Almighty with great vigor... quoting from Scripture all the promises I could remember, that prayers should be granted, and said that he must grant my prayer, if I was henceforth to put faith in his promises."[11]
- **Pray with assurance** that God hears and answers prayer. Whether we feel weak or strong in our prayers, our hope is built on the promises of God. "You hear, O Lord, the desire of the afflicted; you encourage them and you listen to their cry" (Psalm 10:17).
- **Give thanks** for a life worth living. In Joni's story about Kim, she was able to offer hope and courage even as her friend faced death. Joni told Kim:

> Life worth living is not found in a set of circumstances—whether pleasant or painful. Life worth living is found in a Person, the Prince of Life. The Resurrection and the Life. Jesus is the Way, the Truth and the Life. He has words of life. And the moments we invest in praying for his will to be done in lives, communities, and even nations will extend beyond this life—and beyond time itself.

Dave and Jan Dravecky wrestled with God's plan after Dave lost his pitching arm to cancer, thereby ending his baseball career. Today, as the founders of Endurance, they encourage people who struggle with life's harsh realities. In the *Encouragement Bible* they share what they have learned about healing:

> Lack of complete physical healing is not proof that our prayers have gone unanswered or that we didn't have enough faith in prayer. The healing may be an extension of life beyond the normal course of

the disease. It may be that fever is suddenly and inexplicably gone. The healing may be emotional or spiritual. It may be instantaneous or take place over a period of time.

Whatever comes, we are simply called to obey God's prompting to pray for healing. We don't tell God how or when. We trust that he is working, perhaps in ways we don't see or understand. We may not know how our prayers for healing were answered until we stand before the Great Physician. This is walking by faith, not by sight, which we know is pleasing to God and is able to move mountains.[12]

ASSIGNMENT

Your pastor called today asking you to speak to a prayer group at church on the topic of healing. List several questions you would expect to get about healing and write out your biblical responses.

Reflections on Lesson 7

Hope: A Proper View of Healing

1. What might be a wrong view of healing?

2. What are the different kinds of healing found in the Bible?

3. What do we learn about God's power over healing from Hezekiah's story in 2 Kings 20:1-6?

4. How is your church modeling a New Testament church by praying for those who are afflicted with physical pain and suffering?

5. Describe the difference between "complete" and "incomplete" healing.

6. What does it mean to pray in the Spirit?

7. According to Romans 8:18-27, what assurances can we offer to people who are not healed of their present suffering?

8. Asking God to show you two people who need prayer for healing, write out a plan to spend time with them in the next month.

The Gospel of *Luke*:

A Framework for a Theology of Suffering and Disability

OBJECTIVES

Studying this lesson will help you:

✔ Describe an overview of the Gospel of Luke and its significance to the topic of suffering and disability.

✔ Explain the chiastic structure in the Central Section of Luke, and its implications in ministry among people with disabilities.

✔ Appreciate the implications of Luke's Gospel in understanding the rest of the New Testament's teaching on suffering and disability.

✔ Understand the Luke 14 Mandate.

Take a mental stroll through a major bookstore in your area. Picture the towering displays of hot-off-the-press bestsellers written by movers and shakers who claim to have new, bold ideas. For only $39.99 you can take a book home or simply download it onto your phone or computer. But in the first century, notable writings were circulated on handwritten scrolls and read aloud in public assemblies. We can assume, however, that Luke's Gospel was not well received by the Jews of his day. Why? Because Luke's fresh idea declared that the Jews had the message of God's Kingdom completely backward. This page-turner announced Jesus to be the Son of God *and* the Son of Man, who humbled the proud and honored the lowly.

Luke, a beloved doctor, was uniquely qualified to write the Book of Luke because he was a man of education and culture—a Syrian of Antioch, not a Jew. As such, he readily observed the chasm between the Jews and Gentiles. Luke's medical knowledge and experience also made him a man of compassion, acquainted with suffering, yet appreciative of beauty and philosophy. No doubt Luke and the Apostle Paul spent hours in lively discourse during their missionary journeys recorded in the Book of Acts. They both cared deeply about the outcasts in society, but Luke is the one who brought us stories of the Good Samaritan (Luke 10:33), the Publican (18:13), the Prodigal Son (15:11-24), and the Thief on the Cross (23:43).

No other Gospel writer captures Jesus' heart for people affected by disability as well as Luke. Five out of the six miracles he records are about healing.[1] In this lesson, we'll focus on what Christians in the disability movement call "The Luke 14 Mandate" and seek to understand its significance to a biblical theology of suffering and disability.

🔑 *Hospitality*

Who doesn't enjoy a glitzy party? But for contemporary Christians there is danger in climbing the popular party ladder. It is easy to bestow gifts on those who can reciprocate and invite those who will return the favor. Such thinking can lock believers into the worldly social order, driven by insecurity and saturated with a drive for status. It's a false scene with distorted values. In Luke 14 Jesus cuts through this system of mutual hospitality and opens our hearts to God's realities and rewards.

I. **Luke's Concentration on the Kingdom of God**[2]

According to Scripture, Jesus came into this world to give his life for the salvation of sinners, to destroy the works of the Devil and to reveal the Father.[3] This third objective is most pointedly displayed in Luke's description of Jesus' humanity and compassion for people from all walks of life, backgrounds and ethnicities, especially those with disabilities. When Jesus walked the earth, he radiated the true character of the Father. Luke's Gospel reveals Christ as the fulfillment of all that was promised in the Law, the Prophets and the Writings.[4] Luke opens the lens through which we come to understand God's full nature as Father, Son and Holy Spirit—and his compassion toward outcasts and sinners. He also anticipates the ministry and mission of the church, beginning with the Messianic Prophecies.[5]

A. **Messianic Prophecies Found in Luke and Acts**

Luke makes at least 32 references to Messianic Prophecies, many of which have to do with Christ's ministry to the Gentiles, the broken and outcast.

1. Ministry to the Gentiles—Luke 3:4-6

2. Light to the Gentiles—Luke 2:32; Acts 13:47-48, 26:23

3. Invitation to all—Acts 13:34

4. God's Spirit poured out on all—Acts 2:16-21

5. Inclusion of Gentiles in the church—Acts 15:16-17

6. Jews' rejection of the Gospel, Gentiles' acceptance of it—Acts 13:40-41

7. Ministry to the broken—Luke 4:16-21

B. **Major Themes in the Gospel of Luke**
Luke's overarching theme is clear throughout the text as he declares that Jesus is the Savior of all regardless of ethnicity, gender or socioeconomic status. Luke's secondary themes are:

- **Salvation for All People**: With a special focus on outcasts and sinners (Luke 2:10-11, 19:10).
- **The Holy Spirit**: No Gospel writer mentions the work of the Holy Spirit more often than Luke (Luke 1:15,35,41, 2:25-35).
- **Prayer**: In many instances throughout the book, Jesus is praying (Luke 5:15, 9:18, 11:1).
- **Recording Christian History**: Luke's intent was to write salvation history. Taken together, Luke and Acts display the sovereign work of the Lord in bringing salvation to the ends of the earth.
- **Jerusalem**: Though Luke is considered the Gospel to the Gentiles, Jerusalem is of central importance to him. Jesus resolutely sets out for Jerusalem to fulfill his earthly destiny (Luke 13:22).
- **Stewardship of Material Possessions**: Throughout his Gospel, Luke emphasized that Christ's disciples are not to store up treasures for themselves on Earth (Luke 12:13-21, 16:19-31).
- **Women and their Role in Christ's Ministry**: No other Gospel mentions the role of women more often than Luke (Luke 1-2, 7:36-50, 8:1-3, 13:10-17).

C. **Jesus' Teachings in the Shadow of the Cross**
If you knew that you only had a short time to live, what message would you most want to leave with your family and friends?

Outline of Luke-Acts[6]

Imagine yourself standing among the crowds listening to Jesus tell stories with powerful truths. In each of these passages Jesus begins with a healing on the Sabbath, followed by two parables and finally concludes with a narrative concerning who will or will not enter the Kingdom of God.

Who understood Jesus' message?

What things were most important to him as he approached his death on the cross?

Jesus in Galilee
In Samaria and Judea
In Jerusalem

The Heart of Luke-Acts _____ **X** _____ **Resurrection & Ascension**

Church in Jerusalem
In Judea and Samaria
Throughout the Gentile world
The preaching of the Gospel by Paul extends as far as Rome

1. **Luke's Use of the Chiastic Structure**—Throughout his Gospel and the Book of Acts, Luke makes use of chiastic structure.[7] The chiastic or inverted structure is a literary device used in antiquity to highlight parallel ideas or thought patterns. It also aided in memorization. The chiastic structure is shaped like the letter X, which in the Greek alphabet is the letter Chi.

   In the outline above, Luke begins with a global perspective, dating the birth of Christ to the reign of the Roman emperors in Luke 2:1-3:1. From there we see Jesus' ministry in Galilee, an area that had a large Jewish population, but which was primarily a Gentile region.[8]

Beginning in Luke 9:51-56, we see Jesus' focus shift toward Jerusalem. His purpose was to save the world which required him to go to Jerusalem and suffer on the cross. The next section takes place as Jesus travels from Galilee to Jerusalem, passing through Samaria, traveling through other villages in Judea.[9] Luke places the bulk of Jesus' teaching in the setting of this journey from Galilee to Jerusalem.

2. **The Central Section of Luke (9:51-18:34)** is itself a chiastic structure that emphasizes the opposition to Jesus' message, the cost of discipleship, and most importantly, the Kingdom reversals:

a. Opposition & the Cost of Discipleship (9:51-62)
  b. Mission of the Seventy (10:1-24)
    c. Love of Neighbor, Love of God (10:25-42)
      d. Teaching on Prayer (11:1-13)
        e. Leaders Resist Christ's Message (11:14-54)
        f. Judgment to Come (12:1-13:9)
          g. Kingdom Reversals (13:10-14:24)
        f' Cost of Discipleship (14:25-35)
      e' Seeking and Saving the Lost (15:1-32)
    d' Use and Abuse of Riches (16:1-31)
  c' Teaching on Faith, Loving Neighbor & God (17:1-19)
  b' The Coming of the Kingdom (17:20-18:8)
a' The Requirements for Entering the Kingdom (18:9-34)

The material found in this section is not systematically paralleled in Matthew and Mark. While some of the sections are found in Matthew and Mark, Luke's arrangement is unique. The material in this section is arranged topically, not chronologically. Luke may have intended to relate Jesus' teachings in such a way as to reveal what things were most important to Jesus while he was living under the shadow of the cross.

Several scholars have argued that many of the passages in this section closely parallel some of the themes found in Deuteronomy. If this is the case, Luke may have been portraying Jesus as the Prophet who was to come (Deut. 18:15). Some of the themes significant to Luke—the acceptance of the Kingdom by the outcasts of society; and the foreshadowing of the

Gentile mission—can also be found in many sections of Deuteronomy (Deut. 28-33).

The Kingdom reversals focus on the group of people who would count the cost to follow Jesus, and they are the poor, the crippled, the lame and the blind. A closer look at Luke 13:10-14:24, which form the apex of the central section, communicates what was most important to Jesus while he was living under the shadow of the cross. Once in Jerusalem, Jesus presents himself as the Jewish Messiah (Luke19:28-21:38), and then offers himself up as the Savior of the world (Luke 22:1-24:53).

After the resurrection, Luke does not mention Jesus' appearances in Galilee, keeping the action in Jerusalem. This is done to tie in the geographic outline of Acts. The Book of Acts follows just the opposite motion, taking the scene from Jerusalem (chapters 1-5), to Judea and Samaria (chapters 6-9), then traveling toward Rome (chapters 9-28). This "chiastic" structure emphasizes the centrality of the resurrection and ascension to Luke's message, while emphasizing the universal nature of the Gospel.[10]

II. The Luke 14 Mandate: A Closer Look

The Luke 14 Mandate is more than an open invitation to come to God's banquet table or to fill up Christ's Church. It is the definition of God's Kingdom on earth as it applies to Christ's universal Church and what is yet to come in heaven. It is the Kingdom's door swung open for all—the strong and the weak, the rich and the poor, the healthy and the sick, and people with or without disabilities.

In Luke 13 and 14 Jesus spends time away from the urban markets of Jerusalem and in villages where common, country folk resided. But even there he finds religious leaders who are increasingly jealous of him and his so-called kingdom. Jesus clearly shows that no person or community is too small or insignificant for his ministry (nor for ours).

In Rev. Dan'l Markham's paper "The Lost Great Commission," he writes about the climax of these two conflicting kingdoms and the importance of the Parable of the Great Banquet. Markham notes:

Jesus' teaching in Luke 14:1-24 comes at the climax of a running debate between Jesus and Israel's religious leaders, revealing their increasing jealousy and hatred for Him, highlighting two kingdoms in conflict—one religious, i.e. self-serving, legalistic, judgmental, power hungry, money hungry, and insensitive to human need. The other is the Kingdom of God, guided by mercy, justice, faith, righteousness, peace and joy in the Holy Spirit (Rom. 14:17; Mt. 23:23)... The ultimate prize of the two kingdoms in conflict is the number of souls whose destiny becomes eternally entwined with Christ the King.

 READ: "The Lost Great Commission: Luke 13:10—17:10" by Rev. Dan'l Markham

What does Rev. Markham say is required to attend the Great Banquet Feast?

How is the Great Banquet similar or different from banquets you have attended?

A. **The Contrasts and Reversals of the Kingdom**

Steve Bundy, Vice President of the Christian Institute on Disability at Joni and Friends, travels nationally and internationally teaching in churches, colleges and seminaries. He regularly observes the lack of understanding regarding the Kingdom of God among believers, including those in the clergy. In Bundy's paper "The Kingdom of God and Disability," he explains the importance of the contrasts and reversals found in Luke 14. In this lesson, we will closely examine three of these reversals, which ask these important questions:

  · Who is the greatest in the Kingdom?
  · Are you part of the Kingdom?
  · What is the community of the Kingdom?

 READ: "The Kingdom of God and Disability: A Commentary on Luke 14:1-24" by Rev. Steve Bundy

B. **Who Is the Greatest in the Kingdom? Luke 14:7-11**

1. In the parable Jesus told in Luke 14:7-11, what opportunities did the guests miss out on when they chose the honored seats for themselves?

2. Who makes the final decision regarding seats of honor?

The irony here cannot be overlooked. Jesus has just healed a man with a disability who was not invited to the meal. Rather than celebrating with this man over a miraculous intervention by inviting him to the table, the guests tried to gain recognition for themselves by claiming the best seats. The guests missed the opportunity to reverse the social segregation that this newly-healed man had experienced due to his disability. Jesus' actions claimed this man for the Kingdom, reversing religious traditions.

Jesus likely chose a wedding feast as his example because places of honor were more clearly delineated there than at a meal in a Pharisee's house. The parable provided a segue for Jesus' teaching on whom to invite to a feast and the importance of the host's final decision in the seating arrangements. As we saw in the parable in Luke 13, God is the host who assigns seats of honor in his Kingdom.

3. What virtue was missing in the hearts of these guests?

The problem of this group was not a problem of knowledge, but of the heart. Though they knew full well the teaching of Scripture, they were full of pride and arrogance. Jesus ended his parable with these words, *"For everyone who exalts himself will be humbled and he who humbles himself will be exalted"* (Luke 14:11). This is very similar to his conclusion in Luke 13:30, *"Those who are last will be first and the first will be last."* In the minds of these religious leaders, the man with a disability was last, and they were first. But in the words of the Master Teacher, this is not so in the Kingdom of God.

C. **What is the Nature of the Kingdom? Luke 14:12-14**
In this section Jesus turns his attention to the host. Speaking directly to him, Jesus gives what may be the most descriptive explanation of the nature of God's Kingdom found in the entire Book of Luke. Similar to his pattern in Luke 13, Jesus moves from ministry to those with disabilities (vs. 1-6), to a lifestyle of humility,

which places others first (vs. 7-11), to a lifestyle of including the disabled, the Gentiles, the poor and outcast. He concludes with an eschatological view of the Kingdom.

Jesus instructs the host using a personal pronoun: "When you give a banquet, invite the poor, the crippled, the lame and the blind" (Luke 14:13).[11] Jesus also made his commission personal to the host of a luncheon or dinner in the earlier verse. This is a clear instruction to the Church to include people with disabilities in both our personal lives, as well as in our faith communities.

- His first commission is to us, individually. If our lives are to reflect the Kingdom of God, we must live our King's lifestyle, inclusive of those with disabilities.
- His second commission in Luke 14:15-24 is to the Church as the representative of God's Kingdom, which we'll discuss in the next section.

When Jesus uses both of the terms *luncheon* and *dinner*, he is indicating a comprehensiveness that encompasses one's overall hospitality. In other words, Jesus doesn't suggest this commission applies only for special occasions. We should be including people from outside of our comfort zones and traditional associations, those we may consider "lowly" as part of our day-to-day lives. Jesus goes so far as to name people on a typical Pharisee's guest list: *"friends, brothers, relatives and rich neighbors"* (Luke 14:12).

1. What does this text say about the Church's understanding of the nature of the Kingdom?

2. If the Kingdom is one in which those with disabilities have a seat of honor, how can the Church honor the King's heart for the overlooked in our society?

Author and Pastor John Piper observed that even the most faithful followers of Jesus must fight the natural tendency toward reciprocity. In a sermon he delivered one Thanksgiving Sunday, Piper addressed the Luke 14 Mandate:

There is in every human heart a terrible and powerful tendency to live by the law of earthly repayment, the law of reciprocity. There is a subtle and relentless inclination in our flesh to do what will make life as comfortable as possible and to avoid what will inconvenience us or agitate our placid routine or add the least bit of tension to our Thanksgiving dinner. The most sanctified people among us must do battle every day so as not to be enslaved by the universal tendency to always act for the greatest earthly payoff.

The people who lightly dismiss this text as a rhetorical overstatement are probably blind to the impossibility of overstating the corruption of the human heart and its deceptive power to make us think all is well when we are enslaved to the law of reciprocity, the law which says: always do what will pay off in convenience, undisturbed pleasures, domestic comfort and social tranquility. Jesus' words are radical because our sin is radical. He waves a red flag because there is destruction ahead for people governed by the law of reciprocity... Why does it make such an eternal difference whom you invite to Thanksgiving dinner? It... reveals where our treasure is. Is Jesus, with His commands and promises, more valuable to us than tradition and convenience and earthly comfort? Is He our treasure or is the world? That question is not decided during an invitation at church. It is decided at Thanksgiving dinner, and hour by hour every day by whether we are willing to inconvenience ourselves for those who can't repay or whether we avoid them and so preserve our placid routine. It matters whom you invite to Thanksgiving dinner because it matters where your treasure is.[12]

This mandate of including people with disabilities is not simply a ministry of benevolence. Though they may have limited financial means, the Church will be blessed as a result of their inclusion. Though the Pharisees viewed reciprocity in terms of what they could anticipate receiving from those with riches and influence, make no mistake about it—people with disabilities are also able to repay with their presence and lives. In Luke 14:14 we find that not only will there be an earthly blessing, but a heavenly one as well: *"...you will be repaid at the resurrection of the righteous."* As William Hendriksen comments, "What minister cannot bear testimony to the fact that some of the finest lessons he ever learned were given to him by the poor... the small, the sick, the handicapped, the dying?"[13]

D. **The Great Banquet – Who Fills the Seats at the Table? Luke 14:15-24**

1. What did the Jews at the table expect the coming Kingdom to reflect?

2. What were Jesus' expectations of the coming Kingdom?

As Luke creates dialectic between human responsibility and God's priorities of grace and initiative, we once again see an emphasis on parallels in chapters 13 and 14 with a focus on contrast and reversal. The reversal here is of the expectation of those who experience the earthly ministry of Jesus and expect to be present at the banquet of the eschatological Kingdom.[14]

As soon as Jesus brought up the resurrection of the righteous, someone at the table jumped on the topic of the feast in the Kingdom of God.[15] From the context and Jesus' response, it is clear that the tone of the one speaking was quite pious. Yet, having just been rebuked by Jesus over not caring for those with disabilities and the outcasts, this guest tried to restate his (and the other guests') position in the Great Banquet of the Kingdom. This only added fuel to Jesus' fire. His response seemed to go something like this: "You want to talk about the Kingdom? Okay, let's talk about the Kingdom." Jesus then launched into a parable that is unmistakably a climactic point in his Gospel.

In Chapters 13 and 14 Jesus had already...

- ministered to two persons with disabilities
- twice rebuked religious leaders for their hypocrisy and greater concern for their animals and personal affairs than for the outcast children of God—all in his name

- foretold of Gentiles and outsiders becoming "insiders" in the Kingdom of God and "insiders" becoming outsiders
- communicated that a Kingdom lifestyle, which they claimed to represent, was a lifestyle of inclusion of those with disabilities

Jesus then throws the final punch! All he had been teaching up to this point was simply a reflection of the Kingdom to come. To his audience, a discussion of the feast in the Kingdom of God had a clear meaning. The Jews viewed the Messianic Kingdom of God in all its fullness as that of a great banquet, with lavish amounts of food, drink and fellowship, with God ultimately ruling all the earth, including the Gentiles:

> "On this mountain the Lord Almighty will prepare a feast of rich food for all peoples, a banquet of aged wine—the best meats and the finest wines" (Isa. 25:6; see also Ps. 23:5; Matt. 8:11-12; 22:1; 26:29; Mark 14:25; Rev. 3:20; 19:9).

Turning to the self-righteous pious man, Jesus used a parable to reiterate what he had already told them about seats of honor and guest lists. He said the feast of the Kingdom that the Jews had put such self-confidence in would be filled with those he had listed in Luke 14:23.

In those days, it was not uncommon for a host to first invite a great number of guests to a banquet and then send a reminder. The story does not indicate that any had declined the first invitation, so they were expected to attend once the banquet was prepared. As the host eagerly waited for his guests to arrive and enjoy the well-prepared feast, his servant returned with the message that no one was coming. It was as if they were of one mind not to participate in the banquet.

Luke makes it clear that they *"began with one (consent) to excuse themselves all."*[16] As Alfred Plummer comments, "There was no variation; it was like a prearranged conspiracy: They all pleaded that they were at present too much occupied to come. And there was not a single exception."[17] Not one of the excuses given was a legitimate excuse that would justify disgracing the host. What a powerful analogy for those who will not partake of this great eschatological feast! It is as if something in their hearts led them to conspire together to hide behind excuses in order to avoid honoring the host, or, in this case, "The Host of hosts, King of kings and Lord of lords."

Throughout the parable Jesus spoke from the perspective of the host. As he ended the parable, however, it is clear in Luke 14:24 that Jesus switched from the perspective of the host to himself, speaking directly to those present: *"I tell to you* (plural)." Jesus made it a personal address to those listening: *you* are the guests who made excuses; those who did *not* make excuses are the poor, the crippled, the blind and the lame (v. 21).

When the host became angry at the excuses, he ordered his servant to go out into the streets and bring in the poor, the crippled, the blind and the lame. The servant had to go past the downtown urban homes and into the alleys where one would find beggars who were poor and disabled. Notice the segregation of those with disabilities from the mainstream—the servant had to go out past the neighborhoods, hotels, schools and even the synagogues to find the disabled. The master told the servant to *"bring them in."* Hendriksen observes:

> This was probably necessary, not so much because, for example, the blind would not have been able to find the banqueting hall unless they were taken by the hand and led, but rather because all of the groups here mentioned might well entertain serious doubts with respect to the question whether a sumptuous banquet could really be for them.[18]

The servant was told to *"make them come in"* (Luke 14:23). The language conveys a strong urging or compelling, something that was necessary for them. The host desired that his house be full of people who were poor, crippled, blind and lame; he would not start the banquet until they were all gathered in and had a place at the table. Those who in the comfort of their lifestyle and self-confidence made excuses would in no way participate in the banquet. But for those with disabilities and the outcast, the host made it clear: the Kingdom was made up of *"the least of these brothers of mine"* (Matt. 25:40).

III. Hosting a Luke 14 Banquet

One of the disability models that Joni and Friends recommends to churches is the Luke 14 Banquet.[19] It is a great outreach to the disability community and builds relationships between volunteers and families in your church. This idea also follows the principle of Isaiah 58:7-8 which says, *"Is it not to share your food with the hungry and to provide the poor wanderer with shelter—when you see the naked, to clothe him... Then your light will break forth like the dawn... your righteousness will go before you and the glory of the Lord will be your rear guard."* Here is how to host a banquet in your church:

> Design a banquet in the manner of Luke 14. Recruit volunteers to prepare food and decorate tables. Design centerpieces for the tables and create small gift baskets. Then, invite a set number of people with disabilities and their families to attend. After dinner, give away door prizes or gift certificates. Hold a short program highlighting someone's testimony. Declare the Gospel at the close of the banquet.

LISTEN TO: "The Banquet Table" by Joni Eareckson Tada, a Joni and Friends Radio Feature
http://www.joniandfriends.org/banquet-table/

Jesus' teachings on Luke 14 were radical and revolutionary not only for his day, but continue to challenge Christians today. He reverses our fundamental human value systems and calls us to lives of courtesy, hospitality and radical inclusion. This is not simply good advice that makes nice people nicer. This is living out one's faith in such a way that it exemplifies the saving rule of God through which mankind comes to repentance and faith. When our daily lives reflect the attitude and behavior of Jesus himself, we can say like the Apostle Paul, "Follow me as I follow Christ."[20]

Reflections on Lesson 8

The Gospel of Luke: A Framework for a Theology of Suffering and Disability

1. In the shadow of the cross, what teachings were central in Jesus' mind?

2. Describe the "chiastic structure" of Luke 13 and 14.

3. What is the Luke 14 Mandate?

4. Why is an understanding of kingdom reversals and contrasts so critical to a Christian's core values, as well as those of the Church?

5. Why does Rev. Markham call Luke 14 the "Lost Great Commission"?

6. What implications do Luke 13 and 14 have for a theology of suffering and disability?

7. What can we assume from the parable of the Great Banquet about the final Wedding Supper of the Lamb in Revelation 19:7-9?

8. Describe a time in your life when you have truly lived out Jesus' message of the parable of The Great Banquet.

MODULE 3

The Church and
Disability Ministry

The Church and Disability Ministry

Get ready to roll up your sleeves.

We're going to cover the nuts and bolts of disability ministry in the church. How do you get your church leadership and church onboard? Where do you find volunteers and how do you recruit them? What are the important topics for training? What ministry models do you begin with?

God's intention is that we embrace our own suffering and those who are experiencing suffering. We'll study Paul's letters that admonish all believers to build one another up in love, sharing one another's burdens and joys through fellowship and genuine community. We're going to study what Scripture says about the mature church; how ministering to people with disabilities, the broken and suffering, is not a burden or an obligation, but a privilege and ministry to Christ himself.

People affected by disability are one of the world's largest unreached people groups in every culture of the world. Part of the strength of Joni and Friends over the years has been strategic partnerships with churches and ministries, as well as social and governmental organizations to meet needs and help empower people with disabilities. We'll look at how disability ministries can network strategically with other ministries and organizations to meet the physical and spiritual needs of individuals and families affected by disability.

Finally, throughout this module you will be introduced to friends of Joni and Friends who have been transformed by God's amazing grace. God bless you as you seek to obey his wonderful mandate.

Rev. James Rene

Major *Challenges* of the Church on the Path to *Maturity*

OBJECTIVES

Studying this lesson will help you:

✔ Explain from Scripture a brief overview of ecclesiology and the importance of its theological framework.

✔ Explain the main images the Bible uses to define the nature and function of the Church.

✔ Describe the Church as the Broken Body, Suffering Body and Mature Body of Christ.

✔ Understand the seven movements of disability ministry.

✔ Explain how a "mature church" understands God's plan for disabilities and responds.

We have this treasure in jars of clay to show that this all-surpassing power is from God.—2 CORINTHIANS 4:7

A church is comprised of ordinary people with extraordinary potential for both good and evil. Thus, a church must function as a living and moving *organism* with the ability to love, forgive, encourage and support. At the same time, a church is an *organization* in which divine work is accomplished. God calls leaders, pastors and teachers to service, which requires strategic planning and implementation. Leaders must also be faithful stewards of the finances and resources that the Lord has entrusted to them, which requires accountability.

Problems arise when a church is unbalanced in either function; i.e. *organism* or *organization*. If a church operates as an organism, with no structure or organization, it risks ministering without responsibility or direction, resulting in all sorts of spiritual abuse within the fellowship. On the other hand, if a church functions strictly as an organization, it can become insensitive to the leading of the Holy Spirit, relying solely on the wisdom of men. This can result in the church becoming an "institution" rather than a family with a heart for God and a hurting world. Disability ministry doesn't fare very well with either scenario.

In Module 3 we'll discuss biblical and contemporary models of the church's role in reaching families affected by disability. We'll examine the challenges that can prevent these families from joining the mainstream of church life. We'll discover that when a church fails to welcome the disability community there's a high price to pay—Jesus said, "I tell you the truth, whatever you did not do for one of the least of these, you did not do for me" (Matt. 25:45).

♪ *Unity*

The phrase "United we stand—Divided we fall" is attributed to Aesop's fables, but it originated in the heart of God. He created all people, with and without disabilities, to live in unity with him and in fellowship with one another. The counter image of this would be to divide and rule, which causes chaos in our lives, as well as in our churches. Unity—"one body called to peace" (Col. 3:15)—transforms our brokenness and builds mature faith communities.

I. **Identifying the Church's Theological Framework**

People describe the church in many different ways depending on their personal experiences. The church is complex, because it's made up of people, who themselves are complex. Therefore, we must first define the church from a biblical point of view, rather than a sociological standpoint. In Millard Erickson's book, *Christian Theology*, he describes a modern, societal shift to a more secular train of thought regarding the church, as well as how people view God. For thousands of years it was believed that God related to the world solely through the supernatural institution of the church. However, Erickson observes that the church is no longer seen as God's special agent which solely embodies his divine presence. He sees the results of this shift as worrisome. Erickson writes:

> There is a widespread conception that God dynamically relates to the world through many avenues or institutions. The emphasis is upon what God is doing, not upon what he is like... As a result of this change in orientation, the church is now studied through disciplines and methodologies other than dogmatic or systematic theology... The new emphasis applying non-theological disciplines and methodologies to study of the church poses a danger as the church struggles to understand itself theologically. The major problem with attempting to define the church in terms of its dynamic activity is that such a definition avoids making any kind of statement regarding the nature of the church.[1]

With the foregoing in mind, the rest of this lesson is devoted to the task of developing an explicitly *biblical* view of the church as it relates to people with disability.

A. **Ecclesiology: The Doctrine of the Church**

The church is a "chosen people." The term "ecclesiology" comes from the Greek word *ekklesia—ek*, which means "out of," and *kaleo* means "to call." Thus, the church is "a called out group." In the Old Testament the term is used in Deuteronomy 9:10 as "the day of the assembly." *Ekklesia* appears 114 times in the New Testament, and the phrase "called out people belonging to the Lord" was a familiar term for New Testament writers, especially Paul who used the term 111 times.[2] Even the origins of the English word for church can be traced back to the Greek word *kuriakon*, which means "belonging to the Lord."

Chuck Colson, Founder of Prison Fellowship and The Chuck Colson Center for Christian Worldview, spent years observing the Church and powerfully challenged the worldviews of today's Christians. Speaking during the 2009 Joni and Friends President's Retreat, Mr. Colson said this about the church:

> The single greatest need of the Christian Church is to understand that Christianity is not just a relationship with Jesus. But it's a way of seeing all reality... I am convinced that the biggest single weakness of the Church is that we have a reductionist view of Christianity—it's just me and Jesus. We think we're in good shape. Jesus is taking care of me, and I've got a great relationship with Jesus. That's an abomination!

 READ: "Love, Life and Worldview" by Chuck Colson

What direction does Mr. Colson provide in his paper for moving from a "me and Jesus" perspective to a biblical worldview of the Church?

B. **The Biblical Nature of the Church**

We must recognize that historically the church has not always reflected its true nature. As saints or "holy ones" we are called to reveal God's character by our love for

John 21

others.[3] Our nature—infused by the power of the Holy Spirit—should reflect the images, figures, functions, and purposes of God in the world. The Bible uses three primary images to describe the church.

1. **The People of God**—We belong to God and he belongs to us. When God commands us in Exodus 20:7 to not take his name in vain, he's asking us not to claim his name and then live contrary to his character. In Matthew 5, he calls Christians the "salt of the earth" and a "city on a hill" which means we are to display his words and works through our lives and testimonies. When nonbelievers look at the church, they should say, "These are a people who belong to a holy God."

2. **The Body of Christ**—This image means that the church is the focus of Christ's activity on earth. The church is his body; though made up of many parts, it forms one union: *"Now you are the body of Christ, and each one of you is a part of it"* (1 Cor. 12:27). A body cannot reject a part of itself and still function as a complete body. Christ is the Head of the Church since God has placed all things under his feet and has appointed him over everything concerning the Church. [4]

3. **Temple of the Holy Spirit**—The Spirit gave birth to the Church at Pentecost (1 Cor. 12:13), and the Spirit continues to give life to churches today. The Spirit is not a "tool" that God uses simply to "repair" his people—rather, the Holy Spirit of God relates to our spirits and it is by him that we call God our "Abba" Father (Rom. 8:15). We are indwelt by the Holy Spirit both individually (1 Cor. 3:16-17, 6:19) and collectively (Eph. 2:21-22). In him we live and move and have our being (Acts 17:28).

C. **The Biblical Functions of the Church**
Any effective organization has a set of well-defined statements of its purpose and goals; if it has no purpose, it will have no direction. Many people have different opinions regarding what the church is called to be and do in the world. But the Bible specifically identifies the following functions of the church in its call to minister to the Lord, to one another, and to the world.

1. **Worship**: individual attitude of the heart (Matt. 5:23-24; Rom. 12:1-2; 1 Tim. 2:10, 5:4) and corporate (1 Cor. 14:26; Eph. 5:19; Col. 3:16)

2. **Instruction**: Early Church model (Acts 2:42, 5:28, 18:11) and correct doctrines (1 Tim. 1:3; Acts 5:28)

3. **Edification** through ministry and fellowship: breaking bread together (Acts 2:42), prayer (Acts 4:24-31), ministry inside the church (Rom. 12:3-8), and supporting the ministry (Rom. 15:26; 2 Cor. 9:13)

4. **Evangelism**: ministry outside the church (Acts 8:4, 11:19-20)

5. **Organization**: appointing leaders (Acts 14:23; Titus 1:5)

6. **Ordinances**: baptism and the Lord's Supper (Acts 2:41; 1 Cor. 11:23-24)

D. **Koinonia—The Ingredient for Community Life**

Koinonia is a New Testament Greek word which means "communion" or "fellowship" among Christian believers. Paul's letters to the churches admonished them to build one another up and commune with one another and with God. Church was never meant to be a "place" people simply visit for worship, but rather a shared community where friends knew one another's joys and burdens. Throughout the New Testament, *koinonia* is used to communicate:

1. Unity and bond between believers—Acts 2:42; Philem. 1:6; 2 Cor. 8:4

2. Unity with Christ—1 Cor. 1:9, 10:16; Phil. 3:10

3. Unity between the Trinity and the Church—2 Cor. 13:14; 1 John. 1:3-7; Phil. 2:1

4. Partnership in the Gospel—Gal. 2:9; 2 Cor. 8:23; Phil. 1:3-5

In "doing" church we can often forget to "be" the church. In the following skit, we will visit Pastor Pickle's study as

> *Koinonia is not simply a matter of transferring a piece of knowledge or material possession, it communicates a deeper sense of relationship; in biblical times it was also used to communicate commitment, sacrifice, partnership or even intimacy in marriage.*[5]
>
> JAMES STRONG

he prepares for his Sunday sermon. It seems that his faithful parishioners are having some difficulty with their deeper sense of commitment to one another.

READ: "Pastor Pickle" A Skit Based on Ezekiel 34
(Appendix B)

Who do you most identify with in this skit?
Who was having a difficult time with *koinonia* in this skit?
How would this same challenge play out in your own church?

II. Where Is the Church Today?

A. Why Are Many Churches Missing the Mark?

According to Erik Carter in his book *Including People with Disabilities in Faith Communities*, "Numerous faith groups have acknowledged their failure to respond to people with disabilities in ways that reflect their calling to be caring, loving, and responsive communities."[6] Although it is difficult to quantify the precise degree of involvement of people with disabilities in churches, various statistics reveal a need for churches to become more active in ministering to families affected by disability. Below are some U.S. statistics:[7]

1. According to one study which queried parents of children and youth with disabilities, fewer than one-half of children and youth with autism, deaf-blindness, intellectual disabilities, or multiple disabilities had participated in religious activities at any point during the previous year.

2. When 200 parents of adolescents and young adults with autism were asked about their child's attendance at religious services, less than one-third reported their child attended on a weekly basis; only 11% attended religious social activities.

3. One-third of children and adults with intellectual disabilities who live in foster care or small group homes rarely attended religious services; only one-fourth "sometimes" attended religious services.

4. In a survey of 91 Christian, Jewish and Muslim congregations, 71% said they had a general awareness of the barriers to inclusion for the disability community; 69% said they *had not yet started* or were just beginning to transform their church family into a place of inclusion; 53% said they were in the process and only 28% had explored partnerships with community agencies or organizations serving the disabled.

Even with the abundance of biblical teaching on the image and function of the church, we still fall into the trap of wanting our churches to appear "successful" and "to have it all together." We prefer members who wear the right clothes, drive the right cars, and know the right vernacular. But this is an illusion and a misunderstanding of what God truly desires—***our brokenness.***

Bible teacher Dr. Michael Beates says, "For us to understand the power of God working through His people, we must understand two things: first, brokenness forces us to see God as the ultimate and only reliable source of power; secondly, God, through His Holy Spirit, brings about brokenness in the people He intends to use for His glory." In the following paper, Dr. Beates discusses the church as a broken body, a suffering body and finally, by God's grace, a maturing body.

 **READ:** "Major Challenges of the Church on the Path to Maturity" by Dr. Michael S. Beates

What are the sources of brokenness according to Dr. Beates? (Ps. 119:67; 1 Cor. 1:27-31; 2 Cor. 12:7-10)

B. **The Church as a Broken and Suffering Body**
Identification is one of the most powerful tools God uses in the lives of believers to bring about brokenness. Through relational ministry to and with broken people (disabled, poor, marginalized) God breaks, blesses and gives away a transformed and selfless life. Christ is the ultimate example of identification.

- John 1:14—The Incarnation—"The Word became flesh and dwelt among us..."

- Hebrews 2:17—"Therefore he had to be made like his brothers in every way..."
- Matthew 25:40—"When you've done it to one of the least of these my brothers, you've done it unto me..."

Throughout world history Christian believers have suffered for various reasons, but with a single purpose—brokenness! And the early church was no exception. It grew and expanded as a result of suffering. God allowed suffering to enter the life of the church just as he allows it to enter the lives of individual believers. God's intention for his church is that we embrace our own suffering, and embrace those who suffer. To the degree that we exclude them from our faith community, we exclude ourselves from the depth of God's grace.

1. **Jesus, the Suffering Servant**—In Isaiah 54 Jesus was described as a *Man of Sorrows* who was acquainted with grief and who carried our sorrows. He felt abandoned by God (Matt. 27:46). In Revelation 5:9-12 Jesus was *"the Lamb that was slain"* who became a curse for us (Gal. 3:13).

2. **Paul's Call to Suffering**—*"I will show him how much he must suffer for my name's sake..."* (Acts 9:15-16). He also suffered for the Gospel (Col. 1:24).

3. **The Church's Call to Suffering**—We are to *"share in Christ's suffering..."* and to be used by God to spread the Gospel (1 Pet. 4:12-13; Acts 8:1-4). Suffering and brokenness produce character (Rom. 5:3-6), maturity (Jas. 1:2-4), faith (1 Pet. 1:6-7) and trust (2 Cor. 1:8-11).

C. **The Church as the Mature Body**
"Being a Christian is more than just an instantaneous conversion—it is a daily process whereby you grow to be more and more like Christ."
Dr. Billy Graham

The path to Christian maturity is a slippery slope; one that should not be traveled alone. For this reason, every church has its "saints" who model faith in the midst of weakness. We are privileged to watch these saints and grow from their example.

The mature church understands the role of brokenness and suffering in the lives of believers and responds in positive ways. It recognizes that God is at work and counts ministry to the broken, disabled and suffering not as an obligation, but as a privilege—as if ministering to Christ himself.

1. **The privilege of ministry to the broken:** Many cultures stress the importance of being *independent*, that is, not needing anyone to help or assist one on one's journey. Being "self-made," in this view, is a sign of competence and strength. Being *dependent* on anyone or anything is a sign of weakness. In reality, this is an illusion—we all need each other, and we all need God. No one "makes it" alone. We are, in fact, *interdependent* upon God and one another. Disability helps us see that we are all broken and all part of the same body, needing to give and receive from one another. This in turn keeps each member of the body *accountable* to Christ and one another. People with disabilities have much to contribute to the Body of Christ—and when they are not present, the body is incomplete.

   God's intention for the Church, his body, is that it would *"grow up in all things..."* (Eph. 4:15). Part of growing up is having a proper understanding of serving and accountability to others. Disability is one way God shows his church how to become his *complete* body.

2. **The privilege of joining in the priesthood:** In 1 Peter 2:5,9 we are reminded that through Christ we are now a holy priesthood. The "priesthood of believers" means that we as believers have direct access to God, where once only a qualified minority (i.e., a priest, under Old Testament law) represented God to the people and the people to God. As a priesthood, we also are now ministers to one another through natural, spiritual, and "calling" gifts (Rom. 12:1-8; 1 Cor. 12:1-11; Eph. 4:7-16). As Peter went on to emphasize in 1 Peter 4:10, "Each one should use whatever gifts he has received to serve others, faithfully administering God's grace in its various forms."

3. **Understanding our calling to serve:**

In light of these privileges, should the church then function as an organism or an organization? Both are essential to a mature church. The New Testament Church is a practical model in both Luke and Acts. Paul's letters also emphasize the "one another" aspect of the Christian lifestyle. He uses active verbs such as accept one another, love one another, build one another up and bear one another's burdens (Rom. 14:19, 15:7; Eph. 4:2; Gal. 6:2). Just as the early church struggled to live out this kind of unity, especially in accepting Gentiles, today's congregations must stretch to extend their love to all people. God's love is transformational. It moves us to action, as the early church lived out in Acts 2.

READ: Acts 2:42-47

 VIEW: Joni at Foundations

In Joni Eareckson Tada's message to a disability ministry class, Joni discussed Colossians 2:19 and pictured Christ as the head of the Church. She stressed that "each member" of his body has a gift that should be used to serve one another and honor the Lord.[8] Joni says, "If the lines of communication between the head and the rest of a physical body are disrupted, then certain parts of that body will be ignored or neglected. This can also be true of the Church."

Discuss the four key words Joni uses to help Christians better understand their calling to serve.

III. **Practical Applications for the Church**

In Rev. Steve Bundy's paper, "Modeling Early Church Ministry Movements," he cautions us that the success of a church's ministry is not necessarily defined by the size of the congregation. It's the church that prayerfully seeks God for a sensitive heart toward those who are in need that finds opportunities for the richest ministry.

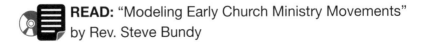 **READ:** "Modeling Early Church Ministry Movements" by Rev. Steve Bundy

Where does your church fall in the seven movements of ministry described in Rev. Bundy's paper? "We must take a personal inventory, look at our hearts and determine our true motivation... For ministry to take place among those affected by disability, the church and individual believers alike must intentionally move toward seven specific areas of ministry," says Rev. Bundy.

A. **Seven Movements of Ministry to Persons with Disability**

1. **Ministry of Fellowship**—Movement from Program to Presence

2. **Ministry of the Word**—Movement from Quantitative Ministry to Qualitative Ministry

3. **Ministry of Obedience**—Movement from Ministry of Convenience to Ministry of Conviction

4. **Ministry of Identification**—Movement from Being Understood to Understanding

5. **Ministry of Prayer**—Movement from Being Important to Being Available

6. **Ministry of the Spirit**—Movement from Being Heard to Listening Intently

7. **Ministry of Reciprocity**—Movement from Teaching to Being Taught

B. **The Tale of Two Families**
Church growth specialists tell us that we have seven minutes to make a positive first impression when a family visits our church for the first time. Churches that understand this concept have elaborate plans such as parking lot attendants, door greeters, welcome centers manned with smiling helpers, coffee bars, class escorts, clear directional signs, well-trained ushers, pre-service videos or music, and exit greeters at the end of the service. In other churches, visitors can park, enter, worship and leave without a smile or handshake from a single person.

For families affected by disability, going to church can be one of the best or one of the worst experiences of their whole week. Unfortunately, many families are turned off by their first visit to a church. But, occasionally, they're pleasantly surprised by the warmth and welcome they receive.

Family A—When Thom and Blanca Siebels' third child, James, was diagnosed with autism they found it increasingly more difficult to maintain *normal* family life. James' condition sometimes required 2-3 therapy sessions per day in their home and going out to dinner after church on Sunday was nearly impossible due to James' behavior problems. Church friends had always been an important part of their lives so they determined to take turns volunteering in James' class... until one day when the teachers failed to show up and the Siebels were left alone to teach 21 third-graders. Unfortunately, James bit a classmate that day before his busy parents could stop him. A church leader called the Siebels a week later asking them to stop bringing James to class because 10 families had vowed to stop coming if James was there. Thom and Blanca were devastated.

Family B—Dan and Marisol Jaramillo and their daughter, Meghan, were accustomed to being stared at and feeling alone in public, where no one identified with a 17-year-old wheelchair user. Meghan's birth defect, Arthrogryposis Multiplex Congenita, caused reduced mobility in many of her joints. But everything changed for them when they found a church with a support group for parents with special needs children and a welcoming youth group for Meghan. Dan and Marisol knew they needed to be closer to God, so when they began meeting with other couples who prayed about the same fears and concerns they had for their child, it was obvious they'd found the right church for their family. Another confirmation came when a group of girls invited

Meghan to a sleepover. Her father couldn't believe it! "They knew what it took to take care of Meghan's needs, and they wanted her anyway... just as she was!" said Mr. Jaramillo. "Outside of church it's a cruel world out there, but in the church we've found comfort, love and hope for the future."

 VIEW: Siebels Family/Jaramillo Family

In Lessons 10-14 we'll break down the steps to starting a church disability ministry, as well as age-group ministries for children, youth, adults and the elderly with special needs. You'll hear from everyday experts who serve in the trenches of this ministry offensive and witness families being transformed by God through the church's strength as a growing *organism* and a unified *organization*.

ACTIVITY CHALLENGE

Search for a church in your community that has a support group for couples and/or families affected by disabilities. Ask permission to visit the group or to talk to some of the couples who attend. Remember to respect their need for privacy, but share with them that you're taking a course to better understand disability ministry. After your visit, compare the biblical framework of the church with the experiences of these families.

Reflections on Lesson 9
Major Challenges of the Church on the Path to Maturity

1. Discuss the growing shift in how our modern society thinks about the church.

2. How does Chuck Colson's description of a "reductionist view of Christianity" conflict with the biblical nature of the church?

3. Identify the biblical function of the church.

4. What are some true signs of "koinonia" in a local church?

5. According to Dr. Michael S. Beates, what are the major challenges of the church on the path to maturity?

6. Reflecting on the privileges of striving to be a part of a mature Body of Christ, how are you being stretched in your faith?

7. Discuss the importance of the seven movements of ministry described in Rev. Bundy's paper as they relate to persons with disability.

8. Write a prayer using Acts 2:42-47 as a model for your church's disability ministry.

How to Start a *Disability Ministry* in the Church

We often hear the questions, "Can one person really make a difference? And if so, where does one begin?" You may be surprised to learn that one person with a disability has often been God's change agent in a church. The first step is simply showing up with a desire to belong. That's how it happened on Joni Eareckson Tada's first Sunday back to her church after a lengthy recovery from a tragic diving accident. Joni recalls that day:

> There I was, out of the rehab center only a few weeks, sitting upright and awkward in my bulky wheelchair and wondering what to do about Sunday morning. I knew my church had been praying for me since my diving accident two years earlier in 1967, but facing people terrified me. Would they stare? Would I know what to say? Would I have to sit next to my family in the pew, half blocking the middle aisle? And what if I had to wheel into the restroom—would I fit?
>
> What I discovered that Sunday morning, after my family lifted me out of the car and into my wheelchair, changed my entire outlook on church. Someone had hammered together a few pieces of plywood to make a ramp. People smiled and asked me how I was doing at college. Old friends asked me to sit with them and held my Bible and hymnal. The feeling was warm and friendly. I felt welcome. I belonged.[1]

What happened in Joni's church can happen in any congregation, but it doesn't happen overnight. Even the most mature church can be immobilized by fear when it comes to adding a disability ministry on the shoulders of over-extended pastors and volunteers. However, when the church sign out front reads, "The Friendliest Church in Town," and a wheelchair ramp or large-print Bible is nowhere to be found, we must admit that our words don't match

OBJECTIVES

Studying this lesson will help you:

✔ Detect the myths about disability ministry.

✔ Enlist pastors and leaders in disability ministry.

✔ Explain the steps to becoming a disability-friendly church.

✔ Describe effective disability ministry models.

✔ Communicate the vision to the congregation and community.

our actions. No church wants to turn individuals and families with special needs away, but it happens far too often.

In Lesson 8 we examined the clear directive of the Luke 14 Mandate to bring in the "poor, the crippled, the lame and the blind." And in the book of James we read that faith without works is no faith at all.[2] So in this lesson we will roll up our sleeves and delve into some practical strategies that can open church doors to welcome those with disabilities. Successful ministries begin with a clear mission statement, so here are some examples of disability ministry goals.

The Goals of Disability Ministry

- A disability ministry and outreach opens the door to share the Gospel with people with disabilities and introduces them to a personal relationship with God.

- A disability ministry and outreach integrates people with disabilities into the life of the church and gives them the opportunity to have active roles in serving God.

- A disability ministry and outreach enables the church to serve as a witness or model to the community for meeting the spiritual, physical, and social needs of people with disabilities.

? *Inclusion*

If you have ever been picked last for the ball team or missed out on an invitation to a party, you know the pain of rejection. Maybe you once visited an unfamiliar church and felt alone, until someone struck up a conversation or invited you to lunch or a special event. That new friend flipped a PA switch announcing, "You belong here!" and that made all the difference. Full inclusion in the family of God should always be an open invitation!

I. **Addressing Concerns about Disability Ministry**

Before we can build awareness for a disability ministry, we must shine some light on several misconceptions church members may have due to a lack of education. These common misunderstandings can keep churches from acting on their biblical values and convictions. Perhaps people in your own church have expressed concerns or fears about ministering to people with disabilities. Here are some typical ones:

> *Our church doesn't have the resources or volunteers for a disability ministry.*
> *Is disability ministry part of our church's vision or core values?*
> *Volunteers need disability experience or a background in Special Education.*
> *We don't have people with disabilities in our church.*
> *People with disabilities will be a burden and can't contribute to our church.*

The truth is that congregations are filled with people whose gifts and talents are divinely designed to meet every need within the church family. Jesus showed us by example that all people should be treated equally. He spent time "hanging out" with people from all walks of life, doing simple activities and getting to know them. God's love and mercy qualify Christians to reach into their communities where an estimated 20 percent of their neighborhoods are affected in some way by disability.[3] We naturally fear the unknown, yet all types of ministry are a risk to some degree. If we don't take the risk, we don't love people.

The Father's House video discusses seven misunderstandings people have about disability ministry in the church. As you watch, make a list of the positive aspects that result from starting such a ministry.

VIEW: Watch **Section 1** of The Father's House: Welcoming and Including People and Families Affected by Disability. Pause at 17:15, after "The Blessings." (Joni and Friends DVD005)

A. **Moving from Conviction to Action**
   In Matthew 17:20 Jesus said, "If you have faith as small as a mustard seed, you can say to this mountain, 'Move from here to there' and it will move." Starting a new disability ministry can seem like a steep, upward climb. Before you begin, seek the Lord's direction through prayer and Bible reading. Ask God for the right timing and focus for this ministry. Enlist the support of the church's prayer teams

and develop prayer guides to encourage others to pray for the needs of individuals and families affected by disabilities. Begin praying about how to inspire your church leaders and congregation to understand that people with disabilities belong in God's family and to take new steps of faith to begin a disability ministry.

Use the following Action Assessment Chart to consider your congregation's stage of commitment. It may be helpful to conduct a special church survey to detect needs and ways to move the congregation to a higher level of involvement. For a sample survey see Appendix C.

Action Assessment Chart [4]

4. Action
The special needs ministry is recognized and supported by the church and is an integral part of the vision and mission.

3. Ownership
It's taking shape. Church members are working on a special needs ministry.

2. Value
Reaching, serving and including people with disabilities reflects the mission and value of our church.

1. Conviction
Some churches should have a disability ministry, but maybe not our church.

Stage 1—Conviction is a belief that something should be done by someone, but not necessarily by your church. At this stage, churches are content to let the church across town offer a disability ministry.

Stage 2—Value is the next step toward action. Churches begin to value a ministry when they recognize that it is in line with their church's mission statement. Leaders begin to consider how a disability ministry could help them accomplish their vision and reach their community.

Stage 3—Ownership happens when one or more people volunteer to take responsibility for the ministry with the approval of church leaders. Until someone says, "I'll do it!" ownership may only be a mirage.

Stage 4—Action occurs when church leaders give their blessing to a plan and the plan is implemented. Goals are set and reported on. Families affected by disability feel welcome and included at church.

B. **Barriers to Participation**

While some fears about disability ministry are unrealistic, there are legitimate barriers that can keep people with disabilities from full participation in the church, such as:

1. **Architectural Barriers**—These include issues of accessibility for the physically disabled: sanctuary, classrooms, fellowship hall, etc.

2. **Attitudinal Barriers**—Even greater than the architectural challenges are the challenges of attitude. Many people, even Christians, are prejudiced or biased against people with disabilities, particularly with respect to their ability to learn. This is especially true when an individual has intellectual and developmental disabilities.

3. **Theological Barriers**—As we discussed in Module 2, "Theology of Suffering and Disability," many church members may not see the necessity for a disability ministry. In their eyes individuals with disabilities need to be "delivered" or "healed." Handicaps are simply not part of the "real" Body of Christ.

4. **Communication Barriers**—It can be challenging to talk with people whose communication style is different due to deafness, blindness or other intellectual and sensory disorders.

5. **Pragmatic Barriers**—Enabling individuals with disabilities and/or their families to connect to the church

may require practical assistance, such as adapted educational materials, special equipment or changes in meeting locations.

6. **Liturgical Barriers**—Some sacramental practices and rituals (such as communion or baptism) may exclude people with developmental disabilities. Some pastors or leaders may be unwilling to adapt or alter long-held practices.

Church pastors and leaders, who understand Christ's biblical mandate to include families affected by disabilities, must educate their congregations to address and overcome these barriers.

II. **Everything Rises and Falls on Leadership**

When starting a new ministry, it is critical to share your vision with your pastoral team and ask for their support and blessing. This is not a time to guess about financial resources for the ministry. Disability ministry is often seen as costly with little return; this is simply not the case. When you reach one person with a special need, you reach a whole family, as well as their friends and neighbors. Using Scriptures and testimonies from this curriculum will help leaders articulate the benefit of ministering to those with disabilities.

The disability director has an important role in ensuring that good policies, procedures and practices are established and followed. He or she acts as a bridge or liaison with groups inside and outside of the church such as community homes and organizations. Confidentiality is also crucial in leadership and ministry to people with disabilities. Individuals, parents and caregivers may provide the director with sensitive personal and medical information that is private and must be carefully protected. Ministry leaders that use this information for volunteer training should only share the necessary information in the strictest of confidences.

In the following paper, "All Things Possible," Stephanie Hubach shares the biblical importance of calling leaders to disability ministry, while providing a practical approach to addressing issues that may arise.

READ: "All Things Possible: Calling Your Church Leaders to Embrace Disability Ministry" by Stephanie O. Hubach

"Ministry is messy. God plops people with disabilities in the midst of a congregation— a hand grenade that blows apart the picture-perfectness of the church. But these disenfranchised folks are the 'indispensable' part of the body."

Joni Eareckson Tada

162

Discuss the scriptural reasons Ms. Hubach cites for calling leaders to disability ministry.

A. **No "Lone Rangers" in Ministry**

Disability ministry is not a solo act. God places within the Body of Christ all of the gifts and skills needed to minister to one another. Recruit a team of leaders which includes people with and without disabilities. Share your vision with the team and lead them in developing a mission statement. Allow your team time to pray and own the ministry.

B. **You Need Not Look Far to Find People with Disabilities**

1. **Start with the need.** Who are those with disabilities in your community that are attending church or want to come? Start small and build from there. Trying to reach every age level and type of disability all at once can strain your team and cause burnout before you really get started.

2. **Choose a model.** Decide what kind of disability ministry model works best in your church. Although full inclusion is usually recommended, there may be instances where a special classroom or separate meeting time is appropriate.

3. **Decide what program(s) you might start with first.** If children with disabilities attend your church, you may begin ministering to those families by adapting teaching materials and starting a support group for parents. If you have adults with developmental disabilities, you may begin with Bible study groups and social events.

C. **What Will Disability Ministry Cost?**—There may be some costs involved in making needed adaptations to your church facilities or programs. These must be considered and appropriately presented to the church leaders.

D. **Many Are Called But Few Are Chosen**—As you recruit volunteers, put the call out for anyone who has a heart for ministry. Most people do not feel qualified to minister to people with special needs. Encourage church members to spend some time with you and others to simply observe and see how they might fit in. Once they get past the fear factor, they will likely enjoy the ministry.

At first I thought we didn't have the resources to reach out in an intentional way to people and families affected by disability. Now I can't imagine having a church without ministry to them. Our church has significantly grown in Christ-likeness and in numbers as a direct result of disability ministry. —Pastor Steve Pope

---

III. **Ten Practical Tips for Becoming a Disability Friendly Church**

Many churches already have an ideal character and environment for reaching out to individuals and families with special needs. There is a strong spirit of unity and fellowship, as well as a desire to share God's love through acts of service and mercy. There is a heart of expectancy among church leaders even when they're not sure of the direction God is leading. Then one person with a vision for the disability community has courage to speak up, and a new ministry is born. As you watch the second half of *The Father's House*, check these tips to assess the readiness of your church for a disability ministry.

 VIEW: Watch **Section 2** of The Father's House. Begin at 17:15, "10 Practical Tips for Becoming a Disability Friendly Church." (Joni and Friends DVD005)

1. **Provide a warm, friendly, welcoming environment.** Greet people with disabilities as you would anybody else. Communicate that people affected by disability are loved, belong, and are included in your church.

2. **Provide basic disability awareness training for your church staff and volunteers.** Review basic disability etiquette. Invite a Joni and Friends representative or disability expert to your church. Obtain disability ministry resources from Joni and Friends.

3. **Improve accessibility. Make modifications where necessary.** Imagine yourself in a wheelchair or having difficulty

with mobility and make necessary changes. If necessary, modify access to the main entrance, the sanctuary, restrooms and classrooms.

4. **Provide serving opportunities for people with disabilities.** Utilize people with disabilities to serve as ushers and greeters. Ask people with disabilities to help serve communion. Call upon people with disabilities to read Scripture. Include people with disabilities on the worship and prayer teams, or ask them to share their testimony.

5. **Provide disability-friendly materials.** Have large print or Braille Bibles available. Print song sheets for those who are visually impaired. Consider providing assistive listening devices for the hearing impaired.

6. **Provide space for wheelchair users throughout the sanctuary.** Shorten a few pews or take some chairs away from rows so wheelchair users can sit with their families and friends.

7. **Provide a sign interpreter for people who are deaf or hard of hearing.** Place a sign interpreter in a well-lit area that can be seen throughout the entire sanctuary.

8. **General communication and interaction tips.** Treat people with disabilities as you would anyone else. Speak directly with the person with the disability, not through their parents or caregivers. Be relaxed around people with disabilities, not awkward. Don't get caught up with fancy euphemisms, such as "physically challenged" or "differently able." Put the person first, not their disability.

9. **Provide assistance in the handicap parking area.** Have an attendant available to help people with disabilities from their vans. Offer to push their wheelchair if needed. Have a wheelchair available to assist those with difficulty in mobility.

10. **Provide a "buddy" or mentor for those who might need assistance.** Utilize assistants to help people with disabilities participate in worship service. Have a buddy system for children with disabilities in Sunday school classrooms.

IV. **Selecting Effective Disability Ministry Models**

Generally, people with disabilities wish to participate in the same activities in the same way as any other member of the community. Most of them want to be members of a welcoming church family. Therefore, church leaders and members must work hard to make their churches fully-inclusive of all people, whatever their disability, in all aspects of church life, including worship services, social events, classes, and small groups. The following paper presents six training ideas and 15 ministry models.

READ: *Successful Models of Disability Ministry* by Joni Eareckson Tada and Jack S. Oppenhuizen. This paper is a summary from the Lausanne Occasional Paper, No. 35 B. Section 7 (2005). You can download the complete presentation paper at: http://www.joniandfriends.org/static/uploads/downloads/Successful_Models2.pdf

Select one of the models in this paper that you feel would be well received in your church and discuss it with a friend or pastor.

One Pastor's Story

The Living Springs Community Church in Glenwood, IL, launched their Friendship Ministry for people with disabilities shortly after moving into their new church, which was designed with disabilities in mind. When the church scheduled a Disability Awareness Sunday, the planning committee asked Pastor Chris Spoor to preach from a wheelchair and he readily agreed. In an interview with Pat Verbal for the book, *Special Needs Special Ministry*, Pastor Spoor shared that the experience went beyond his expectations.

I got into a wheelchair as soon as I arrived at the church that day. During the first service, I pushed myself onto the platform. But in the second service, a member of our Friendship Ministry team pushed the chair for me. I found that a little more difficult to accept. To be passively dependent on someone else was a very humbling experience. We don't have a special needs ministry to grow numbers. We do it because it's the biblical mandate of the church of Jesus Christ. One of our core values is 'intentional inclusion' in every area.

Some people think that just refers to race, but it also means abilities...

Now, I tell other pastors how important it is to make up your mind to start a disability ministry and do it![5]

V. Going Beyond a Sunday Ministry

Jackie Mills-Fernald, Director of Access Ministry at McLean Bible Church in McLean, Virginia, is a great example of steadfast leadership in this area. She has inspired her church and many others to go beyond a Sunday program to fully include the disability community in Christian fellowship and service.

 READ: "Beyond Sunday Morning: Creating a Truly Inclusionary Culture" by Jackie Mills-Fernald

What advice does Mills-Fernald offer for managing a disability ministry?

Disability ministry may have some challenges and barriers, but as we have seen, they can be overcome. As we seek to obey Scripture to include people with disabilities in the life of the church, the Lord will guide us in creating a vibrant ministry with God-honoring, growing relationships.

For more information on starting a disability ministry contact one of the Joni and Friends Field Ministries across the U.S. through the church relations page on the Joni and Friends web site. *http://www.joniandfriends.org/church-relations/*

CREATE AN ACTION PLAN

Write three action steps you will take to assist your church in including people with disabilities in your church's ministry. Share your list with a friend who will pray with you and hold you accountable.

Reflections on Lesson 10
How to Start a Disability Ministry in the Church

1. What is your church currently doing to serve the disability community? If your answer is "very little," why do you think more is not being done?

2. What do you see as the biggest barrier to starting or improving a disability ministry?

3. Have you heard church members express any of the attitudes discussed in *The Father's House* video? If so, how have these attitudes been successfully addressed?

4. Where would your church fall on the Action Assessment Chart and why?

5. According to Ms. Hubach, what does the progressive transformational process of getting your church leadership onboard look like in the context of disability ministry?

6. List four practical tips from this lesson for becoming a disability-friendly church.

7. Why isn't a Sunday morning disability ministry enough?

8. If you volunteered for one of the disability ministry models in Mrs. Tada's paper, which one would it be and why?

Ministering to *Children and Teens* with Special Needs

OBJECTIVES

Studying this lesson will help you:

✔ Describe the challenges and effects of disabilities on children and teens.

✔ Understand the spiritual needs of children with special needs.

✔ Support parents as the primary models of faith in their homes.

✔ Create training opportunities for teachers, volunteers, and parents.

✔ Adapt church programs to meet the unique needs of the children and teens with special needs.

✔ Help typical children welcome children and teens with special needs.

When God separated light from darkness to create the first day, how bright that light must have been. The contrast of an early sunrise can still take our breath away if we slow down to enjoy it. We often witness this same kind of contrast in the lives of children with disabilities. The depths of their struggles can make their smallest success glow with heavenly light. And those of us who are fortunate enough to know these amazing children experience the warm rays of God's love shining through their smiles.

All children remind us that ***God is good***. In Romans 8:28, God promised to share that goodness with us. Yet, when Katie was born with a neurobiological disorder, the doctors said she would be mentally retarded. But one day this toddler looked out the car window and read a street sign. Katie's parents gave her a book, which she also read. They soon discovered that Katie was hyperlexic, meaning she had an exceptional, untaught reading ability from a young age. As a fourth grader, Katie, who has Asperger's syndrome, taught herself Japanese. She continued to amaze her family with God's perfect plan for her life.

Children remind us that ***God is faithful***. Cole was afraid of the rough neighborhood where he and his mom lived. He often cried himself to sleep thinking about the bullies who made fun of him because he couldn't walk. But Cole learned to pray for bad people and to trust God for protection. He even requested prayer at church for his neighborhood, which eventually lead several members of the congregation to reach out to the bullies and share Christ with them.

These children show us that the image of ***God is within us***—not on the outside. Christy discovered this concept when she cared for

Elliot at camp. His multiple disabilities kept him locked in a crippled body, sitting almost motionless in his wheelchair. He never spoke, made eye contact or responded to her touch. Early in the week, Christy stood by watching Elliot as the other campers swam, made crafts and giggled. By midweek she felt content to push Elliot's chair down quiet paths under the trees, where she would read poems to him and sing songs. She came to appreciate the serenity of their times together and was sad to say goodbye.

The Bible speaks of our need for childlike faith—a faith that surrenders our "grown-up" efforts to understand and fix things. As we minister to children and teens with special needs, we may be tempted to question Romans 8:28. We may even question God's goodness and power to make all things work together for good for children like Katie, Cole or Elliot. And that's when children with special needs will become your teachers![1]

ℙ *Vulnerability*

Jesus said, "Whoever welcomes a little child like this in my name welcomes me" (Matt. 18:5). Jesus taught more than just a particular preference for children; he insisted that the youngest, the weakest, the most vulnerable are the ones to whom we should give special honor. For when we do, we give him that same honor. It is easy to like nice kids and fun to be around well-disciplined children. However, they do not always come that way.
—Joni Eareckson Tada

I. **Growing Up with Special Needs: The Elementary Years**
You've heard it said that children are resilient, bouncing back in tough times. If that's true, it must be due to their God-given sense of hope and wonder. Children help us to see spotted lady bugs resting on green leaves, talk us into joining them for a bike ride when we're tired, and entertain us with delightful, imaginative stories. And their prayers make us smile... even on the toughest day. But what about children who can't see or speak or move their arms and legs? What is life like for them?

A. **The Effects of Disabilities on Children**

In Lesson 2 we discussed a broad-range of disabilities and identified some of their characteristics. These descriptions become even more diverse when we consider a child's age, developmental level, personality, health and environment. Young children are often unaware of their own disabilities or the special needs of their peers. By school-age, however, various kinds of disabilities become evident in some of the following common traits:

+ Hyperactivity with short attention spans
+ Distractibility and impulsiveness
+ Poor visual or motor skills; limited large muscle or fine muscle coordination
+ Rapid and excessive changes of mood and reasoning
+ Faulty perception with repetitious thoughts and/or actions
+ Problems with social interaction; inconsistent and unpredictable behavior

While these characteristics can be especially challenging to teachers and volunteers at church, there is good news! Children with special needs are often the most exciting children to teach because many are eager to please and willing to serve others. They can sense when teachers truly care and eagerly express their love and appreciation.

 VIEW: Making Sense of Autism, Part 1 (Joni and Friends DVDTV30)

What did you observe about the adults who interacted with the children in the video?

Children Ask Hard Questions about Faith

All children have problems. Children with special needs don't necessarily have more problems than their peers, but their challenges and experiences are unique. These children can get depressed dealing with limitations or pain. They often feel lonely, because people may not take the time to get to know them. Sometimes adults treat them as if they can't learn, when they may actually have above average IQs. Children with disabilities need to

age

development level

personality

health

environment

___

hyperactivity

distractibility

poor motor skills

rapid excessive mood changes

faulty perceptions w/ repetitious thoughts

inconsistent / unpredictable behaviors

173

know that Jesus understands their feelings and that he cares about their problems. Here are five of the questions we should be prepared to answer. Keep in mind that discussions should be appropriate for a child's age and level of comprehension.[2]

1. *Does Jesus know when I'm hurting?*

[handwritten: mocked false identity]

Jesus came to earth as a baby because he wanted to feel everything you experience. He was even your age once. Jesus knows how you feel when others call you names like "cripple" or "retard." People called him "liar" and "blasphemer" (one who speaks against God). Jesus also understands your pain because men nailed his hands and feet to a cross and stuck a spear into his side. Jesus will comfort you in hard times and use you to comfort others.[3]

2. *If Jesus loves me, why doesn't he fix my disability?*

Perhaps you've read stories in the Bible about how Jesus healed people. He touched a blind man's eyes so he could see. He told another man to pick up his bed and walk, and the man's crippled legs became strong. But Jesus didn't heal everyone he met. He knows that people are much more than their disability. When Joni Eareckson Tada dove into a lake at the age of 17, she broke her neck and severed her spinal cord. It wasn't easy for Joni to accept the fact that she would never walk or use her hands again. Yet from her wheelchair, she leads a worldwide ministry. Maybe you don't need "fixing," because you are more than your disability. Just as he did for Joni, Jesus has a plan for your whole life.

3. *Is Jesus disappointed in me when I'm not brave?*

You probably wish you'd never have to take another treatment or see another doctor. Maybe you worry that you'll have to stay in the hospital again. Jesus doesn't expect you to be brave all the time—everyone gets scared sometimes. It's normal to be scared about serious health problems. It helps to talk to your parents and doctors about your concerns and ask questions.

You have a right to know about your condition. If you feel scared, you can also call friends and ask them to pray with you. (Psalm 56:3)

4. *If I can't do very much, does Jesus still want me?*

Jesus cares more about who you are than what you can or cannot do. He loves you, and he cares about who you are on the inside. Are you honest and kind? When someone takes time to help you, do you say "Thank you"? Are you grateful for everything you have, or do you envy others? Your disability doesn't give you the right to be rude or act out. Be willing to try new things, and do what you're able to do. Jesus only expects you to do your best. Don't compare yourself to others—instead, encourage them and pray for them.[4]

5. *Does Jesus know when I'm going to die?*

Yes! Jesus not only knows when you will die, but he has already prepared a heavenly paradise for you. One day all sadness and suffering will end for those who know Jesus as their Savior. There won't be any more pain or tears. In eternity, *every* child will get a perfect mind and body, and life there will be much better than it is here. Then, you'll understand things that confuse you now. Best of all, Jesus will welcome you into his kingdom and show you around the New Earth. You can read about it in the Book of Revelation.

II. The Unique Challenges of Teens with Disabilities

Sometimes we think youth ministries have all the fun, but we know today's adolescents are a challenge. Among these media-driven, pro-green multi-taskers, 13 is the new 16. They are the brightest and the best, but many also experience divorce, abuse, drugs, depression and rage. For teens with special needs these years can also pose the biggest hurdles. Parents and youth volunteers at church are equally as challenged.

Michael, a 14-year-old with autism, likes attending the fifth-grade Sunday school class. Some preteen parents insist he is too big and should be promoted, but Michael's mother is afraid for him to join the youth group. On the other hand, Ashley's mom expects her to be promoted to the youth ministry as soon as she turns 13. But the youth leaders are not sure Ashley will fit in with the 7th-12th graders because she is very low-functioning due to her Down syndrome.

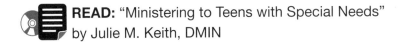 **READ:** "Ministering to Teens with Special Needs" by Julie M. Keith, DMIN

Who decides where teens with limited social skills belong?

How can youth leaders love and support all of the teens in their church?

Discuss the In His Image Guidelines for volunteers and one-on-one buddies in Appendix D.

A. **Adolescence Relational Maze**

The journey through "teenagedom" requires finding one's way along a confusing path of social realities. Most teens face emotional turmoil, but those with disabilities try especially hard to belong. When they are able to connect with Christian friends, their lives can be much easier. This includes adult friends such as pastors, teachers and volunteers. Here are some ways you can help:

1. Your attitude toward special needs ministry is crucial. The comments you make about teens at church stick! Don't act like this is the hardest ministry you've ever done. Your attitude will be contagious.

2. Educate youth leaders and other teens about special needs, as well as about their talents and spiritual gifts. Encourage adults and peers to invest time getting to know a teen's strengths and weaknesses. But be respectful—always seek parental permission before discussing a teen's disability with anyone.

3. Foster good communication between parents and youth leaders; host an introductory meeting or special events for families and volunteers.

4. Use students' interests to assimilate them into youth programs. Some enjoy baseball, computer games, music, etc. Interests can be shared in a small group of

teens before students with special needs are thrust into large group activities.

5. Provide a flexible transition period, allowing adolescents with special needs to visit between the children and youth departments for a few weeks. Assume they are doing their best, and don't push. Remember that for teens without disabilities welcoming classmates with special needs may be a new experience. Encourage everyone to not give up.

6. Help all departments in your church adopt a zero tolerance for hurtful language regarding those with disabilities. Teach teens to reject vulgar movies such as *Tropic Thunder* where the word "retard" is used 17 times in five minutes. Post Ephesians 4:29 above the youth center entrance: "Say only what will help to build others up and meet their needs."

You may be asking, "Why should I do all of this when our youth leaders just don't seem to understand special needs?" That is what Doug Fields, former youth pastor at Saddleback Church in Southern California, once thought—until some kids changed his mind.

"The highlight of my week at camp was hanging out with the students from our group who had special needs," said Doug. "I hate to tell you this, but I didn't really want them to go. I thought the spots they were taking could be filled with other students. Was I ever wrong! These few students with special needs impacted everyone at camp. Their smiles. Their unique way of communicating. Their appreciation for the little things. Not only did I fall in love with them, but our students were drawn to them and cared for them in ways I couldn't have dreamed of."[5]

Like Doug, youth leaders at your church can learn to welcome teens with special needs— and be proud to share stories like this one from Sizwe David Mabowe, an African-American teenager.

By age 13 Sizwe had overcome more obstacles than most kids. As a preschooler he was diagnosed with autism and learning disabilities. In elementary school he had constant seizures, limited language skills and behavior problems. But thanks to Sizwe's church, he found acceptance and a place of service. In his own words, he shares his story.

> When I am confused, my brain really hurts, and I can't respond to anything. My confusion makes me sad sometimes, but it is wonderful when people are patient and praise me when I do get things right. I love Jesus. He has given me the gift to pray. You may not always understand everything I am saying, but the Spirit does, and Mommy is always shouting hallelujahs when I am praying. Often I read my teen Bible and thank God for healing my mind. Two Sundays a month, I am a youth assistant for the kindergartners. We paint, perform plays, read God's Word and sing songs. They love to make paper models, especially paper balls and birds of paradise. I am happy when they are excited to see me. I also sing in the gospel choir every three months. I am so glad God protects me and helps me to think, speak and understand.[6]

The success story here is not about Sizwe learning to fit into the typical church mold, but rather that his church leadership understood and made changes to meet his needs. They were not content to allow him to sit in a corner and just learn to act "right." They challenged him and praised him when he served others. What is your church doing to include teens like Sizwe?

III. **Small Adaptations Pay Big Dividends**

A. **Preparing Your Church to Welcome and Serve All Children**

Volunteers often hesitate to work with children with special needs. How can we inspire them?

People fear and avoid what they don't understand. That is why families affected by disability often feel isolated. As you recruit volunteers, assure them that 1) they only need to become knowledgeable about one child's needs, 2) parents are great teachers, 3) they will make new friends, and 4) they can touch a whole family for Christ.

Pray about inviting volunteers and families with special needs to your home for a meal. Fellowship is the key to breaking down walls and inspiring loyalty.

Pat Verbal is the Manager of Curriculum Development at the Christian Institute on Disability at Joni and Friends. She writes and speaks from a broad Christian education background which includes starting special needs ministries in several churches. In the following paper Pat offers helpful ideas for teachers and volunteers who seek to adapt church programs to meet the unique needs of children with disabilities.

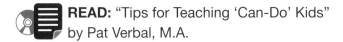 **READ:** "Tips for Teaching 'Can-Do' Kids" by Pat Verbal, M.A.

Using the tips discussed in this paper, consider how you might adapt a lesson plan to teach the Christmas story in Luke 2 to a third-grade girl with muscular dystrophy or a first-grader with Down syndrome.

B. **Serving the Unique Needs of Every Child**

Children have unique strengths, abilities and learning styles. A teacher's goal is to present God's Word to children in ways that allow for understanding and life application, so any program or curriculum must be evaluated with the students' abilities in mind. Most students with special needs are able to use existing children's ministry resources with minor adaptations. James, who is hearing impaired, benefits from picture symbols that illustrate the story's sequence. A large-print Bible allows Dustin, who has low vision, to participate during the Bible reading. Children with developmental disabilities need curriculum, music and activities modified to their level of understanding. Here are a few suggested resources that will help.

1. *Special Needs Smart Pages* by Joni and Friends (2009) contains over 150 articles with advice and answers on ministering to children with disabilities. This comprehensive guide answers many questions on classroom management, curriculum adaptation, communication and safety challenges and outreach projects. It comes with a reproducible CD-ROM to help you

create training tools for teachers and volunteers. This resource is available at www.joniandfriends.org/store.

2. *Joni and Friends Kids Corner* is an interactive website for children with special needs. Kids can sing and blog with Joni, share art and stories, get help on book reports and join others in prayer. www.joniandfriends.org/kids-corner

3. *On a Roll for Jesus! Mission:Unstoppable* and *Camp Lean-on-the-Lord* by Diane Monreal are two disability awareness programs for ages 4-12. Each kit includes five kid-friendly lessons that help children move from uncertainty to understanding. They also include mission projects to help kids support children and adults with disabilities. www.joniandfriends.org/store

4. *Special Buddies Curriculum for Children with Special Needs* is just right for a child spending time with a one-on-one caregiver or in a class of his peers. It is designed for two Bible stories per month allowing time for needed adaptations and repetition. www.Lifeway.com

IV. **Home and Church Go Hand in Hand**

A large part of disability ministry involves strengthening parents, as they seek to provide physical and emotional nurturing at home. It begins with building a relationship with them so we can eventually point them to God's Word for answers through the natural stages of grief that accompany a child being diagnosed with a disability. For many, worry and exhaustion can stall the faith process, but God's plan for them is just as real as his plan for their children. He wants parents to grow deeper in their faith and to trust him more. Without these two things families are susceptible to Satan's temptations to separate or divorce and blame God for their struggles.

Like many men, Jon Ebersole, Director of Field Ministry at Joni and Friends, found himself in a new role as the father of twin daughters with cerebral palsy. He provides an intimate look into the heart of a father, and a touching example of what we hope and pray for every parent affected by disability.

 **READ:** "A Parent's Journey from Weakness to Power" by Jon Ebersole

How was Jon able to find the plan God had for his life?

Is there a parent in your church who needs to read Jon's story this week?

A. **Meeting with Parents**

There are some critical steps to interacting with parents of teens with disabilities. Nathan Gunn, Area Director for Young Life Syracuse East & Urban, NY, suggests these steps:

1. Before you share your plans, meet with each family to see what their own experiences and dreams are for their teen.

2. Approach parents with a compassionate and open mind. Make yourself a student of their experiences as a family.

3. Ask what would be important to avoid and what would be essential to including their teen in your church.

4. Inquire about what kind of social interaction and learning environment works best for their teen.

5. Ask about their schedules. What locations and times work best for their families?

"In each instance where I've had these intimate conversations with parents," says Nathan, "I've asked them to approach me directly if we let them or their child down in any way. Our highest hope is that their teen's time in our group would be a blessing, but at the same time, we can't offer perfection. The goal is to learn from the families about their lives and their child while creating an open door for future feedback that will help us serve their child."

V. **Helping Classmates Understand Disabilities**

Disability Awareness Activities: "Inclusion Walk"[7]
Take children on a walk around your church facility to see if it would be easy or difficult for someone with a disability to attend services, classes or other activities there.

*Don't just see my
legs not running;
Don't just see my
hands not writing;
Don't just see my
mouth not talking;
These broken
pieces are not me.
See instead the light
in my eyes;
See instead the loving
soul; See instead my
thinking mind;
These inner pieces
are the real me.*

JOE BISHOP
A teen with cerebral palsy

Before the walk, discuss with the children how they feel about being included when they go to school or church. Point out that people with disabilities want to be included too, but sometimes even the building and grounds make it difficult for them to be a part of things.

On the "Inclusion Walk" take a wheelchair along if possible. Have the children look for stairs, curbs, narrow pathways, steep hills, etc. Discuss whether or not a person in a wheelchair could get around easily. Think about the places people might go such as the parking lot, through the front door, to a classroom, restroom, playground, snack or refreshment area, gym or main office. When the group returns from the walk, discuss their observations.

"God is looking for people who will go the extra mile, make the extra effort, and do it all in a spirit of humility, and I can't think of a better place to selflessly serve than among families affected by disability. So, if you're a volunteer, 'Thank you!'"
—Joni Eareckson Tada

Reflections on Lesson 11

Ministering to Children and Teens with Special Needs

1. List some of the behavioral traits of children with special needs.

2. Choose one of the questions children have about faith and write a scriptural response.

3. What were some important factors that helped teenager Sizwe David Mabowe accept his learning disabilities?

4. What are some ways you can reassure volunteers who are insecure about serving children with special needs?

5. Discuss the three stages God led Jon Ebersole through to overcome his weaknesses as a parent to children with disabilities.

6. Anticipating that there may be adjustments needed along the way to be most effective in ministry, what does Nathan Gunn ask of the parents of the children in his youth group?

7. If you were to volunteer to work with a special needs ministry, describe the children you would be most comfortable serving.

Ministering to *Adults and the Elderly* with Special Needs

OBJECTIVES

Studying this lesson will help you:

✔ Explain life stages and faith formation for adults affected by disabilities.

✔ Describe successful teaching methods for adults with intellectual disabilities.

✔ Plan ways to use the spiritual gifts of those in the disability community.

✔ Minister to the unique needs of older adults with late onset disabilities.

✔ Support and encourage marriages and caregivers.

Hollywood is not silent on adults with disabilities, and unfortunately, its impact on our culture finds its way into our faith communities. Academy Award winning movies such as *Rain Man, I am Sam,* and *Forrest Gump* feature actors who attempt to enlighten us about disabilities, but often leave us with negative, inaccurate portrayals.

Raymond, the main character in *Rain Man,* is referred to as an "autistic savant." Upon his father's death, Raymond inherits a multimillion dollar trust fund. In order to steal the money, Raymond's selfish brother kidnaps him, shattering his well-ordered life in a care facility and driving him across the country. This emotionally-charged adventure reveals the many sides of autism for everyone involved. While the film was the highest-grossing movie of the year, it left the public with the misconception that all adults with autism are geniuses in math.

In the movie *I am Sam,* a loving father with intellectual disability fights Child Protection Services for custody of his daughter Lilly. As Sam struggles to get a job and an apartment, the audience is moved by his fatherly care and protection toward Lilly. In the end, Lilly's foster mother recognizes their unbreakable father-daughter bond and agrees that Lilly belongs with Sam. This satisfying conclusion, however, is more of the exception than the rule for parents with low IQs.

The portrayal of Forrest Gump in the original novel is notably different than the film. In the novel, Forrest is shown to be somewhat cynical and abrasive—he is a more placid and naive person in the popular film. Forrest is also described as being "socially and mentally slow" yet displaying extraordinary talent in many areas. While his innocence is endearing, what does he really teach us about people with developmental disabilities?

If Raymond, Sam or Forrest came to your church, would they find friends? Would they be fully included in all religious and social events?

Adults with disabilities are in every neighborhood and their numbers are growing due to advances in medicine and geriatric care. Young people with autism are likely to live into their senior years, requiring life-long care. Middle-aged adults are receiving disabling diagnoses such as Alzheimer's, Parkinson's, Multiple Sclerosis, and mental illnesses. Some become impaired due to cancer, strokes or accidents. In this lesson we will consider the realities they face every day and consider how we can include them in our faith communities.

⚷ *Friendship*

To discover a person's true nature, look at his friends. The deepest friendships are forged in the fire of adversity. When darkness besieges you, a true friend holds the light at the end of the tunnel that beckons you forward. In Proverbs 17:17 David described a friend as one who "loves at all times." It may be humbling when that friend sits in a wheelchair or mumbles his words. Yet, his light is equally bright when Jesus Christ shines through him.
—Pat Verbal

Open Hearts, Open Doors

Visitors to University United Methodist Church in San Antonio, Texas, are often surprised to be welcomed by a smiling greeter with Down syndrome. Once inside, they are directed to a hospitality cafe where coffee and breakfast burritos are served by volunteers with cerebral palsy and autism. They notice in the bulletin that a mid-week fellowship brings in van loads of adults from community care facilities. And by the time visitors enter worship, they are not surprised to see several robed choir members in wheelchairs.

Churches like UUMC have learned the joy of including adults with disabilities in their congregations. They don't simply see disability ministry as a benevolent, one-way care program. This view dishonors God's plan for the abundant life he promises to every person who accepts eternal life through his Son, Jesus Christ. Thankfully, many of our friends with disabilities are enjoying a deep and abiding faith and using their talents in places of service. Why? Because caring Christians have intentionally shared God's Word with them and have lovingly discipled their families.

I. **How Life Cycles Affect Families with Disability**[1]

We often describe our lives in terms of stages or cycles. These are normal, age-appropriate "rites of passage" or transitions from one circumstance to another. But when children are born with special needs or adults become disabled, the world does not slow down for their families; life continues moving at the same frantic pace. This can result in confusion, isolation, despair and hopelessness, as some get frozen in one or more life-stage. For example, consider the adult transitions for a child born with a disability.

A. **Marriage and Childbirth:** It is natural for couples to marry and start a family. They have big dreams and high expectations about their lives together. When a child is born with or develops a disability, "normal" life can come to a halt. The future seems lost and their daily activities change. They may find it difficult to participate in religious, social and community activities. They deal with communication barriers, transportation problems, adequate education, societal rejection, behavioral challenges and medical problems.

B. **Families with Young Children and Adolescents**: At this stage, children with severe intellectual disabilities do not develop past early childhood. Children with physical disabilities may struggle with health and mobility issues. The teen years can also be difficult due to puberty and the lack of social acceptance. While many teens are filling out college entrance forms or getting driver's licenses, a teen with developmental disabilities may still be learning how to use the bathroom or cross the street.

C. **Launching to Adulthood**: This is normally a time for young people to "test their wings" by going to college, starting a career or living on their own. But what happens

Jesus said, "I came that they may have and enjoy life, and have it in abundance— to the full, till it overflows."

JOHN 10:10 (*AMP*)

187

when they still need their parents' help to count money or ride the bus? Employment can be difficult to find and adequate housing may be unavailable. And since they may desire to be responsible for themselves, like their siblings, the pressure to be "independent" can be overwhelming. The stress often extends to their parents, siblings and grandparents as well.

D. **Middle Adult Years**: For most parents, this cycle is marked with looking forward to preparing for their own freedom and retirement. But adult-children with a severe disability may continue to struggle with how to live with little or no assistance (if that is even possible). Marriage is probably out of the question for them and day-to-day activities that should have become routine years ago are still a toilsome part of life. Whether adult-children live at home, in a care facility or independently with help, they can remain very dependent upon mom and dad.

E. **Elderly Parenting and Adult-Child Years**: In this stage most parents look forward to the "golden" years when they'll watch grandchildren at play. But for parents of adults with developmental disabilities, these years are met with increased fears and concerns. Parents realize their growing inability to care for their sons or daughters as they once did and wonder who can take over upon their death. Some find peace in this frustrating process in the compassion of supportive siblings and extended family members. Others suffer great anxiety and depression.

F. **Death of Parents**: For many parents and children, the most difficult aspect of this cycle is simply the knowledge that death is coming. If the adult-child with disabilities has no siblings and or other support, that family's life cycle may come to an end with a parent's death. In such cases, the adult-child may be confined to an institution or care facility and may face extreme isolation and loneliness. Even in the best of situations, nothing can replace a parent's presence in a child's life.

However, just as God, our Creator, designed us to mature throughout the family life cycle, he also planned stages of faith development to help us know Jesus Christ better and grow to be more like him. We'll discuss more how people with disabilities can come to know Jesus in Lesson 13 on outreach and evangelism. Here, we'll consider how to effectively welcome and teach individuals with disabilities in our churches.

II. Facilitating Faith Development in People with Disabilities

Peter describes new believers as babies who need food to grow: "Like newborn babies, crave pure spiritual milk, so that by it you may grow up in your salvation, now that you have tasted that the Lord is good" (1 Peter 2:2,3). People with disabilities have the same spiritual needs as people without disabilities, but their learning process may be different.

Dr. Jeff McNair and his wife, Kathi, teach adults with cognitive disabilities at their church and have a passion to see class members grow in their faith. They have also committed their lives to building meaningful friendships with people who have disabilities by interacting with them as often as possible. In their paper, "Faith Formation for Adults with Disability," the McNairs discuss the effects differing types of disabilities can have on a person's faith development.

> **People with intellectual disabilities** may be limited in their ability to understand, evaluate and synthesize information. They depend on others to explain things in ways they can understand. For those with even more severe intellectual disabilities, learning about God may come through their functional skills rather than their understanding. They can know they are an important part of a loving group who talk to God or Jesus, who carry Bibles and visit them at home. "The development of this trust and connection with the Body of Christ is the primary focus of their structures-based faith development, impacting the way faith is both perceived and developed," say the McNairs. "Faith is evidenced in their desire to have a Bible to carry, or requests for prayer for their bus driver or teacher, or having total access to anyone in the group independent of what they are doing."

SPIRITUAL NEEDS OF ADULTS WITH DISABILITIES[2]

To know the truth of the Bible

To experience salvation

To have a relationship with God and His Son

To fellowship in a community of faith

To know that we're uniquely created

To understand our unique purpose

To be accountable

To demonstrate the fruit of the Spirit

To pray and serve others

People with physical disabilities may see faith differently depending on the severity of their disability. They may question God's sovereignty and need a supportive church to show them acceptance and support as they grow to trust God. Due to physical limitations, they might struggle to access usable information. People with visual or hearing impairments may not know where to find Christian materials adapted for their needs.

 READ: "Faith Formation for Adults with Disability" by Jeff McNair, Ph.D. and Kathi McNair, M.A.

According to the McNairs, how does a person's perception of their own disability affect their faith?

III. **Principles for Teaching Adults with Disabilities**

A. Bible Study

"We proclaim him...teaching everyone with all wisdom, so that we may present everyone perfect in Christ." (Colossians 1:28)

One mistake pastors and teachers often make is talking down to adults with disabilities. These adults have the same needs and desires for self-worth, security and companionship as all adults. They can become easily frustrated or embarrassed when treated like children. While some teachers use stuffed animals, toys, coloring pages and picture books with adults with low cognitive function, these practices are discouraged by disability specialists and families of those with disabilities.

Most adults with physical disabilities participate well in Bible studies, and group activities with little adaptations. For adults with intellectual or developmental disabilities, here are some general teaching tips.

1. Use simple, concrete terms when teaching spiritual truths and avoid symbolism. Remember that these adults take things literally, wondering how Jesus can be a "door", the "bread of life" or a "way" to heaven.

2. Use vivid, hands-on, sensory objects to help learners experience the truth you are teaching; e.g., smelling

flowers in the Garden of Eden, stacking bricks to build the temple or knock down the walls of Jericho.

3. Dramatic skits or videos that show Bible heroes in action.

4. Change activities every 5-10 minutes due to their short attention span.

5. Give directions one at a time for games, crafts or dramas, being careful not to rush and allowing questions.

There is no substitute for getting to know the adults in your class. Their learning styles and interests provide unique options for group activities. Special Educator Linda Smith directs programs for the Joni and Friends Boston Field Ministry. She says this about teaching:

"Teaching adults with intellectual disabilities about Jesus is a privilege, not only because they are generally appreciative, affirming and enthusiastic, but because of their potential. Since spiritual truths are spiritually—not intellectually—discerned, these students have the same potential for spiritual growth as other church members. Spiritual maturity may look different...but it is just as real."

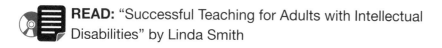 **READ:** "Successful Teaching for Adults with Intellectual Disabilities" by Linda Smith

Why does Ms. Smith feel it is so important to get to know each student?

B. Worship

Have you ever had the thought that it would be easier to sleep in on Sunday than to go to church? Think about the effort it takes some families affected by disability. So from the moment a van with a handicap tag enters the church parking lot, we should be ready to warmly greet these friends. This requires regular volunteer training. The manual, *So My House Will Be Full* (Joni and Friends 2008), is packed with helpful guidelines, as well as a reproducible chart of do's and don'ts for greeters and ushers.[3]

Sermons or liturgies are part of our worship, as are music, drama, dance and Bible reading. Worship helps us connect mind, body, soul and spirit with God. People with physical or cognitive impairments are capable of worshiping the Lord because their feelings, instincts and intuitions are active. Worship can also be a very positive and comforting experience for individuals with emotional or health problems. Even senior adults with advanced dementia can participate with some assistance from caring and compassionate church members.

The key is to make them feel welcome in worship. If people with disabilities are not encouraged to participate in the service, or if they are seated in an undesirable location in order to see or use a hearing device, they will feel excluded.

1. Prayer Time—People with hearing limitations may have difficulty when speakers bow their heads and lower their voices. If a person with speech problems prays aloud, fellow-worshipers should be patient. A caregiver may want to interpret the prayer so others can benefit. There is value in training the congregation to know when and how to respond. If they are comfortable, newcomers will be as well. Incorporate clear transition cues into the worship service such as a song following prayer time.

2. Print Material and PowerPoints—People with visual limitations, learning difficulties, and dyslexia may have difficulty with written material in print. Others may be functionally illiterate, so handing them a service program, song sheet or hymnbook may not help. Ask people what works best for them. Additional materials can take extra time, but the effort can enhance worship for everyone.

   For various reasons, a number of people with disabilities have difficulty reading words projected onto a screen. Provide printed copies of all words projected onto a screen. This is also helpful for anyone who cannot stand during worship.

3. Music and Sound—Loud music can cause physical pain to some people with hearing aids, sensitive hearing or tinnitus, to the extent that some may even stop attending church. Adults with autism may be hypo-

or hypersensitive to light and sound. Similarly, having to dodge waving flags and banners can cause emotional stress for people who are disabled, elderly or nervous. Some may opt out of worship for the comfort of a small group class experience.

4. Baptism and Communion—Depending on your church's doctrine and tradition, participation in these sacraments can be vital for people with disabilities. Churches should give careful thought to enabling all believers, even those with profound disabilities, a way to affirm their faith and to be embraced by their church family. Those with physical disabilities may need extra help managing the communion elements. Small individual cups can tip in unsteady hands causing embarrassment. The bread or wafer can easily be dropped or can choke a person who is trying to rush. Most of these issues can be overcome with careful planning and a "trial run" beforehand will build confidence. Here are some adaptations to consider:

   a. Use a separate cup or a straw for a person who cannot manage a small cup.
   b. Use gluten-free wafers for those with celiac condition.
   c. Serve communion from a more accessible place, if altar steps are barriers for wheelchair users.
   d. Serve people with disabilities and the elderly in their seats before others have been served.
   e. Announce that people may stand or kneel during communion, if kneeling is a traditional position.

Similarly, churches that practice believers' baptism by total immersion will need to use creativity to solve the practical difficulties faced by people with disabilities. One church borrowed the pool at a local special education school for a baptismal service. The ramped access made it much easier for the person being baptized, and everyone appreciated the warm water! For people whose condition prevents immersion, another creative method of baptism should be considered.

IV. Serving Alongside Friends with Disabilities

"The body is a unit, though it is made up of many parts: and though all its parts are many, they form one body." (1 Cor. 12:12)

A. All Christians Are Gifted by God

As part of the Body of Christ, we are all called to serve and to be served by others. Yet, many churches are missing an untapped well of volunteers—people with disabilities. Sadly, they are often overlooked for service. Some are just waiting to be invited to use their God-given gifts and talents.

Jerry Borton has cerebral palsy and sees it as his part-time job. It takes him and his wife about three hours to perform the daily services that keep him healthy. The rest of Jerry's days are spent running a multi-faceted Joni and Friends area office and teaching at a local college. His spiritual gifts and passion for ministry are unmistakable in the following video interview with Jerry conducted by Steve Bundy, Managing Director of the Christian Institute on Disability at Joni and Friends.

 VIEW: Jerry Borton, Director of Joni and Friends Greater Philadelphia

Sometimes church leaders automatically allocate the role of the prayer ministry to people with limited mobility or visual impairments. This is a mistake since it fails to consider that some of these friends have excellent financial, organizational or administrative skills that are often scarce in a church. They may be skilled artists, singers, musicians, designers, carpenters or seamstresses. They may be excellent youth workers or Sunday school teachers. Make it a rule to always ask individuals with disabilities about their interests and abilities. Like Jerry Borton, most of them will surprise you!

Disability Ministry Director Connie Hutchinson has been putting people with disabilities to work at her church for years.

 READ: "Exciting Ways to Use the Spiritual Gifts of People with Disabilities" by Connie Hutchinson

List some of the various ways people with disabilities serve in Ms. Hutchinson's church.

Once a church masters teaching adults with disability and involving them in the work of the ministry, families begin to look to the church for help with questions about marriage, disability benefits, and network support. The Christian community has a challenge here. We can stay in what some have called a "Holy Huddle" or we can become educated on these issues and learn to partner with other groups, which will be addressed further in Lesson 14, "Networking with Disability Ministries and Organizations."

V. **Marriage with a Disability**

What advice would you give to men and women with disabilities who are considering marriage?

Ken and Joni Tada, who have enjoyed a happy marriage for almost 30 years, get many questions on the subject of marriage from women and men. Some are looking to marriage as a means of making them feel whole because they struggle with a low self-image or feel dissatisfied with God's plan. They falsely assume that if they are "marriageable" they'll have equality with their peers. In the following paper, Joni shares some excellent advice on the key to a successful marriage.

 **READ:** "Marriage with a Disability"
by Joni Eareckson Tada

What does Joni mean when she says Jesus is the third strand of the rope in her marriage (Eccl. 4:21)?

VI. **Minister to the Unique Needs of Senior Adults with Disabilities**

A. **God's Promises to Adults in the Golden Years**
"Even to your old age and gray hairs I am he, I am he who will sustain you. I have made you and I will carry you; I will sustain you and I will rescue you." (Isaiah 46:4)

"They shall bear fruit in old age; they shall be fresh and flourishing." (Psalm 92:14)

INCREASE OF
DISABILITY WITH
AGE[4]

Ages 18-24—6.9%

Ages 25-54—14.1%

Ages 55-64—28.4%

Over Age 65—38%

Over Age 85—56%

Women—15.4%

Men—14.6%

Are God's promises only for the young and healthy? No! At the age of 91, Frances Cummins walks with a cane since breaking her hip and uses computerized hearing devices, but she rarely misses worship at her neighborhood church. After teaching Sunday school for over 50 years, Frances began writing for an annual devotional book that her family publishes. She averages about 100 devotions per year. Her 27 grandchildren and great grandchildren call her "inspiring!"

Just as God promised to sustain the elderly, so the church should find ways to partner with God in the ministry of encouragement and support for the elderly. Productivity does not stop at age 65 for people with or without disabilities. According to the Christian Association Serving Adult Ministries (CASA) Network, 40 percent of the average North American congregation is over 55 years of age.[5]

Dr. Jim Pierson, founder and president emeritus of The Christian Church Foundation for the Handicapped (CCFH), is a veteran in the field of disability ministry. As an Adjunct Associate Professor of Teacher Education and Special Services at CCFH, Dr. Pierson trains leaders on the importance of serving adults with late onset disabilities. He suggests that one of the most important services churches can provide is to help members know how to be sensitive to elderly adults. "Think about how the disability has altered the person's ability to carry out his or her everyday life," says Dr. Pierson. "Start a new section in the church library of materials that provide information on dealing with a new lifestyle, coping with a disability, where to go for help, and a Biblical perspective on disability. Develop a team in the church to do odd jobs for members who can no longer do for themselves."

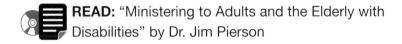 **READ:** "Ministering to Adults and the Elderly with Disabilities" by Dr. Jim Pierson

Dr. Pierson lists 10 ways to be sensitive to the needs of the elderly. Consider how you might discuss these ideas with the pastors and teachers in your church.

Born during World War II with cerebral palsy, Cordell Brown built a life of no limitations. He started a camp for people with disabilities in Ohio and built a second camp in Africa. Today, Cordell is almost 70 years old and serves as a member of the Joni and Friends International Disability Center Board of Directors. "Cordell's life is like a delicious chocolate treat that's good for you," says Joni. "His story is full of laughter, of discovery and understanding and most importantly, faith." Are there stories like Frances' and Cordell's in your church that need to be told?

Reflections on Lesson 12

Ministering to Adults and the Elderly with Special Needs

1. Describe how disabilities can potentially affect the family life cycle.

2. According to the McNairs, how does society's perception of people with disabilities affect their faith development?

3. In Linda Smith's paper she gave three important principles for teachers to keep in mind. Which one stood out to you? Why?

4. List five creative changes that could be made in your church to include people with disability in worship services.

5. How was Ms. Hutchinson able to change her congregation's attitude in order to use the giftedness of people with disability in places of service?

6. Should you encourage and support couples to marry when one has a disability? Why or why not?

7. Describe the kind of support elderly adults with disabilities need from the church.

8. Summarize how the church will be blessed, edified and built up when all God's people are welcomed and used to glorify him.

Outreach and Evangelism to *Families* Affected by *Disability*

OBJECTIVES

Studying this lesson will help you:

✔ Explain the scriptural emphasis on evangelism.

✔ Explain basic doctrines regarding God, Jesus and salvation.

✔ Understand a person's need for redemption and why people with disabilities may reject the Gospel.

✔ Present the plan of salvation to individuals with various kinds of disabilities.

✔ Assist a new Christian with disabilities in their walk with Christ.

✔ Describe some practical outreach models to the disability community.

People with disabilities are one of the largest unreached people groups in the world. Unfortunately, disability ministry can be seen as simply a care giving service, yet it must include a firm commitment to go where children and adults with disabilities are and declare the Gospel to them. If your church is missing the joy of including these precious families in your outreach, this lesson will provide a variety of evangelism models.

Joni Eareckson Tada is the first to admit that she has never heard of one certain style of sharing the Gospel with others. In fact, it may surprise you to know that it is Joni's wheelchair that initiates many of her opportunities. "People don't expect me to be happy in this wheelchair. Saying 'I have a reason for living' in response to their remarks about my singing or my smile, always evokes a curious look," says Joni. "That's when I add, 'Jesus has blessed me! By the way, what's your reason for living?' Sure it catches people off guard, sometimes delighting them, sometimes making them curious, and sometimes sending them running for the nearest exit. But one thing's for certain... it got them thinking."

Joni has learned to trust the Holy Spirit's work in people's hearts. She encourages us to prayerfully watch for opportunities to cultivate relationships and to rely on God to change people's lives.[1]

🔑 *Grace*

Friends with disability remind us of God's grace. Without Christ, we were once disabled spiritually, unable to move into his kingdom, blind to his purposes and deaf to his voice. By his grace we are made whole, and it is often the disabilities in others which serve as God's physical, audiovisual aid of how he's working spiritually in the lives of us all.

I. **God, Open Our Eyes to People without Christ**

Someone once suggested that all lack of evangelism was a lack of love on our part as Christians. Do you believe that is true? Why or why not?

When Samantha met Robert, she instantly felt compassion for him. His contorted body, blank stare and lip-drool made her want to back away from his wheelchair. Surely, Robert couldn't understand the message that he had come to church to hear. Samantha couldn't help thinking that his parents might have saved him an uncomfortable van ride and mercifully left him at home. However, being a well-trained church greeter, she touched Robert's shoulder and warmly welcomed him and his parents into the sanctuary.

During the service, Samantha prayed for God to strengthen Robert's parents. She asked that if they were not believers, God would help them receive the Good News. She glanced at Robert several times during worship as his head dropped further down his chest and his father gently wiped his mouth with a handkerchief. From what Samantha could tell, Robert seemed oblivious to his surroundings—until her pastor asked the congregation to raise their hands if they had an unspoken prayer request. With great effort, Robert clearly lifted a shaky hand from the arm of his wheelchair and kept it up as the pastor prayed.

Samantha's eyes filled with tears as she witnessed Robert's display of faith in God. In his simple way, he expressed his trust in the One who had created him in his mother's womb. She realized Robert *could* hear the message. His body was still, but his mind apparently reached beyond this disability. In her effort to be a "good" Christian, Samantha had prayed for Robert's parents, his siblings, and for church members to show him kindness, but she had not prayed for Robert's relationship with God. It would have never occurred to her to ask Robert to remember her needs in his prayers.

That day opened Samantha's understanding of how people affected by disabilities know God. With her prompting, it also expanded the vision of her church's outreach team.

Is it more difficult for a person affected by disabilities to have faith than it is for you? Why or why not?

When our eyes are opened to see the spiritual needs of people with disabilities, God's Word informs and motivates us to action.

A. **Scripture Illuminates Our Mission**

Three significant passages help us understand God's heart for evangelism to those affected by disability and encourage us to join him in his work: Luke 4:18-21, Matthew 28:18-20 and Luke 14:21-23. They give us a clear understanding of the mission of Jesus and the mandate to evangelize all people—men, women and children, able-bodied and those affected by disability.

1. **The "Mission Statement"—Luke 4:18-21**

   Luke 4:18-21 has been called a "mission statement" for the ministry of Jesus, quoted from Isaiah 61:1-3. This mission models what the preaching of the Gospel should include. Jesus' "mission statement" asks us to lay down our lives to bring deliverance (salvation) to the captive. God desires to work through us to evangelize the marginalized—the poor, the brokenhearted, the captives, the blind and the oppressed.

2. **The Great Commission—Matthew 28:18-20**

   As disciples of Jesus we speak with and operate under Christ's authority. Therefore, we have the right and the responsibility to make disciples of Christ in all nations (literally, "all ethnic groups"), which involves baptizing and teaching them the Word of God while modeling the ways and character of the Master, Christ Jesus.

This Commission is not completed "until the end," when Christ physically returns to Earth for his church at the end of time. Meanwhile, he is with us at all times—whether in triumphs, trials, or testing—as we bring the Gospel to all nations, especially to the marginalized.

3. **The Luke 14 Mandate—Luke 14:21-23**

As we've already seen in Lesson 8, Luke 14:21-23 is at its core the essence of the heart of God. Rev. Dan'l Markham, Former Director of Joni and Friends Field Ministry, teaches that it is also central to the preaching of the Gospel:

"The Great Commission is the distillate of the core theme of the Gospel of Luke. It is one of the first Great Commission texts and given with such passion by our Lord Jesus, perhaps the Holy Spirit might be saying something like this: 'Go out with my fervor to bring the lost into my house, my Church. And make sure you go with priority, with haste, and with the greatest zeal to those who are the most marginalized—the poor and those affected by disability, the poorest of the poor. There is no more important task for you to undertake for me.'"[2]

Mission, Commission and Mandate

	"Mission Statement" Luke 4:18-21	The Great Commission Matthew 28:18-20	Luke 14 Mandate Luke 14:12-24
Connection	How Jesus was directed by the Holy Spirit to preach and express the Gospel in thought, word, and deed	Based upon Christ's sacrifice and mission	The passionate part and a key essential of fulfilling the Great Commission and the Mission Statement
Spokesperson	God the Holy Spirit	God the Son	God the Father (Master of the House)
Audience	Jesus as the example for all disciples to do accordingly	Apostles' model for the Church to carry out	"Servants" (Christians) and the "House" (the Church)
Focus	The hurting and marginalized, including those in the disability community	The world—all ethnic groups	The poor and those affected by disability, who are the poorest of the poor
Action	Preaching, healing and delivering	Making disciples, baptizing, teaching	Passionately compelling (evangelizing) people with disabilities to come into the Church

B. **Acceptance Shines Light in Our Hearts**

When Doug Mazza's son, Ryan, was born with severe multiple disabilities, he and his family experienced darkness like they had never known. Doug, a businessman who had already mastered the corporate world, felt helpless and hopeless when doctors described his son's prognosis. Thankfully, God's plan extended far beyond the best of medical minds to love and transform Doug and his son.

 READ: "Trading Control for God's Grace" by Doug Mazza

If we judge the faith of our friends with disabilities by a faulty understanding of what faith actually is, we see them as "incapable" of becoming Christians who can share their faith with us.

Since faith can be observed in simple words and acts, people with mental disabilities are not hindered in their ability to feel and express love for God and others.

In *Expressing Faith in Jesus*, Ronald C. Vredeveld provides a beautiful description of the hearts and minds of those with limited cognitive abilities.

> Our friends' minds are not cluttered with concerns that preoccupy others or with the need to understand and know all about faith. But theirs is not a childish, wobbling, unfounded faith; it is deeply trusting, informed by hearing the stories of God's people and by living in a broken world. Their faith may not be informed by knowledge of a creed or statement of faith that they have studied, but their faith is nurtured by relationships that reflect the love of Jesus. Their responses to God's love, which arise from their inner being and are nourished by the Spirit of God, express a simple but very rich faith in Jesus. When the faith community encourages new members with cognitive impairments to express their faith in Jesus, the emphasis is on the belief of the heart rather than the level of knowledge.[4]

II. **God, Open Our Mouths to Speak the Gospel**

Salvation only comes through a correct belief in and about Jesus. Whether affected by a disability or not, the preaching of the Gospel is the same for all. All must come to Christ in

Faith is . . .

Not mere mental assent.

Not allegiance to a church or denomination.

Not hereditary endowment.

Not an emotional state.

Not a system of good works.

Not a passive, inert condition.[3]

repentance and faith, which is the common salvation and faith delivered *"once for all"* to the saints (Jude 1:3). The Apostle Peter declared that we are *"born again... through the word of God"* (1 Pet. 1:23); that is, we receive our spiritual birth into Christ's kingdom through faith in God's Word. This implies a correct understanding of God's Word, which fundamentally includes an understanding of who God is, who Christ is, who man is, and what is the way to salvation.

A. Salvation Is Based upon Proper Beliefs

1. Who Is Jesus Christ?

Jesus Christ is fully God (Son of God) and fully man (Son of Man).

In 1 John 4:1-6, the Apostle John gave us guidelines to ascertain who is and who is not a Christian. He wrote that the "spirit of error" is indicated by any doctrine excluding the humanity or divinity of Christ. This is confirmed in John 1:1,14 and Colossians 2:9.

Jesus' own statements indicated that he saw himself as having full humanity and full deity (John 8:24, *NASB*). According to Greek scholars, the phrase "I am He" (*ego eimi*) is the Greek form of the Old Testament personal name of God, the great I AM, or Yahweh, meaning that Jesus claimed to be the Timeless One (see also Ex. 3:14).

2. Who Is God?

He is a Person and the Trinity.

Biblical theology reveals that God is a Trinity of three Persons. He is neither some impersonal force in the universe nor is he merely human, though in Jesus Christ he took on humanity in order to relate to us through his sacrificial death. He is Creator; there are no other gods beside him, he being the one and only God who reveals himself as Father, Son and Holy Spirit. Christian orthodoxy (correct belief) acknowledges God to be beyond what human thought can fully comprehend—for example, he is omniscient (all-knowing) and omnipresent (present everywhere), he is Spirit, and he is eternal (Gen. 1:26-27; Matt. 3:16-17; 28:19; John. 3:16; 4:24; Phil. 2:5-11).

3. **Who Is Man?**

Man (all humanity) is not God or a god, but is made in God's image and likeness. Man is also fallen and in need of a Savior.

a) Created by God
As many theologians and Bible teachers have articulated, all good and bad theology comes from the statement "God is God and we are not"—or, as Ray Pritchard put it, "He's God and We're Not."[5] Genesis 1:26-27 clearly states that man was created by God in the "*image and likeness*" of God, that man was the pinnacle of God's creation, designed to think and act like God yet not an equal of God.

b) Fallen by Choice
Man fell out of fellowship with God through disobedience (sin) and thereby lost full dominion over creation (Gen. 3). He lost his status of being fully in the likeness of God, and lost the full favor of God.

Since Adam, every man and woman has sinned (Rom. 3:10-12; Eph. 2:3; Ps. 51:5; Jer. 17:9) except for "Jesus Christ the righteous" (1 John. 2:1, *NASB*). Christ's sinlessness versus man's sinfulness is affirmed in Hebrews 4:14-16. Romans 3:24-25 declares that we are redeemed from our sinful state by God's gift of love through faith in the sacrificial work of Jesus Christ, who bore God the Father's wrath upon the cross, that we might be "justified," or declared not guilty.

The Bible states that man's basic nature is inclined toward evil, is sinful in nature, and can *never* become God. Man can become a child of God but never equal with God (Isa. 43:10; 44:6, 8; Hos. 11:9; Num. 23:19). Man cannot save himself through his own effort (Eph. 2:8-9; Titus 3:5; Gal. 2:16; Isa. 64:6).

B. **What Is Salvation?**
Salvation is through—and only through—Jesus Christ: "*Jesus said to him, 'I am the way, and the truth, and the life; no one comes to the Father but through me'*" (John. 14:6, *NASB*).

"If you confess with your mouth Jesus as Lord, and believe in your heart that God raised him from the dead, you shall be saved; for with the heart man believes, resulting in righteousness, and with the mouth he confesses, resulting in salvation" (Romans 10:9-10, *NASB*).

Various non-Christian religions declare that man earns his own way to eternal life and/or becomes God or a god. The Bible repudiates such heresy by teaching that we are saved by grace (undeserved, unearned favor from God) through faith in Christ and his atoning sacrifice on the cross. Salvation is a gift of God, not something earned by our good deeds (Eph. 2:8-9). Confession and belief are the critical requisites for a person to become a true believer in Christ.

The Bible reveals that we get one chance at life and eternal life, with no future reincarnations (Heb. 9:27). *Thank God*, our salvation is based not on what we do or do not do, but rather on who *Jesus* is and what *he* has done! Our performance vacillates, but Jesus *"is the same yesterday and today, yes and forever"* (Heb. 13:8, *NASB*). Becoming a Christian and growing in Christ requires complete and sole commitment to Jesus Christ (Mark 8:34-38; Matt. 10:32-40).

Following a violent attack, Vicki Olivas knew she needed something to break the chains of depression and bitterness in her life. Heart-wrenching questions haunted her, causing her to mistrust everything she thought she knew about life and even about God.

 VIEW: When Life Isn't Fair, (Joni and Friends DVDTV07)

Today Vicki is a vibrant, productive woman with a new life in Christ. What made the difference?

III. **God, Show Us How to Live What We Proclaim**

There are two primary ways to proclaiming the Gospel—word and deed.

Ken and Joni Tada have traveled the world over sharing their faith in Jesus Christ. Ken is especially known for taking every opportunity to share a Gospel tract with strangers along the way, those with disability and without. He also shows them every kindness in the name of Jesus, believing that even a glass of cold water can start conversations with eternal results.

Where does Ken's soul-winning spirit come from? Some believe it has been nurtured in his heart as a caregiver.

 READ: "Caregiving: A Cause for Christ" by Ken Tada

A. **Word: Hearing and Reading**
Proclamation in word without deed leads to an irrelevant Gospel.

> *"What things?" he asked. "About Jesus of Nazareth,"*
> *they replied. "He was a prophet, powerful in **word and***
> ***deed** before God and all the people"* (Luke 24:19, emphasis added).

The Gospel proclaims the Word of God regarding who Christ is and how one comes into a personal relationship with God through Jesus Christ. But proclamation in word is hollow without proclamation through deeds that reflect Christ's character and ministry. People learn primarily through *hearing-reading* and *seeing-experiencing*. Hearing-reading is the result of someone proclaiming the Good News of Jesus Christ, that is, hearing the Word, or reading about the Good News in the Bible or a Gospel tract.

B. **Deed: Seeing and Experiencing**
Proclamation in deed without word results in a powerless Gospel.

> *"You know what has happened throughout Judea, begin-*
> *ning in Galilee after the baptism that John preached—how*
> *God anointed Jesus of Nazareth with the Holy Spirit and*
> *power, and how he went around **doing good and healing***
> ***all** who were under the power of the devil, because God*
> *was with him"* (Acts 10:37-38, emphasis added).

Seeing-experiencing results from Christians and churches that demonstrate the Good News through acts of love, mercy, and kindness—i.e., how we reflect the character of Christ in our everyday lives (also known as "lifestyle evangelism").

C. **Joining the Kingdom Work**
In "Kingdom Matters in Disability," Joni Eareckson Tada describes Christians as kingdom builders and the church

as a training camp for the kingdom. At church we are equipped to go out into the world to make Christ real and reclaim territory from the devil under the banner of Christ. But Joni makes it clear that the church is not the same thing as the kingdom of God:

> The church is the elect of the Father, the redeemed of the Son, and the renewed by the Spirit—in Matthew 16:18, Jesus calls us His church. The church helps people worship God according to the Word, encouraging them to love Jesus Christ as they should. A disability ministry within a church does the same thing. We call and disciple people with disabilities in the Word. We evangelize and disciple them, mentor and encourage them, and help them discover their spiritual gifts and their roles of service and leadership within the church. But that's not the only role of disability ministry. We have a kingdom role—all people with disabilities in the church have a kingdom role. Unlike the church, the kingdom is not a group of people. It is a reign, the rule of Jesus our Lord.

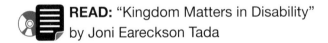

READ: "Kingdom Matters in Disability" by Joni Eareckson Tada

According to Joni's paper, what does it mean to be a *transformational* Christian?

Where does evangelism fit into the view of the church and the kingdom?

IV. **God, Help Us Share the Gospel in Word and Deed**

   A. **Principles in Adapting the Message for our Friends with Disabilities**

   1. **Friends with Intellectual Disabilities**—These friends may have low, medium, or high cognitive functions. They think in concrete terms about spiritual matters and come to know Christ according to their mental age. In the book, *Expressing Faith in Jesus: Church Membership for People with Intellectual Disabilities*, author

Ronald C. Vredeveld shares methods for preparing a person with intellectual disabilities for church membership. While there may be some doctrinal differences between church traditions, the book is recommended here for examples of how to address common issues to fully include these friends in your faith community.[6]

Eighty-nine percent of people with mental disabilities can understand Scripture on a third-grade level.
Dr. Jim Pierson, *Exceptional Teaching*[7]

---

2. **Friends with Developmental Disabilities**—The spiritual needs of friends on this wide spectrum are often first met through the loving nurture of Christian parents, caregivers and friends. One teacher described her witness to a student with autism like this: "When he has a meltdown, I whisper a prayer or sing a quiet song. Then when he calms down, I celebrate his uniqueness, telling him how important he is to God and to our church family. I always let him know that I am his friend."

   • Relational evangelism happens when we "hang out" with these friends and "do life" together.
   • These friends may be able to participate in worship or may be more comfortable in their own special class.
   • Use age-appropriate picture cards to share the Christmas and Easter message.
   • Adapt church membership and baptism classes to include their needs and welcome them into the Body of Christ.
   • Create a *discipleship plan* that addresses one faith concept or goal at a time.

3. **Friends with Hearing or Visual Impairments**—If you do not know sign language, seek the help of a family member who can sign as you witness to someone who is deaf or hearing impaired. Use a simple explanation of the plan of salvation. For people who are visually impaired, give them the Bible in Braille or a Bible CD.

You can also have your faith story translated into Braille so the person can read it (with their fingers).

4. **Friends Who Are Nonverbal**—Just because a person is nonverbal does not mean that he or she is incapable of talking with you. Ask if the person uses a message board, computer or signs for "yes" and "no." Take time to become acquainted with the preferred method of communication before you share your faith story or teach a simple Bible lesson with pictures or objects.

5. **Friends with Physical Impairments**—As in the case of friends with hearing or mental impairments, as well as those who are nonverbal, it is important to remember that physical impairments can vary widely in their degree of severity and in their effects on individual functioning. Never assume that a person with a physical impairment either *can* or *cannot* participate in a given activity; it is always better to inquire as to the specific needs of particular individuals.

B. **Evangelism Tools**

1. **Romans Road**: The Romans Road to salvation is a way of explaining the Good News of salvation using verses from the Book of Romans. http://www.gotquestions.org/Romans-road-salvation.html

2. **Wordless Book**: This small booklet consists of several blocks of pure color that, in sequence, represent a nonverbal catechism of basic Christian teachings for the instruction of children, adults with illiteracy or people from different cultures. http://www.berean.org/bibleteacher/wbpage.html

3. **Gospel Bracelets:** This bracelet uses colored beads like the Wordless Book to present the Gospel. http://www.joniandfriends.org/store/product/gospel-bracelets-poster/

4. **The Four Spiritual Laws:** Developed by Campus Crusade for Christ, this tool is now used (with variations) by many churches, evangelistic and missionary

organizations. http://www.campuscrusade.com/four lawseng.htm

5. **Created In the Image of God:** This Gospel tract was written and published by Joni and Friends specifically to communicate the Good News of Jesus Christ to people affected by disability. http://www.joniand friends.org/static/uploads/downloads/CreatedImage God09.pdf

V. God, Open Our Lives to Outreach and Discipleship

One of the best ways to reach out to individuals with disabilities is to care for the whole family. Dr. David Deuel, Academic Director of the Master's Academy International, finds that family support groups are vital to seeing people affected by disability turn to God in both sad and happy times. Churches that successfully use support groups as an outreach strategy see families remain together through the power of creating extended families within the church. Dr. Deuel cites the following reasons for family support groups in your church.

Why start family support groups?

1. To help families see the Church as a caring place where emotional and practical needs can be met.
2. To provide a safe place where parents can share information, as well as their pain and victories.
3. To love people by giving them the Gospel. This should never be far from our thinking or conversation.
4. To model for parents ways to help their children through the stages of life and faith development.
5. To mobilize the congregation to compassionately serve in venues they may otherwise have missed.

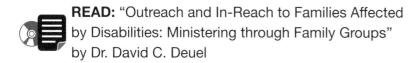

READ: "Outreach and In-Reach to Families Affected by Disabilities: Ministering through Family Groups" by Dr. David C. Deuel

Earlier in this lesson, we asked if it was more difficult for people affected by disabilities to have faith than those without disabilities. The answer is yes and no. Their fears and angers may cause them to reject the Good News or seek God with greater fervor. It depends on the nurture or rejection that they experience in their lives. And in that way, they are no different than the rest of us. Christians can make a tremendous difference in the trajectory of a family's life if they are ready to care and provide support. As Joni says,

> We are about transforming the kingdoms of this world to become the kingdoms of our Lord and of his Christ... Whenever people spent time with Jesus, they experienced a hunger for his message. When in the world, we live as Christ would have us live, it prompts the question of "What must I do to be saved like you?"[8]

Reflections on Lesson 13

Outreach and Evangelism to Families Affected by Disability

1. Someone once suggested that all lack of evangelism was a lack of love on our part as Christians. Do you believe that is true? Why or why not?

2. Why are proper beliefs essential in sharing the Gospel message among those with disabilities?

3. Look again at part three of this session. Why is it essential to communicate the Gospel in both word and deed? What results when either of these essentials is neglected?

4. In "Joining the Kingdom Work," a clear difference is mentioned between the church and the kingdom of God. What is this difference? What significance does this make in serving those in the disability community?

5. Ken Tada's story shares a powerful example of caregiving to share the Gospel message. In what ways does caregiving open opportunities to share our faith?

6. Part four of this session discusses various principles for adapting the Gospel message to individuals with various types of disabilities. What are some additional positive examples you have seen or experienced of adapting the Gospel message to these various groups?

7. What are some of the reasons provided for offering support groups for family members of those with disabilities? What are some ways these support groups offer opportunities to share the Gospel with family members?

Networking with *Disability Ministries* and Organizations

OBJECTIVES

Studying this lesson will help you:

✔ Understand the need for strategic partnerships with a variety of organizations to better serve the disability community.

✔ Describe the barriers to networking with organizations to relieve suffering and empower people with disabilities.

✔ Know how to locate and exchange ideas with government and private agencies.

✔ Share with your church the importance of being involved in community efforts to serve families affected by disability.

✔ Develop a broader networking strategy to better serve people with disabilities.

Better Together...

One key phrase that can transform how we serve the disability community is "better together." Part of the strength of Joni and Friends over the years has been the ability to further our mission through a variety of strategic partnerships with churches, mission organizations, nonprofits, schools, social service providers, corporations, and civic organizations to build on the unique strengths each provides in changing the lives of families affected by disabilities.

In this lesson, our goal is to provide insight and instruction into the vital area of networking with disability ministries and organizations. You'll find there is often a tremendous need for strategic partnerships with a wide variety of individuals and groups. Part of our time together will also focus on the sometimes challenging barriers of networking with outside organizations, especially those that may not share our faith values. One particular area of discussion will include ways to obtain the knowledge required to locate and exchange ideas with government and private agencies.

Further, you'll see the importance of helping churches become more involved in their community's efforts to serve families affected by disability. Ideally, your church can become known as "the place" people think of first when asked about churches serving the disability community. Doing so will require a broader networking strategy, intentionally designed to make connections with those in the community who are also serving individuals affected by disability.

Each partnership is unique, just as each friendship is different; no two relationships are exactly alike. However, through a clearly stated purpose in partnership and a broad networking strategy with the groups that best fit the calling of your ministry, you will have the potential for greater impact than would otherwise be possible.

🔑 Strategy

In talking about changing the world, Mother Teresa said, "I may not be able to change the world, but I can cast a stone across the waters to create many ripples."[1] This life strategy allowed one woman to impact nations on behalf of the poor. Satan's scheme is to build self-serving Christians who think community involvement is too heavy a "stone" to carry, thus keeping the Gospel inside the church walls. But Jesus said, "As the Father has sent me, I am sending you"[2] and if we go into our communities in Jesus' name, we cannot fail!

I. **Understand the Need for Strategic Partnerships with a Variety of Organizations to Better Serve the Disability Community**

A strategy is a plan or method to accomplish a specific task. In serving the disability community, the strategy should include a holistic plan to best develop each person's abilities so people can live to their fullest God-given potential. In this process, you will often find that collaborating with another organization or agency in specific areas can be a tremendous benefit. Partnerships are never simply for the sake of partnering, but rather to benefit those people who are served, as well as those doing the service.

The church is defined as the people of God. We are a community. God has designed us to function better with one another than apart from one another. In disability ministry, this is true for at least four important reasons:

A. **We're More Effective When We're All Connected**

A child who attends a local church is often only in church programs between one to three hours per week. He or she spends significantly more time with parents, teachers, and others outside of the church on a regular basis. A child with a disability may be even less involved in your church due to physical issues and stress on the family, but will spend many hours with others, including a wide range of health, social service, and educational providers. Simply put, disability ministry is more effective when we are more connected with multiple areas of a person's life.

Pat Verbal shares the example of a man named Ramero. When Ramero was in elementary school, reading was challenging for him, which made school very difficult at times. As an adult, Ramero's desire was to connect with similarly challenged children that he could assist. Sharing his dream with fellow church members, Ramero recruited several children's ministry volunteers to serve as mentors in a local school. After passing the required background checks, they were each given the opportunity to visit a child once a week.

The mentors met together at church on Sundays, encouraging each other and praying for the children they served. It wasn't long before word traveled into the community that Ramero's congregation cared deeply about children with special needs. Several families began to attend the church, and a teacher from the school became a member of the congregation.[3]

This is just one example of how connecting with the other areas of a community through strategic partnerships results in better outcomes for all involved. The school gained helpful volunteers, the church became known for its ministry to those with learning disabilities, and the children received better care.

B. **Intentional Partnerships**

Whether we choose to develop strategic partnerships or not, there are other organizations influencing those we serve in the disability community. We can either benefit by working with these individuals and groups whenever possible or rely solely on our own efforts.

Frequently, the result of not partnering with others involved in the lives of those we serve is that we do not have an accurate picture of reality. If we are not working as partners with family members and caregivers, we might not be aware that our friend's medication was changed last week or that they had a discouraging doctor's appointment. In the case of a child, he or she might share something and we may not know if it was a recent experience or something that happened in the past if we don't have the full picture of their day to day lives.

The answers to these and other questions can often be resolved through building relationships with others. While we need to be sensitive regarding a family's privacy, parents are our primary connecting point to children and teens. They are usually pleased when we ask what school, clubs or activities their family members are involved with, and reflect a genuine desire to understand their daily lives.

This interconnectedness can lead to conversations with teachers, social workers or other professionals, and on occasion, have surprising results. For example, one local church surveyed parents of children with special needs to find ways to better serve their families. The results showed that nearly half of those who responded had recently transitioned their children to a relatively new school that served special learners. That discovery led to a fruitful partnership between the church and school that has fostered great benefits for the parents and their children.

Strategic partnerships with both the families and other professionals serving our church members can lead to some unexpected results. However, what should come as no surprise is that intentionally connecting with other disability services can make our work more effective for Christ.

C. **Practical Partnerships**

Disability ministry uniquely recognizes the importance of meeting emotional, physical and spiritual needs. Through unified partnerships with other disability care providers, we are able to offer more specific care to those we serve.

When Lori Lucore sought to overcome the obstacles of Individualized Education Program (IEP) meetings for the education of her 12-year-old daughter with Down syndrome, the daunting task required more than one person or even one organization. First, Joni and Friends' Christian Institute on Disability (CID) helped by providing Lori with the necessary information to challenge an inadequate response from her local school system. Second, her journey included multiple meetings with a variety of school officials to share this information and seek an appropriate solution.

In the end, the solution Lori sought—to involve her daughter in an integrated classroom—was a success. Though not without difficulty, Lori's willingness to partner with a wide range of people and organizations was essential to her achieving her goal, which will ultimately have a daily impact on her child's education.

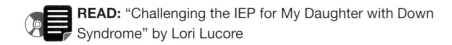

READ: "Challenging the IEP for My Daughter with Down Syndrome" by Lori Lucore

"Pray continually; give thanks in all circumstances..." (1 Thess. 5:17). Take time to pray for the parents, administrators, teachers and counselors who strive for the highest quality education available for every child with special needs. Consider how you might encourage them with a kind word or deed.

D. **Disability Ministry Is More Relational When Partnerships Are Developed**

Christ-centered ministry is built on relationships. Disability ministry is no different. For our service to be more effective, it must ultimately become more relational. Partnerships are one way to accomplish this objective.

How? *First, networking itself is a relational effort.* It requires meeting new people, making connections with organizations different from us and rising to the challenge of relating to people with a variety of interests and perspectives.

Second, building partnerships involves our participation in other areas of the lives of those we serve. It is one thing to ask, "How was school this week?" It is quite another to ask, "How was your meeting with Mrs. Ralston on Tuesday?" or to say, "It was great to see you at lunch last Thursday."

Third, disability partnerships build community among volunteers who serve in disability ministry. This is often overlooked, but important to making a long-term impact. As volunteers and caregivers in unique roles, our goal is to help families affected by disabilities. It is essential over the long haul to build friendships with coworkers who can relate with our services in ways other friends cannot.

221

> *"In all my prayers for all of you, I always pray with joy because of **your partnership in the gospel** from the first day until now, being confident of this, that he who began a good work in you will carry it on to completion until the day of Christ Jesus."*
> Philippians 1:4-6

How did the Apostle Paul rely on a variety of partners to communicate the Gospel and accomplish his mission? Can we expect to function any differently?

II. Understand the Obstacles to Networking with Organizations

Networking is important, but that doesn't mean it is easy. Many barriers exist in our attempts to collaborate with organizations that serve people with disabilities. Knowing these potential barriers is essential in order to avoid the inevitable problems that could arise in the partnership process.

Rev. William Gaventa describes two specific categories of importance to those working in disability ministry. The first relates to people with disabilities and their families. The second category relates to outside people and organizations we must consider as possible partners.

A. Obstacles to Collaboration

Gaventa shares a profound story that illustrates the complexities of this barrier:

> At a recent small conference in Lancaster, Pennsylvania, the key speakers were individuals with disabilities and their family members. Two mothers of children with disabilities, one with autism and the other with psychiatric disabilities, relayed their faith journeys which included being asked to leave a church—seven times for the first mom and thirteen times for the other. The first woman shared how she persevered until finding a welcoming congregation. In the second story, the grown son with mental illness got involved in a new church plant and invited his parents back in. The obvious (albeit judgmental) question here is, "Who showed the greatest faith?"[4]

Those within the disability community have often been hurt in the past in their relationships with churches and other organizations. As a result, there can be a natural tendency to resist working together with others. Further, as Gaventa shares, those who have been hurt within churches may find their primary community with *another* group. Advocacy groups or social service organizations are their primary source of social connection.

We must diligently seek to overcome this resistance through unconditional love and a willingness to meet people where they are, including outside support groups. Given time, trust can be built and this barrier can often be overcome.

B. **The Hurdles in Working with Social and Human Services**

Often, hurdles stem from our Christian prejudice toward social and human service organizations. "We" are the Church with the right message and others are not. While the Church is the bride of Christ and an essential part of our spiritual growth, this attitude is built on a common misconception—that those in non-Christian organizations are not willing to partner with Christian organizations in a mutually beneficial manner.

First, many professionals in these areas are Christians who serve out of a sense of calling. The organizations they work for may be state institutions, non-religious non-profit groups or businesses, but their desire is to show Christ's love in their particular areas. We can partner with these friends by showing mutual respect, understanding the limitations of the faith expressions they can make in their workplaces and praying for one another's efforts.

Second, many other professionals have a spiritual background that is friendly toward churches and Christian organizations willing to help people in the area they serve. While they themselves may or may not practice our faith, they are supportive of churches taking an active role to help those in the disability community. These allies can be among those we collaborate with and sometime share our faith with as opportunities allow.

Third, sometimes other disability service professionals may not understand the efforts of Christians serving in disability ministry. Maybe they remember a negative faith experience or perhaps never saw good examples of faith that connected with their own lives. As such, we have the

WHAT ABOUT "SECULAR" AGENCIES?

When you partner with agencies, you run the risk of being "unequally yoked" with an organization that has different goals than yours. What's deceptive is that you'll look like soul mates at first: You both care about special needs children or adults, you both want to provide support and respite for parents, and you both may use the same language.

Ask the hard questions at the front end: What are your expectations regarding our sharing the Gospel? About praying with people? About encouraging participation at church services?

There are excellent partnering opportunities out there, but not every opportunity is a match. Be open about your own intentions, and ask good questions about a potential partner's intentions and expectations.[5]

opportunity to not only partner together to serve those in the disability community, but to be "salt and light," living out our faith in a way that points others toward our heavenly Father.

 READ: "Networking with Disability Ministries and Organizations: The Power and Witness of Seeking, Consulting, and Collaborating" by Rev. William Gaventa

Are you able to relate to Rev. Gaventa's statement:

"...strategies for collaboration are traditional acts of outreach and mission into what may feel like a 'foreign' mission field"? Why or why not?

III. **Locate and Exchange Ideas with Government and Private Agencies**

Building a better disability ministry must include knowing what local and national resources exist. Do you know what is available in your area? If not, here is a checklist of questions to help you start:

· Where do families with disabilities in our community turn for help?

· Who are the contacts in our area school district(s) for children with special needs?

· What are the names of the local group homes in our community? What are the names of the leaders there?

· Who are the contacts at our local hospital(s) regarding children and adults with special needs and/or disabilities? What resources do they recommend?

· Which local churches have an existing special needs or disability ministry?

· What local events are already taking place on behalf of the disability community? Support groups? Sporting events? Special Olympics? Educational courses?

· To all of the above questions, what could we do to help with the positive work already taking place in our community?

IV. Helping Your Church Understand the Importance of Partnerships

A. Lead by Example

Jesus often asked others to "Follow me." As we saw in our study of Luke 13 and 14, rather than merely telling others what to do, he showed others through his own actions. In fact, he provided the perfect example when he came to live among us to show us how we are to live our lives for the good of others.

This same principle applies in our efforts to involve our church in community initiatives to serve families affected by disability. Response to your efforts will be much greater if your walk matches your talk.

- If you are not already actively involved in an area of disability ministry, where can you start?
- If you are already involved, how can you find a connecting point outside of your church to show how this involvement can impact your community?
- Who should you meet with to encourage your church to become part of these efforts?

Short-Term Versus Long-Term Partnerships

There are two basic types of partnerships—short-term and long-term.

In a short-term partnership, the collaboration is either a one-time event or a specified period of time. This is often preferred when working with an unknown group or with a large number of organizations.

A long-term partnership should be preserved for a more limited number of groups or individuals that are the best fit for those involved. Because of limitations of time and resources, this type of collaboration must be chosen with discernment by those involved based on how the work together will benefit individuals served within the disability community.

B. Start Small

When asking your congregation to become involved in any new ministry, the ideal approach is often to ask for a small change first. A one-time event to connect with your community in the area of disability ministry can prepare the way for further involvement.

In one congregation, a major change started when people were asked to "just try it once" with the concept of serving at a local group home on a Sunday afternoon. Many who tried it once were moved by the opportunity to minister one-on-one with a person who rarely ventures outside their room and thrives on the smallest conversation with a new person. As a result, a few dozen people now regularly visit this group home, all because of saying "yes" to a one-time request.[6]

Where to Begin?

In the New Testament, the family and friends of those who were disabled were the ones most likely to serve as advocates on their behalf. The same is often true today.

Mark 2:1-5—The "paralytic" and his four friends
Matthew 15:30—Great crowds came to Jesus, "bringing with them" people with various disabilities

---

C. **Share Successes**

Success is contagious. In a world where bad news dominates the nightly news headlines, our congregations rejoice when a church member shares about a personal example of life-change among those beyond the church.

When you see God work in a special way through your efforts to serve the disability community where you live, ask your pastor for an opportunity to share. Whether through speaking, a video, church newsletter, classes or other venues, take every opportunity to tell others the great things taking place. Others will be excited and want to participate. Be ready to tell them how.

Bethlehem Baptist Church's statement on disability ministry shares a moving story that has motivated many in their congregation to commit to this area of service:

Matt and Kathy have two children, one with severe autism. A year ago, they were unchurched and angry. A friend introduced them to Dawn, the director of disability ministry at a local church, who called several times with little response. Dawn's church provided money for the couple to attend a weeklong Joni and Friends Family Retreat. They went as a last resort, since they were on the brink of divorce. There, surrounded by struggling and conquering families, faithful volunteers and a godly pastor, they found Jesus.

Back home, Dawn continued to minister to Kathy and recruited a man to meet with Matt. The church welcomed them and served their needs. This year at the Joni and Friends Retreat, Matt and Kathy were different people. Their anger had been replaced with an obvious joy. Their son's autism is as bad as ever, but they now have a lasting hope. God's power is being perfected in their weakness. And they have a church that understands and loves them.

Matt and Kathy's church is a real church that has embraced Christ's command to reach out to the least, both far and near. They have made a significant investment in people, time, and finances. Most importantly, they have discovered the joy of seeing God at work.[7]

D. **Ask for Help**

Finally, *ask* for help. The Bible tells us, regarding prayer, to "ask and we will receive." We tend to know this, but are often reluctant to ask other people for a commitment due to a fear of rejection.

Be encouraged. Rejection can be difficult, but it is worth experiencing the no's to discover those who say yes. Often, those who agree to help are those we would least expect. God has an interesting way of surprising us with those he uses to do his work.

V. **Develop a Broader Networking Strategy**

To reach your community, you must connect with your community. Two specific ways to serve on a community-wide scale are through building a community network and participating in community-wide events.

A. **Build a Community Network**

Upon investigating other groups in your area who serve

the disability community, you will likely find a variety of groups operating apart from one another, wishing they could help a broader array of individuals at a deeper level. One way to help everyone in this process is to build a community network for those who serve the disability community.

How does this take place? Erik Carter offers some of the following guidelines to assist in preparation:

1. Develop a directory of local congregations and organizations that could serve as potential partners.

2. Compile a list of people who are willing to share their expertise, perspectives, talents and time to equip organizations to include people with disabilities.

3. Design a simple website as a connecting point for your network.[8]

4. Offer periodic workshops and training relevant to the disability community.[9]

Make a Promotional Video

You may be surprised at how much information can be shared about your ministry in a three minute video. As you view the Joni and Friends Promotional video, list the positive objectives which are highlighted in this short clip.

 VIEW: Joni and Friends Promotional DVD

B. **Participate in Community Events**

Your community may already have organized events for those with disabilities. Some examples include:

- *The Special Olympics:* Where is the nearest Special Olympics to your church? This is an excellent opportunity to volunteer and be involved in a significant event for those in the disability community. Find out how at www.specialolympics.org.

- *The National Wheelchair Basketball Association:* If your church has a gym or access to one, you can sponsor a league through this organization. Find out more at www.nwba.org.

- *Local Group Homes:* Local group homes can be found in most communities. Find the ones nearest you. Contact the appropriate person and ask about events they may have where you and your church can help.

- *Big Brothers Big Sisters:* Many communities have a branch of this organization. Often, children with special needs are enrolled that you can ask to mentor. For those preferring to help someone on a one-to-one level, this can be a life-changing opportunity. Find out more at www.bbbs.org.

- *Other Special Events:* Your community likely hosts numerous events, ranging from 5K runs, golf tournaments, concerts and more. Find out about an event in your area and seek to partner together in a way that helps a local disability organization.[10]

Ten years ago, a few men from a small group chose to hold a day where they invited a few children with disabilities to join them for fishing at their church's pond. A decade later, over 800 people attend their annual Fishing Derby for the disability ministry at their church. Why? Because a few people chose to show God's love and networked with many in the process. Now their church is known as a place where those with disabilities and their families can come to experience the love of Jesus Christ.[x]

Disability ministry is rarely easy, but it can be easier—and better—together. As you continue to serve in this area, consider the material in this lesson for ways to better connect with other providers in your area. You can make a greater difference in the lives of the disability community by pursuing partnerships that honor God and show his love to those you serve.

Reflections on Lesson 14

Networking with Disability Ministries and Organizations

1. Of the four reasons shared for partnering with others in the first section of this lesson, which one was the most compelling to you? Why?

_____

_____

_____

_____

2. In Lori Lucore's story, why were a variety of experts and leaders from the faith community and beyond more effective in providing the solution needed for her daughter's education?

_____

_____

_____

_____

3. What are some of the common barriers that keep churches and ministries from partnering with other organizations that serve people with disabilities?

_____

_____

_____

_____

4. What is the difference between a short-term and long-term partnership? Name an example of each.

_____

_____

_____

_____

5. In your church, who are the people you could see joining you to better serve the disability community? What could you do to "start small" together to move forward?

6. How could your church or ministry partner with an existing community event to serve the disability community? Be specific.

7. Does a community network exist where you live to connect those who serve the disability community? If so, do you participate in it? If not, where could you begin to help start such a network?

MODULE 4

An Introduction to *Bioethics*

An Introduction to Bioethics

What is bio-medical ethics?

There is a lot of confusion about bio-medical ethics in our culture and in the church. The term speaks to ethical questions at the edges of life—life in the womb and life at the end. Bio-medical ethics has to do with life and death.

When people fall ill, experience an accident, or receive a terminal diagnosis, their illusion of control is completely shattered, leaving them with many questions. What should they do? Who can they talk to about treatment options? Where will they find help and hope? If Christians become a valid source of knowledge on these issues, we will have an opportunity to share a biblical view of meaning, life, suffering and death. In this way, not only will we provide answers and hope, we will also show how God's Word speaks to these issues.

While topics such as end of life issues, infertility, reproductive technologies, genetics and social justice may seem heavy and overwhelming, this module will help Christians grasp the basics and be ready to engage in meaningful discussion. Case studies in these lessons can bring clarity to these complex situations and give believers confidence to personally walk through some of these issues with a family member or friend.

Biomedical ethics is a complex field and it is in need of Christian engagement. These are life and death issues, and we want you to be confident about what God's Word has to say. We want you to understand biomedical ethics from God's standpoint.

Dr. Kathy McReynolds

What Is
Bio-Medical Ethics?

Fifteen

OBJECTIVES

Studying this lesson will help you:

✔ Define bio-medical ethics.

✔ Discuss why Christians should care about bio-medical ethics.

✔ Describe some of the negative consequences that could take place if Christians are uninformed regarding bio-medical ethics.

✔ Understand the relevance of the history of bio-medical ethics and its importance to the recent development of ethical theories.

✔ Name four ways to be salt and light concerning bio-medical ethics.

✔ Describe "calling" from a theological perspective.

Bio-medical ethics is not a topic that makes the top ten list of things most likely to be discussed at the dinner table. Words like genetic engineering, cloning and biotechnology are more at home in scientific journals. Nevertheless, these words represent life and death issues that many of us face on a daily basis, whether we realize it or not. People with disabilities and chronic illness confront these issues more than the average person. And the reality is that if we live long enough, many of us will experience some level of disability that could involve bio-medical ethics.

In recognizing these pending ethical dilemmas, President George W. Bush said this:

> As the discoveries of modern science create tremendous hope, they also lay vast ethical minefields. As the genius of science extends the horizons of what we can do, we increasingly confront complex questions about what we should do. We have arrived at this brave new world that seemed so distant in 1932, when Aldous Huxley wrote about human beings created in test tubes in what he called a "hatchery."[1]

As Christians, we must deal with these issues from a sound biblical basis. A good starting point in understanding how technology should be used is to remind ourselves that God made us "in his image," as the Bible makes so clear in Genesis 1 and Psalm 8. In this lesson, we will learn the basics concerning what bio-medical ethics is and why believers should be engaged in this field. It is important for us to understand that a fully-developed Christian worldview requires that we know something about bio-medical ethics.

🔑 *Knowledge*

We live in the Information Age, but what passes for knowledge today can vary greatly in its reliability as truth. Unfortunately, much of the information gleaned from the Internet and other media sources is little more than uninformed opinion. As believers, we know that all knowledge and wisdom come from the Lord.[2] We can boldly ask God for discernment regarding the sources we use to inform ourselves about today's important topics.

I. **What Do All of These Situations Have in Common?**

> **READ:** Case Studies #1—Lisa; #2—Brian and Becky; #3—Peter (Appendix E)

   A. All of these situations involve bio-medical ethical decision-making. Bio-medical ethics is a burgeoning discipline dealing with ethical issues that arise in a number of settings in the medical arena, including the physician-patient relationship, withholding and withdrawing treatment, new genetic and reproductive technologies, advance directives, medical futility and many more.

   B. Christians who become a reliable source of information and guidance on these issues may have opportunities to share a Christian view on life, meaning, suffering, and death with both unbelievers and believers in the process.

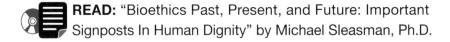 **READ:** "Bioethics Past, Present, and Future: Important Signposts In Human Dignity" by Michael Sleasman, Ph.D.

II. **Why Should We Care About Bio-Medical Ethics?**

   A. Dr. Sleasman takes a historical look at how bio-medical ethics has evolved over the centuries and clarifies the potential dangers that lie ahead for the most vulnerable if believers do not arm themselves with this important body of knowledge.

B. What is clear from Dr. Sleasman's paper is that ideas matter. As a result, knowing where concepts originate has enormous implications on present and future situations. We all make bio-medical ethical decisions frequently, some of us even on a daily basis. Sometimes, however, decisions are made without really thinking through their potentially life-changing implications. In light of this, it is important that we examine these choices carefully from a Christian perspective. Where does morality come from? If it comes from God, what if someone does not believe in him? Can such a person still have a moral compass? What reliable guidelines do we have for making difficult decisions that involve people, their choices, and their lives?

III. What Are Some Important Ethical Theories?

Deontological Ethical Theory

As Dr. Sleasman has pointed out, there are several ethical frameworks used in contemporary bio-medical ethics. Among modern ethical theories, perhaps the most amiable to Christianity is the deontological framework. Eighteenth Century Enlightenment thinker Immanuel Kant is credited with developing this abstract Christian ethic.[3] Kant stated that there was a rational principle that would function as a categorical imperative legitimizing all other ethical judgments. The command would be categorical rather than hypothetical because, for Kant, morality does not depend on our likes or preferences.

Kant's theory is comprised of two primary rules: 1) Always act in such a way that you can also will that the maxim of your action should become a universal law; 2) Act so that you treat humanity always as an end and never merely as a means. The first law demands that moral principle be universal in scope; the second seeks to make a distinction between persons and things.

The Judeo-Christian tradition is similar to a rule-based framework. Both Jews and Christians believe that God actually spoke to Moses, giving him the Ten Commandments. We also believe that he revealed himself to humankind through Scripture, and most completely through the person of Jesus Christ. We believe that we will be held accountable for our actions.

Online Resources for Bio-Medical Ethics

The Center for Bioethics and Human Dignity: A Christian-based research center for issues related to bio-medical ethics (cbhd.org).

The Center for Bioethics— Cedarville University: A bioethics resource center including numerous free resources in this area of research (www.cedarville.edu/Center-for-Bioethics).

The Center for Applied Christian Ethics (Wheaton College): Offers a wide array of academic resources on ethical issues from a biblical worldview, including several free resources on bioethics topics (http://www.wheaton.edu/CACE/).

National Right to Life (NRLC): Lobbies for the fundamental right of life given to every person, including the unborn (www.nrlc.org).

International Life Services: Works to restore a culture of life in our nation and worldwide (www.internationallifeservices.com).

Personhood: Pro-Life & Pro-Human Policy for the 21st Century: Safeguards the personhood of all human beings to protect human dignity (www.personhood.net).

Do No Harm: The Coalition of Americans for Research Ethics: Educates the public and policy makers regarding ethically acceptable and medically promising areas of research and treatment (www.stemcellresearch.org).

The Center for Bioethics and Culture Network (CBC): Sheds light on the bioethics issues that most profoundly affect our humanity—especially among the most vulnerable (www.cbc-network.org).

Utilitarianism

Utilitarianism is another contemporary theory that holds a place of prominence in secular circles.[4] The goal of utilitarianism is to "provide the most benefit for the greatest number of persons." The definition of "benefit" has always been vague and hard to define. In addition, the underlying assumption is that this "most benefit..." is the only rule that applies. All other concepts, such as loyalty, integrity, respect for God, or fidelity are only to be recognized if they are "beneficial."

Peter Singer, who holds an endowed chair in ethics at Princeton University, is probably the most widely known utilitarian today. He takes this position one step further by questioning the definition of "person." According to Singer, a person with an intellectual disability *is not* a person, while baboons and chimpanzees, having the capacity to learn, grow, and establish meaningful social ties, *are* persons.[5] Thus, the seemingly simple concept of "most benefit for the greatest number of persons" may not always mean precisely what we might think. While Singer represents only one form of utilitarian philosophy today, his views manifest the potentially dangerous implications of this view for vulnerable people.

Principlism

A third ethical theory widely used today employs a form of reasoning that utilizes four broad principles. These principles are 1) autonomy, 2) beneficence, 3) nonmaleficence and 4) justice. This approach is otherwise known as "Principlism."[6] Principlism has gone a long way to advance the discipline of clinical bioethical decision-making; but it has, nonetheless, some ethical drawbacks.

For one thing, these principles are anti-foundational; in other words, they are not tied to any philosophical or religious tradition. Therefore, their application can oftentimes become subjective. These principles actually have their basis in traditional, objective morality, but that foundation is no longer recognized by secularists.

Christians, on the other hand, do recognize that morality is grounded in the God of the Bible. That is why Christians ought to always refer back to the four sources of knowledge provided by God himself: Scripture, reason, godly experience, and tradition. Believers armed with these sources of knowledge stand on firm ground as they enter the marketplace of ideas.

However, as we engage our world we must anticipate that many will reject Scripture as a basis for authority and will scoff at our religious experiences and traditions. We must therefore be able to articulate reasoned, essentially religion-neutral arguments if we hope to persuade persons antagonistic to our faith. While we must never abandon our sources of knowledge in forming our position, we may need to create our public discourse based more on reasonable tenets that will immediately have credibility in the secular arena. We must appeal to evidence that those who oppose our beliefs will accept in order to achieve greater success.

IV. **What Is a Christian to Do?**

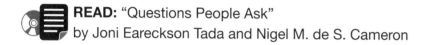

READ: "Questions People Ask"
by Joni Eareckson Tada and Nigel M. de S. Cameron

Joni and Nigel discuss the importance of being able to address the questions that people honestly ask about many bio-medical issues. It is so much better for people with serious questions about medical treatment to come to Christians for answers rather than consulting the works of Singer! What a ministry opportunity! Below is a list of some of the most frequently asked questions. Imagine for a moment what you would say if a friend came to you and asked...

1) Do cloned people have a soul?
2) Should we use assisted reproductive technologies?
3) Are embryos really human?

These and similar questions serve not only as mere conversation pieces, but as life-changing opportunities that God has opened up for us so that we might communicate our God-given biblical beliefs.

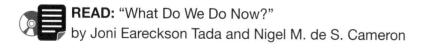

READ: "What Do We Do Now?"
by Joni Eareckson Tada and Nigel M. de S. Cameron

The strategies for the church are relevant for everyone and are certainly not difficult to implement. God may not call many of us to quit our current jobs and work full-time in the area of bio-medical ethics. For most of us, the question will more likely be, "How can I best serve Christ faithfully today?" Hopefully, as we ask this question, we may also consider, "What can I do to be a voice for God in this developing field of bio-medical ethics?" The following are some direct opportunities to become involved in this critical area:

1) Volunteer at a local Crisis Pregnancy Center.
2) Volunteer with a local hospice organization.
3) Find out what your local politicians believe about key bioethical issues and vote accordingly.
4) Volunteer to pray for your local politicians, doctors, social workers, and school counselors.
5) Become a volunteer at your local hospital, and see if there are any open volunteer positions on the hospital's ethics committee.
6) Contact Christian organizations that are working to set policy regarding these tough issues, and offer your prayers, monetary gifts, and time.
7) Read quality books on bioethics so that when you are asked about these issues you can give a reasoned Christian response.

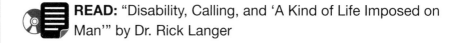 **READ:** "Disability, Calling, and 'A Kind of Life Imposed on Man'" by Dr. Rick Langer

Dr. Langer encourages us to gain a deeper understanding of work and calling. People with disabilities also have a calling and one that is vital to the life of the church. As he writes in the aforementioned paper:

> In Scripture it is clear that not only gifts and abilities come by divine appointment, but also our weaknesses and disabilities. Moses was concerned about his ability to speak, Gideon was concerned about his age, Paul was concerned about his ability to see. But in all of these cases, it is clear that the impediment in question was there by divine intention. They were apportioned to these men by the divine will. And in each of these cases, what might have been a disqualifying disability was actually ordained by God to further their calling in indirect ways. As the motion of the gears of a clock sometimes appear confused, and certain gears may actually turn in opposition to the

hands of the clock, they make an essential contribution to the final purpose of telling time.

People with disabilities are indispensable. At the same time, they are responsible to be faithful to God's calling. As a result, the ways discussed to become involved in issues of bio-medical ethics is not an invitation only to medical professionals or to those who work with the disability community, but extends as an invitation to all.

Reflections on Lesson 15
What Is Bio-Medical Ethics?

1. What is bio-medical ethics?

2. Why should Christians care about bio-medical ethics?

3. What are some of the consequences if we fail to inform ourselves about bio-medical ethics?

4. Which ethical theory do you think is closest to the biblical understanding of ethics? Why?

5. Is the embryo a human person? How would you defend your view?

6. Discuss one way you will practice being salt and light with regard to bio-medical ethics.

7. Discuss calling from a theological perspective. What do you believe is your calling? Why?

8. What is the importance of narration with regard to calling?

Ethical Issues at the *Edges of Life*

OBJECTIVES

Studying this lesson will help you:

✔ Understand some of the curses and blessings of medicine.

✔ Understand key beginning of life issues and why prenatal genetic testing is problematic in some cases.

✔ Understand the theological arguments and relationships between human dignity, disability, and bio-medical ethics.

✔ Identify the divine source of human rights and human dignity.

✔ Define some key end-of-life bio-medical issues and the term "futility of care."

✔ Understand the difference between euthanasia and physician-assisted suicide.

When it comes to medical treatments, one could say that we live in the best of times and the worst of times. It is the best of times because we are living longer, healthier lives due in part to recent medical advancements. But it is also the worst of times because oftentimes medicine is not used for its intended purposes; that is, to bring healing. When healing is not possible, the purpose of medicine is to bring comfort. But in the past several decades, we've seen an attempt to go beyond medicine's intended purpose in order to somehow make us "better" than well.

When medicine fails to heal us, every attempt is made to "relieve suffering," even to the exaggerated point of doing away with the *sufferer*. There is trouble whenever we attempt to distort purpose (right to choose over right to life) or get rid of purpose altogether (withholding or withdrawing treatment simply because of "quality of life").

Purposes become distorted when we fail to understand the sanctity of life. *Sanctity*, as it relates to human personhood, is a word that many in the Christian community have often heard and would readily agree with in terms of its validity. Yet, the nature of some disabilities can cause us to question our understanding of the sanctity of all life. It is evident that in our increasingly secular society, all human life is not viewed as sacred. Now more than ever, it is crucial that believers understand the biblical teaching that all human persons are sacred and valuable, not because of their abilities, but because God's image is stamped on every soul. This stamp can never be erased or destroyed. Human abilities can and will wane, but God's truth on this subject will last forever.

In this lesson, you will begin to understand the key bio-medical ethical issues such as abortion, assisted reproduction, genetics, futility of care, advance directives, physician-assisted suicide and euthanasia. You'll discover that although there is less public protest, human dignity and end-of-life human rights issues are under more attack than beginning-of-life choices. You'll see that the threat to vulnerable people has escalated. You will also have an opportunity to consider the relevance of seemingly abstract and academic terms in the papers and real-life case studies in this lesson.

ᛏ *Sanctity*

What should sanctity of life mean to you personally? According to God's Word, sanctity of life means that no matter what physical or emotional state your mind and body are in at any given moment in your life, you are valuable to God. Young or old, able or disabled…your life need never stop fulfilling the purposes for which God created you, regardless of how others see you or treat you. This sacred knowledge becomes the core of how you ethically treat yourself and others. —Pat Verbal

---

I. **The Sacredness of Life**

In this lesson we'll examine tough issues through the eyes of ordinary people attempting to cope with life's choices. We begin with the following cases, which involve the beginning of life, and observe the subtle and not so subtle trampling of human dignity.

READ: Case Study #4—Dawn (Appendix E)

A. **The Abortion Debate**

Two watershed Supreme Court cases in 1973 changed abortion from a criminal act to a right protected by the Constitution. The more famous case is Roe v. Wade.[1] Norma McCovey claimed she had been raped (a statement she later revealed was a pure concoction), and was pregnant. Texas law at that time allowed abortion only to save the mother's life. Her suit, decided at the Supreme Court, established that a woman had an unquestionable right to an abortion during the first trimester, and after that, with possible restrictions by the state.

Doe v. Bolton, decided the same day, blew the cracked door wide open. Essentially, the court ruled that whenever the "life and health" of the mother was in danger, abortion was legal. And, they broadly defined "health" to include emotional health, undue worry, stress or hardship. With these two decisions, abortion essentially became legal, on demand, for almost any reason, throughout the whole United States. Since that time, over 30 million abortions have been performed in the U.S.A.

A number of court cases followed over the years, alternately restricting or liberalizing abortion parameters. State legislatures have mandated minor guideline changes on a state-by-state basis, but the broad general protection of abortion on demand has been upheld many times.

Thousands of books, articles, laws, and opinions have been published on abortion since Roe and Doe. Many have taken a fairly firm "Life begins at conception," pro-life stance. Others, Christians and non-Christians, have worked hard to keep abortion legal, and protect a woman's right to privacy. Even among conservatives, however, many find cause to consider particular exceptions.

Are there not some legitimate instances when the life and health of the woman should receive preference to that of the unborn baby? What about children who are doomed to severely limited and painful lives? Is there no place for consideration of the quality of life of the baby and the mother? The Roman Catholic Church has stood firmly as one of the staunchest proponents of life at all stages.[2] Many mainline Protestant denominations, on the other hand, have taken pro-choice positions.

READ: Case Study #5—Thomas and Betty Smith (Appendix E)

B. **Assisted Reproduction Issues**

In the last 30 years or so, reproductive procedures have made tremendous advances. Some of these advances have been in medical interventions, such as improved care for mothers with diabetes and hypertension. But many of the advances involve what might be labeled "reproductive technologies." These include: 1) artificial insemination from husband or donor; 2) egg donation; 3) surrogate motherhood; 4) prenatal genetic screening.

Historically, Protestant churches have had little to say about any of this. The Roman Catholic Church, on the other hand, has had a great deal to say. The Catholic Church has based much of their teaching on natural law, which is law based on careful observation and reflection on creation, as opposed to revealed law seen in Scripture. Thomas Aquinas, an influential natural law thinker, summarized this position relative to procreation by stating that every individual marital sexual act must be open to the idea of creating new life.[3] This, then, would forbid any form of contraception.

In 1968, Pope Paul VI clarified this in "Humanae Vitae: On the Regulation of Birth," an official Vatican encyclical. In 1987, "Instruction on Respect for Human Life in Its Origin and on the Dignity of Procreation" further clarified the Vatican position. Any form of sexual expression that separated the sexual union of the couple from the direct possibility of pregnancy was to be shunned. Even within the Catholic Church, however, many feel that these parameters are too strict. Certainly within Protestant Christianity, the idea that all sexual activity must be open to creating new life is not held to be true. While Protestants in general revere the processes of procreation and sexual marital union, few would claim that the two processes must always be linked.

READ: Case Study #6—Bob and Angie (Appendix E)

Most conservative Protestants agree on the Christian's right, and perhaps even obligation, to plan one's family. Permanent sterilization is a non-issue for most Protestants. Many would generally accept artificial insemination with husband's sperm, or manipulations involving the couple's own eggs and own sperm. The use of donor sperm or donor eggs is more controversial.

Surrogate motherhood would be deemed highly problematic and generally unacceptable. Surrogate motherhood may include use of the surrogate's eggs and uterus, or solely her uterus. A number of ugly lawsuits have resulted from surrogate arrangements, and most states now have laws that prohibit or strictly regulate this process.

C. **New Genetics Research**

In 1988, the National Research Council endorsed a mind-boggling research project that had been discussed for several years. The Human Genome Project is an ambitious public plan to map out the entire human DNA blueprint. During this same time period, Dr. J. Craig Venter undertook a parallel project in the private sector. In June 2000, Dr. Francis S. Collins along with Dr. Venter announced the essential completion of these monumental undertakings.[4]

The benefits of these two projects are difficult to fathom. We will soon gain a vastly improved understanding of genetically inherited diseases. With this understanding we could prevent and treat many diseases that are currently unpredictable, inescapable and untreatable. This could completely alter the way we do medicine.

So what is the cause for alarm? There actually are a number of concerns:

1. Could this information be used to discriminate against those who have serious diseases in their gene pool?

2. Who would be responsible for maintaining confidentiality regarding this sensitive information?

3. Would the information provided cause some people to give up on life based on the negative predictions inherent in their genes?

4. Even if the testing is absolutely correct, many diseases are caused by a combination of genetic and environmental factors. Thus, important decisions might be made based on very incomplete information.

5. Even if one has the most gifted gene pool, free will and personality play into his or her achievements.

In contrast, some people with little natural talent have accomplished great things through sheer determination.

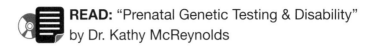

READ: "Prenatal Genetic Testing & Disability" by Dr. Kathy McReynolds

While Dr. McReynolds delves into some of the potential abuses that could result from prenatal genetic testing, clearly discrimination does take place in this arena. Sometimes just the thought of having a child with a disability is enough to make potential parents consider abortion. Thus, these ethical issues surrounding the beginning of life are all related at a fundamental level. Throughout history pessimists have warned that different technological advances would create dire consequences, both foreseen and unforeseen. The unknown effects of electricity, for instance, were thought to cause cancer and dementia. Yet, some technologies *have* caused previously unforeseen problems. Where will all the new genetics knowledge lead us? Only God knows for sure.

Do you agree with the arguments in favor of prenatal genetic testing? Based on your assessment, would you counsel a friend to use this technology?

II. **The Dignity of Human Life**

Dignity is one of the most overused and misunderstood words used in today's society. However, with God's wisdom we can find the road to understanding. We begin with these insights from Chris Ralston, a Ph.D. Candidate at Rice University:

Death with dignity. Human dignity. The dignity of human life. Respect for dignity. These phrases are heard repeated in contemporary, bioethical debates from disputants on opposing sides of the same argument, which begs the question: What do these phrases mean and how can they be used in such seemingly contradictory ways?[5]

READ: "Dignity, Disability, and Bioethics" by Chris Ralston

Chris provides clarity to what are often nebulous concepts, beyond academic thought. As Chris points out, the concept of human dignity has enormous practical implications that call us to take action steps in order to ensure that all people are treated with the respect they deserve—simply because they are human beings. It is clear that human dignity rests on the idea of human rights, but who or what grants human rights?

We must understand where rights come from since many people are vulnerable and their rights are being threatened in today's society. In Proverbs 31:8-9 we, the Body of Christ, are called to be a voice for the voiceless: "Speak up for those who cannot speak for themselves, for the rights of all who are destitute. Speak up and judge fairly; defend the rights of the poor and needy."

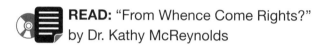

READ: "From Whence Come Rights?"
by Dr. Kathy McReynolds

Dr. McReynolds wants to ensure that human dignity and human rights are protected at every stage of life. In order to protect those who possess rights and dignity, we have to understand from whence rights are derived. If they are from God, no state or government can take them away. If they are from the state, then they are subject to the governing authorities. She makes the argument that rights come from God; therefore, we have an obligation to do what we can to protect the rights and dignity of all. The following cases serve as examples where rights and dignity are most threatened.

READ: Case Study #7—Jarod (Appendix E)

A. **Defining Futility of Care**

Dr. William May, in his book *Testing the Medical Covenant,* argues that the concept of "medical futility" emerged in the middle 1990s as a way of placing a limit on the physician's and the health care organization's medical covenant with a gravely ill patient.[6] Since providers receive fixed annual payments from the insurers, unlike older models of fee services, it is in the provider's best interest to deny full service to patients who need care.

They then disguise this fact by describing full service as unnecessary and futile. Physicians of faith may find Dr. May's analysis unnecessarily cynical.

While the term "medical futility" may be relatively new, the concept was conceived before managed care. Triage, established after World War I, is the placement of wounded soldiers into three classes: 1) Salvageable if acute care is given; 2) Salvageable even if treatment is delayed; and 3) Unsalvageable despite any efforts. This third group was not to be treated. If time and resources were wasted on these patients, they would still die, and so would the patients from the first category. Thus, a functional definition of futility has been used for over 70 years.

Although futility may be hard to define, the idea is straightforward. Physicians are not ethically obligated to provide care that in their best judgment will not have a reasonable chance of benefiting their patient. But ethical questions remain: 1) Whose best judgment decides? 2) What is a reasonable chance? and 3) What does "benefiting the patient" mean? These questions seem somewhat open to interpretation.

B. **What Are Advance Directives?**

Many people remember the media circus that surrounded the life and death of Terri Schiavo. The controversy drew protesters on both sides of the end of life issue, as had similar cases like Karen Quinlan's in 1976 and Nancy Cruzan's in 1990. In each situation there was a question over whether the patient would want to be kept alive through medical interventions. Since none of the patients had left their wishes in writing with their signatures, family members were forced into court to speak on behalf of each patient. However, in the Schiavo case, family members could not agree and the case went all the way to the U.S. Supreme Court.

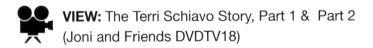

VIEW: The Terri Schiavo Story, Part 1 & Part 2
(Joni and Friends DVDTV18)

The term "Advance Directive" may refer to several different types of documents. The two most widely used are the Living Will (LW) and the Durable Power of Attorney for Health Care (DPAHC). A third scenario, where no specific wishes are delineated, and where no person is denoted as the decision-maker, is accounted for in many states by a surrogate law in some form, usually involving the appointment of a proxy. The proxy is supposed to make decisions for the patient based first on "substituted judgment" which means that the proxy knows for certain what the patient would have wanted.

1. **Living Wills** are legal in most states. Through a LW people may decide and document in advance exactly what medical treatments and interventions they will allow the medical team to do on their behalf. An obvious advantage of this is that if they strongly do not wish to have a specific medical treatment, such as intubation or defibrillation, to be performed, they can exclude these treatments in advance.

   One disadvantage of a LW is that it is impossible to predict all the variables that may come to play in a complex decision at some point in the future. When a LW is written closer to a person's death, it will more closely approximate the patient's true wishes, but even this is not always true. Another problem with LWs is that in most states the LW does not take effect until a determination of terminal illness or persistent vegetative state is made. Because of some of these problems, many find the DPAHC a more suitable document.

2. **Durable Power of Attorney for Health Care** documents specify in advance the person who will be authorized to make health care decisions for the patient in the event that the patient loses decision-making capacity. Thus, the determination of imminent death or persistent vegetative state is not necessary. Some persons include the DPAHC as a separate part of the same document that specifies the LW. Thus, a person could say in the event of imminent death the LW is to take effect, but in the event that the patient is not able to make decisions due to acute injury or non-competence the DPAHC will be in effect. Many Christians find the DPAHC to be more reasonable, but it requires that the patient speak clearly and at length with the designated decision-maker regarding their wishes.

An underlying assumption of the discussion above is that patient autonomy is very important, and should be given first place in authority for deciding difficult questions.

READ: Case Study #8—Paula (Appendix E)

C. **Taking a Stand on Physician-assisted Suicide and Euthanasia**

The idea of euthanasia, "good death," has captured public attention in recent years, particularly due to Dr. Jack Kevorkian, who assisted in killing a number of patients—many with non-terminal diseases. The concept, however, is thousands of years old. Hippocrates, famous Greek physician and founder of a school known by his name, said in his famous oath: "...I will not give poison to anyone though asked to do so, nor will I suggest such a plan."

Terminology is murky on euthanasia, but three distinct categories of death are usually discussed: suicide, assisted suicide and active mercy killing. Suicide and assisted suicide are self-evident terms. Active mercy killing can be subdivided into voluntary, involuntary (against the patient's wishes), and non-voluntary (without input from the patient).

Proponents of legalizing euthanasia in the U. S. often tout the history of euthanasia in the Netherlands. While many Americans assume that the Dutch experience is one of voluntary euthanasia, a major study conducted by the Dutch government revealed that many deaths in the Netherlands fall into the involuntary and non-voluntary categories.

Some use the terms "passive euthanasia" versus "active euthanasia" to differentiate between fatal withholding of treatment versus direct intervention to cause death. Passive euthanasia can also be voluntary, involuntary and non-voluntary. It is within the patient's rights to refuse further medical care or treatment and can be the most humane action to take. To label this action passive euthanasia is a grave disservice to physicians who offer this option and to the patients who accept it. Good people who hold to the sanctity of life are not guilty of compromising their position if they believe that patients have a right to refuse treatment under certain circumstances.

These complex discussions involve a number of overlapping questions:

1. Who owns our lives, anyway? Do our lives belong to us to claim at will, or are they trusts lent to us by God? Are we owners or the fiduciaries?

2. Is it ever moral to hasten someone's death? If it is moral, on what grounds may we base this decision?

3. When does the imminence of death supersede the need to fight death as a bitter enemy?

4. Is it possible to over-treat a patient in an attempt to avoid death? Are we always morally compelled to take all possible action that might temporarily stave off the inevitable?

III. **Quality of Life Versus Sanctity of Life**

What is "quality of life"? This rather abstract concept applies to situations in which decisions about withholding or withdrawing care from a patient are made based on his or her levels of self-awareness, reasoning, communication and activity, as well as the patient's probability of improvement. Quality of life decisions are usually not made by persons in question, but by their physicians, their families, or at times, the courts. Thus, there is an inherent element of uncertainty and guesswork involved. There are a number of reports of people who were seriously injured and made only a limited recovery, but when they reached their final new baseline seemed to be relatively happy. If families and doctors had been asked to predict what the patients' response to their new life would be, they would have underestimated the patients' rate of adjustment and happiness. Observers might think that some patients have a low quality of life, when the patients themselves would rate their quality of life fairly high.

This concept may also be employed in health care rationing discussions. *"After all, we shouldn't waste any more money on this person because their quality of life will be so low, anyway."* Utilitarianism, with its goal of providing "the most good for the most number of people" would typically hold this view. Another concern is: "Whose definition of quality do we use?" This was how Nazi Germany rationalized killing mentally ill and handicapped patients. They maintained that the quality of life they led was not worth saving. It would be an act of mercy to kill them.

"Sanctity of life" advocates usually find themselves on the opposite end of a freewill spectrum from quality of life proponents. Quality of life advocates sometimes support abortion on demand and a patient's "right to die." Sanctity of life advocates usually seek to support the patient regardless of likely outcome. As was mentioned earlier, the extreme sanctity of life position holds that everything possible must be done for every patient regardless of expense in time, money or personal sacrifice.

However, many sanctity of life advocates would support removing feeding tubes from patients in persistent vegetative state, if certain conditions apply. Scott Rae, in *Moral Choices*, suggests that under certain conditions removal of the feeding tube is justifiable for a patient in persistent vegetative state. According to Rae, removal may be considered if: 1) the patient cannot absorb nutrients, 2) feeding is a burden greater than a benefit, 3) there is no reasonable hope of benefit, or 4) if written advance directives dictate.[7]

Finally, on a metaphysical level, what is the purpose of our lives? Is it only to be happy, or is it primarily to glorify God and serve him with whatever means he puts at our disposal? If we answer the former, then we are hedonists, humanists, or utilitarians. If we answer the latter, then we align ourselves with the great Christian creeds of the ages.

God is eternal and sacred, so this life is sacred. The phrase sanctity of life reminds us that life is God's precious gift and cannot be disrespected or exploited. God's laws break down primarily into two commands: 1) to love God, and 2) to love others. This phrase emphasizes the great respect that we are to show for all human life including the newly conceived, up to the aged and infirm. No lack of intelligence, creativity, or beauty on the part of the humans in question should diminish the deep respect that we owe every person simply because they are God's creation, made in his image. In other words, there is not a human disease or disability that could be severe enough to undermine human dignity.

Reflections on Lesson 16

Ethical Issues at the Edge of Life

1. Name the key beginning-of-life/end-of-life bio-medical issues. What are some of the specific ethical issues related to each area?

2. How would you discuss the issues involved with a woman contemplating an abortion because she is afraid of having a child with a disability?

3. What role do the media play in forming public opinion regarding beginning-of-life issues? Please give some examples.

4. If a person begins his or her thought process with the presupposition that there is no God, how will this affect his or her thinking on beginning-of-life issues?

5. Describe the relationship between dignity, disability and bioethics.

6. Why is it important to understand where human rights and human dignity are derived from?

7. Acts 7 reveals that Stephen not only gave up his life for Christ, but he did two things that seem mutually exclusive: 1) He confronted the evil he saw and 2) he continued to love his tormentors. Does this guide our responses to physicians who intentionally put people to death in the name of medicine?

8. Is autonomy a biblical concept? Why do Americans value it so highly? Is this true of people from every part of the world? How does autonomy relate to the concept of human dignity?

9. Discuss one way you will take action in regard to practicing what you have learned about end-of-life issues.

A P P E N D I X   A

Fact Sheet on Persons with Disabilities

Adapted from United Nations Enable, www.un.org/disabilities/documents/toolaction/pwdfs.pdf

Overview

- In countries with life expectancies over 70 years, individuals spend on average about 8 years, or 11.5 percent of their life span, living with disabilities.
- Eighty percent of persons with disabilities live in developing countries, according to the UN Development Programme (UNDP).
- Disability rates are significantly higher among groups with lower educational attainment in the countries of the Organisation for Economic Co-operation and Development (OECD), says the OECD Secretariat. On average, 19 percent of less educated people have disabilities, compared to 11 percent among the better educated.
- In most OECD countries, women report higher incidents of disability than men.
- The World Bank estimates that 20 percent of the world's poorest people have some kind of disability and tend to be regarded in their own communities as the most disadvantaged.
- Women with disabilities are recognized to be multiply disadvantaged, experiencing exclusion on account of their gender and their disability.
- Women and girls with disabilities are particularly vulnerable to abuse. A small 2004 survey in Orissa, India, found that virtually all of the women and girls with disabilities were beaten at home, 25 percent of women with intellectual disabilities had been raped and 6 percent of women with disabilities had been forcibly sterilized.
- According to UNICEF, 30 percent of street youths have some kind of disability.
- Mortality for children with disabilities may be as high as 80 percent in countries where under-five mortality as a whole has decreased below 20 percent, says the United Kingdom's Department for International Development, adding that in some cases it seems as if children are being "weeded out."
- Comparative studies on disability legislation shows that only 45 countries have anti-discrimination and other disability-specific laws.

Education

- Ninety percent of children with disabilities in developing countries do not attend school, says UNESCO.
- The global literacy rate for adults with disabilities is as low as 3 percent and 1 percent for women with disabilities, according to a 1998 UNDP study.
- In the OECD countries, students with disabilities in higher education remain under-represented, although their numbers are on the increase, says the OECD.

Employment

- An estimated 386 million of the world's working-age people have some kind of disability, says the International Labour Organization (ILO).
- Unemployment among persons with disabilities is as high as 80 percent in some countries. Often employers assume that persons with disabilities are unable to work.
- Even though persons with disabilities constitute a significant 5 to 6 percent of India's population, their employment needs remain unmet, says a study by India's National Centre for Promotion of Employment for Disabled People, in spite of the Persons with Disabilities Act, which reserves for them 3 percent of government jobs. Of the 70 million persons with disabilities in India, only about 100,000 have succeeded in obtaining employment in industry.
- A 2004 United States survey found that only 35 percent of working-age persons with disabilities are in fact working, compared to 78 percent of those without disabilities. Two-thirds of the unemployed respondents with disabilities said they would like to work but could not find jobs.
- A 2003 study by Rutgers University found that people with physical and mental disabilities continue to be vastly underrepresented in the U.S. workplace. One-third of the employers surveyed said that persons with disabilities cannot effectively perform the required job tasks. The second most common reason given for not hiring persons with disabilities was the fear of costly special facilities.
- A U.S. survey of employers conducted in 2003 found that the cost of accommodations was only $500 or less; 73 percent of employers reported that their employees did not require special facilities at all.
- Companies report that employees with disabilities have better retention rates, reducing the high cost of turnover, says a 2002 U.S. study. Other American surveys reveal that after one year of employment, the retention rate of persons with disabilities is 85 percent.
- Thousands of persons with disabilities have been successful as small business owners, according to the U.S. Department of Labor. The 1990 national census revealed that persons with disabilities have a higher rate of self-employment and small business experience (12.2 percent) than persons without disabilities (7.8 percent).

Violence

- For every child killed in warfare, three are injured and acquire a permanent form of disability.
- In some countries, up to a quarter of disabilities result from injuries and violence, says the World Health Organization (WHO).
- Persons with disabilities are more likely to be victims of violence or rape, according to a 2004 British study, and less likely to obtain police intervention, legal protection or preventive care.
- Research indicates that violence against children with disabilities occurs at annual rates at least 1.7 times greater than for their peers without disabilities.

"Pastor Pickle"
A Skit Based on Ezekiel 34
By Rev. Steve Bundy

Scene: Pastor Pickle has just settled down in his office to prepare a sermon for the upcoming church service. A TELEPHONE sits on his desk, along with a number of BOOKS and, of course, a large BIBLE.

Pastor Pickle: Oh, let's see...this week's message is in Ezekiel 34... Let's see what this says...

(reading text aloud, in a contemplative manner) "Ezekiel 34:1-4—The word of the LORD came to me: "Son of man, prophesy against the shepherds of Israel; prophesy and say to them: 'This is what the Sovereign LORD says: Woe to the shepherds of Israel who only take care of themselves! Should not shepherds take care of the flock?... You have not strengthened the weak or healed the sick or bound up the injured. You have not brought back the strays or searched for the lost. You have ruled them harshly and brutally."

Whew, this is a strong passage... *(shifting in his seat, getting a little uncomfortable)* "This is what the Sovereign LORD says: I am against the shepherds and will hold them accountable for my flock. I will remove them from tending the flock so that the shepherds can no longer feed themselves. I will rescue my flock from their mouths and it will no longer be food for them."

(Hits intercom button on phone) ... uh, Sally, bring me a glass of cold water and um, turn the heat down. It's awfully hot in here... *(pulling at his collar)*

"As for you, my flock, this is what the Sovereign LORD says: I will judge between one sheep and another and between rams and goats. Is it not enough for you to feed on the good pasture? Must you also trample the rest of your pasture with your feet? Is it not enough for you to drink clear water? Must you also muddy the rest with your feet? Must my flock feed on what you have trampled and drink what you have muddied with your feet?"

Oh boy, this sermon is not going to go over well... I'd better lighten this one up... let's see, where is my book of jokes *(looks around desk area, then hits intercom again)* ... Um, Sally, can you also find my book of jokes? I need to pull some out for this Sunday.

"Therefore this is what the Sovereign LORD says to them: See, I myself will judge between the fat sheep and the lean sheep. Because you shove with flank and shoulder, butting all the weak sheep with your horns until you have driven them away, I will save my flock and they will no longer be plundered. I will judge between one sheep and another.

(a pause.) "I myself will tend my sheep and have them lie down, declares the Sovereign LORD. I will search for the lost and bring back the strays. I will bind up the injured and strengthen the weak, but the sleek and the strong I will destroy. I will shepherd the flock with justice.

(another pause) "I will place over them one shepherd, my servant David and he will tend them; he will tend them and be their shepherd. I the LORD will be their God and my servant David will be prince among them. I the LORD have spoken."

Brother Thorn and Sister Tiffany enter.

Brother Thorn: Um, excuse me, Pastor Pickle, I'm sorry to bother you… is this a good time?

Pastor Pickle *(annoyed)*: Well, not exactly. I'm doing sermon preparation and really need some quiet time.

Brother Thorn *(interrupting, oblivious to Pastor Pickle's response)*: Well good, I'm glad it's a good time; it will just take a minute. I have with me Sister Tiffany. Pastor, we have a concern we need to discuss with you… *(turning to Sister Tiffany)* …go ahead, Sister Tiffany.

Sister Tiffany *(arrogantly)*: Pastor, I don't want to seem like an unloving Christian, but we are having major problems with a number of families in our children's ministry. I don't want to over exaggerate, but I feel our problem is destroying the integrity of our children's ministry… I'm concerned that good Christian families are going to leave.

Pastor Pickle *(concerned)*: Well, my goodness, Sister Tiffany! What on earth is the problem?

Sister Tiffany *(judgmentally)*: Pastor, some children just don't belong with other children—they're just too complicated! Again, I don't want to seem like a bad Christian… I know we are to love everyone… but Pastor Pickle, parents are bringing "special needs" children to church and it's seriously disrupting our children's programs… nobody knows what to do with them!

Pastor Pickle *(calming)*: Now, now, Sister Tiffany, it can't be that bad, can it? I mean, we're only talking about a few children with disabilities, right? How can they be destroying the integrity of the children's ministry?

Sister Tiffany *(arrogant)*: Pastor, I don't want to seem unreasonable, but have you ever tried to teach about Jesus feeding the five thousand using gummy fish and Cheez-Its, when one particular child seems to feel that all the gummy fish and Cheez-Its belong to him? I mean some of these kids act like they've never once been disciplined in their entire lives!

Sister Jane enters, interrupting the conversation.

Sister Jane *(politely)*: Excuse me, Pastor Pickle, could I have a word with you… I was wondering if this was a good time?

Pastor Pickle: Well, Sister Jane, as always it's good to see you, but this is actually my sermon preparation time… in fact, Brother Thorn and Sister Tiffany were just leaving…

Sister Jane *(ignoring Pastor Pickle's response and taking a seat)*: Oh good, it won't take long, it will be just a minute. Good to see you, Brother Thorn and Sister Tiffany; I know you will want to hear this.

Pastor Pickle *(growing impatient)*: Yes, yes, of course. Come on in… have a seat…

Sister Jane *(with passion)*: Pastor, there is a disturbing situation in the children's ministry…

Sister Tiffany *(agreeing)*: Yes, we were just discussing a situation, too…

Sister Jane: The children with special needs?

Sister Tiffany *(strongly agreeing, thinking they are on the same page)*: Yes, can you believe it!?

Sister Jane *(indignant)*: No, I can't! *(turning to Pastor Pickle)* Pastor Pickle… as Brother Thorn and Sister Tiffany have probably already told you, parents are bringing children with special needs to the children's area… and you would not believe…

Sister Tiffany (*leaning forward in chair*): Yes, yes, yes, I was telling him…

Sister Jane (*continuing, with a sense of justice*): You would not believe how un-Christlike parents and volunteers are treating these children with special needs and their parents…

Sister Tiffany and Brother Thorn (TOGETHER) (*Shocked*): Yes, that's right! I mean… what!?! (*sinking back in their chairs*)

Sister Jane (*passionately*): I mean, here these families are coming to our church and instead of welcoming them and ministering to them, we have volunteers complaining, telling parents their children can't participate in the programs and parents talking about finding another church for their children. Can you believe this, Sister Tiffany?

Brother Thorn (*defensively*): Well, maybe it *is* best they find another church…

Sister Tiffany (*upset and defensive*): Well, now, Sister Jane, maybe we just don't see eye to eye on this. I mean, look, we've attended this church for years, we've paid our tithes and offerings, we've helped build this building so our children could come and learn about Jesus, not so they would be assaulted by children that don't belong in the classroom. I don't know where these kids belong. Perhaps they can learn somewhere else—if they can learn at all. What do you think, Brother Thorn?

Brother Thorn (*concerned*): Look, ladies, I'm not going to get into issues of ministry; that's not my role as a board member. (*turning back to Pastor Pickle*) My main concern, Pastor Pickle, is the cost that this is going to have on the ministry… with the building campaign we're stretched to the max already… I mean, this has been coming to a boil for quite some time. We have a number of adults in wheelchairs who have been complaining that Sunday school classes are upstairs and there is no elevator to get them up there. Last week someone complained that the bathroom was not adequately accessible, that the doorways need to be widened and handrails installed around the toilets… we just don't have the resources for this!

Sister Jane (*passionately*): Pastor, back to Sister Tiffany's comments… since when did we decide that decisions around here are made based on who tithes more than others? Can you put a price on ministry to those Jesus loves?

Sister Tiffany (*interrupting and argumentative, voice raised*): Sister Jane, I hate to have to give you a reality check, but people in wheelchairs are not going to support the financial needs of this church!

Sister Jane and Sister Tiffany now both trying to talk over each other… Brother Thorn jumping in, trying to show Pastor Pickle financial numbers… all three trying to be heard above the voices of the others…

Pastor Pickle (*exasperated*): Stop, stop! (*calmer voice, hands raised*) …please, please… nothing is going to be resolved by arguing. We have a board meeting tomorrow night; I'll have the issue placed on the agenda for the board to discuss.

(*pressing intercom button*) Sally, please add to the board agenda for tomorrow night the subject of—oh, what would you call it… handicapped people? …yes, yes, I know the agenda is full. What's the last item on the agenda… what's that, "is fundraising with bingo night godly?"… okay, just place it right after "is bingo night godly." If we have time, we'll get to it.

(*returning his attention to the other three still in his office*) Now, friends… I really do need to get back to my sermon preparation, so if we could please discontinue this conversation until after I meet with the board… and Brother Thorn, please bring the financial costs you have calculated to the meeting with you. We can look over them then.

ALL TOGETHER (*frustrated*): Fine!

Sister Jane (*concerned*): Pastor Pickle, could I please attend the board meeting?

Pastor Pickle (*patronizingly*): Umm, I'm not sure that's a good idea, Sister Jane... these matters are best left up to those of us God has elected to be in charge.

The three finally leave Pastor Pickle's office and he settles back to resume his sermon preparation.

Pastor Pickle (*frustrated, exhausted and overwhelmed*): Ok, finally back to my sermon preparation... let's see now, where was I... oh yes, here I was... verse 20...

"Therefore this is what the Sovereign LORD says to them: 'See, I myself will judge between the fat sheep and the lean sheep. Because you shove with flank and shoulder, butting all the weak sheep with your horns until you have driven them away, I will save my flock and they will no longer be plundered. I will judge between one sheep and another.'"

(*looking upward in prayer*) Oh Lord, this is a confusing passage... you're going to have to show me what this means... send me a sign...

APPENDIX C
Special Church Survey

1. Does a member of your family have a disability? .... ☐ Yes ☐ No
2. Do you have a friend or neighbor with a disability? .... ☐ Yes ☐ No
3. What is your friend or relative's disability? _____
4. Does he/she attend church regularly? .... ☐ Yes ☐ No
5. If not, would he or she like to? .... ☐ Yes ☐ No
6. Does your friend or relative have a need such as:
   - ☐ Weekly shopping assistance
   - ☐ Transportation to medical appointments
   - ☐ Respite care
   - ☐ Medical equipment
   - ☐ Other _____
7. If your friend/family member would like to attend our church, what changes (if any) should be made?
   - ☐ Parking
   - ☐ Accessibility (please specify):
   - ☐ Sign-language interpreter
   - ☐ Large-print Bibles
   - ☐ Better sound equipment
   - ☐ Better lighting
   - ☐ Wheelchair space that does not obstruct aisles
   - ☐ Special class for people with intellectual/developmental disabilities
   - ☐ Special care for child while family is in church
   - ☐ Other
8. We would like to help your friend/family member. Please let us have his or her name and address, or ask him or her to contact us.
   Friend/relative name: _____ Phone ( ) _____
   Address: _____
   City _____ State _____ Zip _____
   Additional comments: _____
9. Your name: _____ Phone ( ) _____
   Address: _____
   City _____ State _____ Zip _____
   Additional comments: _____
10. Our church is interested in starting a disability ministry/outreach. Would you like to become involved?
    - ☐ Yes, please let me know about opportunities for involvement.
    - ☐ No, I'm not interested in becoming involved at this time.

In His Image

Sample of Shadow/Buddy Guidelines
Volunteer/One-on-one Buddy Guidelines

In His Image wants to assure that church is a safe place for all children of all ages to have the opportunity to learn about the love of God in a way that they best understand. For some children, that will come through a specialized classroom that includes mainstreaming opportunities. This allows children a structured environment with age-appropriate teaching modified for their development while also allowing for some interaction with other typically-developing children. A one-to-two ratio of volunteer to children is acceptable. If the ratio ever becomes greater than this, parents will be expected to participate in the classroom. Classes meet every Sunday morning at 9:15 and 10:30 AM. All volunteers need to report to assigned classrooms a minimum of 15 minutes before classes begin.

- Assist Special Needs students with participation in typical ministry programs.
- Keep up to date on important information for each child.
- Keep open communication between Special Needs Pastor and parents.
- Report any incidents and/or observations to Pastor/Director.
- Attend training specific to "Buddy's needs."

The role of the buddy is to serve as a support for the special needs child. Occasionally using the buddy to help with regular classroom activities may be permissible if the special needs child functions well in the mainstream environment. However, when a buddy is utilized as a regular volunteer for the class, it may compromise the buddy's support role to the child that he or she is there to serve.

The buddy will meet the child at the designated area at check in time and should at no time be alone with the child, unless given permission by the Special Needs Pastor or coordinator.

* Used with permission of First Church of the Nazarene, Pasadena, CA.

Case Studies for Module Four
By Kathy McReynolds, Ph.D.

Case Study #1—Lisa

Lisa is a 17-year-old water polo player with big dreams to go to the Olympics. Her father is not involved in her life but Lisa's mother works very hard to pay for her coaching and pool time. Lisa has been successful in several tournaments, which has given her the confidence to believe that she could actually fulfill her dream. She has been asked to join an international team and to begin training at an Olympic level. Both she and her mother are thrilled.

Not long after joining the international team, Lisa met a young man named Jim who plays for the men's water polo team. With similar interests in many things both in and out of the pool, they hit it off immediately. Within six months, Jim and Lisa decided to live together, with plans to marry the following year. Not long after moving in together, Lisa found out that she is pregnant. She and Jim are sure they cannot have a baby right now because of their dreams and aspirations to participate in the Olympics while they are still young. They are in no way prepared financially or emotionally to have a child now. Lisa made an appointment with Planned Parenthood. The nurse informed her that they can remove the "product of conception" next week and that she will be back in the pool two days later. Lisa is encouraged that she will not have to lose too much time and that all will be back to normal soon.

Case Study #2—Brian & Becky

Brian and Becky have an ideal marriage in almost every respect. They have wonderful jobs that provide excellent financial security, are active in their church, and both come from supportive warm families. However, they remain childless. They have been trying to become pregnant for four years. So far, infertility treatments have not been successful, and they simply cannot afford them any longer. Sensing their discouragement, their doctor tells them that there is another option that could be made available to them. She then suggests that Brian consider using his sperm to fertilize a donor egg. The doctor described how she would fertilize the egg in a Petri dish and implant it in Becky's uterus. She says the success rate is not as high as she would like it to be, but this method may just give them the desire of their hearts: a child.

The doctor goes on to explain that the donor could be anonymous. She has a large pool of eggs to draw from which were donated by highly intelligent and beautiful young women. If Becky and Brian wanted further assurance, the doctor could perform a procedure called PGD, pre-implantation genetic diagnosis, in which she could assess the DNA of the potential child before it was implanted. This way they could avoid any adverse outcomes such as disability.

Case Study #3—Peter

Peter is extremely sensitive to social injustices not only in the United States, but also in developing countries. Thousands of children die every day as a result of starvation, violence, and neglect. What could he possibly do to help? The problem seems so overwhelming. One day Peter hears about an organization that endeavors to feed, clothe, and house children for as little as a dollar a day. Intrigued by their ministry model, Peter does some research on the organization and finds that 90 percent of the monies donated go toward the work of the ministry. He starts giving as much as he can. He stops going to Starbucks every day and starts to apply the money to this worthy cause. Still, he cannot help but wonder: Why do these injustices occur in the first place? Isn't there a loving God who controls all events in the universe? If that's true, why do we still encounter so much suffering?

Case Study #4—Dawn

As Dawn walked to her car in the darkened parking lot she had a vague uneasiness. She should have waited for the security guard escort, but if she had, she undoubtedly would have been late for her meeting at the office. Hastily, she unlocked the car, yanked the door open, jumped in and was trying to shove the key in the ignition when a hand from the back seat covered her mouth and jerked her head viciously into the head rest. "One sound out of you, and you are dead," he said.

The next 10 minutes would be seared into her mind forever. With a knife at her throat, the stranger sexually assaulted her in the back seat of the car, beat her savagely, and left her for dead. When she finally came to her senses, she drove herself to the nearest emergency room. Over the next few weeks the physical wounds healed. The emotional healing would take much longer. The nightmare continued. Four weeks after the assault, the clinic confirmed Dawn's worst fears. She was pregnant.

Surely God wouldn't demand that she carry this criminal's baby to term. The rape was terrible enough, but there was no way she could endure the pregnancy. Dawn's mind was numb but her heart felt untold anguish as she drove herself to the abortion clinic.

Case Study #5—Thomas & Betty Smith

Thomas and Betty Smith were heartbroken. After eight years of marriage and high hopes for a large, loving family, the Smiths were still childless. Six pregnancies were each followed by a miscarriage. And then the bleeding began. A tumor the size of a grapefruit was removed from Betty's uterus. In the process, Betty ended up receiving a complete hysterectomy, leaving only her ovaries. Now they would never be able to have children together...or would they?

Not long after the surgery, an opportunity to make everything right again was made available to them. Betty's cousin, Kim, offered them the chance of a lifetime. Using Tom's sperm and Betty's eggs, fertilization could be achieved in a Petri dish. The six to eight embryos could be frozen and stored in a lab. Then two or three of the embryos could be implanted into Kim's uterus. The embryos would grow, and later on, if more than one was viable, the other embryos would be removed. This way, disability could be avoided. The remaining healthy embryo would grow to term in Kim's body, and then would be given back to the Smiths at delivery. *What a great opportunity*, Betty thought, *and how relatively simple. How sweet Kim was to offer her help in this way.* "Let's do it!" she urged Tom.

Case Study #6—Bob & Angie

Bob met Angie on the campus of a major Midwestern university. He was drawn to her instantly, and soon they were planning marriage. Bob had grown up in Chicago, and Angie in St. Louis. Bob's family had originally come from the UK, and Angie's from Brazil. Bob had always dreamed of a large family. As he and Angie began discussing their hopes and dreams, however, Bob got a big surprise.

Several of Angie's relatives had died from Huntington's Disease (HD). HD is an autosomal dominant disease that has no cure. Symptoms can begin as early as the late thirties or early forties with peculiar behaviors and limb movements. It is progressive and eventually affects the mind, causing bizarre limb movements that gradually grow worse and inevitable death after 15 to 20 years. Angie did not know if she was a carrier for HD. If she was, it was only a matter of time until she was affected, and she had a 50 percent chance of passing this illness on to each of her children.

Bob did not know what to think. As he checked a genetic website on the Internet that night, he learned more. There now was a DNA blood test that could prove long before any symptoms occurred if a person had Huntington's Disease. All they had to do was obtain the appropriate testing, and they would know if Angie had the gene. Bob was shocked at what he read next: 10-12 percent of all HD victims kill themselves. And another study revealed that 30 percent of those at risk said they would kill themselves if they discovered they had the disease. Did Bob really want to have to deal with these problems? Perhaps he was wisest just to break it off with Angie and walk away before he got in any deeper.

Case Study #7—Jarod

Jarod never knew what hit him. Jogging along the sidewalk in his suburban neighborhood, he thought nothing of the blue sedan that drove slowly past him. Neighbors, sitting on their porches, heard a muffled gunshot and the sound of the car as it sped away. When they looked up, Jarod was lying in a pool of blood.

By the time his wife, Jane, got to the hospital, Jarod was intubated, and in the Surgical Intensive Care Unit. Dr. Braun, the neurosurgeon, had already examined Jarod, and told Jane there was nothing he could do. The bullet fragments had exploded inside his head, and the brain was a swollen, bloody mass. "Can't you do something?" Jane wailed. "He can't die like this. We have three children, and I am six months pregnant. Do something! Take him to surgery! Transfer him to a bigger hospital!" "I wish we could help," Dr. Braun responded, "but all further intervention at this point would be futile. We could call your pastor or your family for you, but there is nothing else to be done medically."

Case Study #8—Paula

Paula had always been an energetic woman. When her children were young, their friends always loved to come to their house to play because Paula made everything seem like such an adventure. Backyard games, craft projects, story hour, even watching videos together became times of excitement and fun under Paula's magical touch. Now she had terminal cancer. The physical pain was not too severe, but the crushing sense of despair was overwhelming. First chemotherapy, then radiation was tried, but neither was able to stop the spread of the illness. Her doctor suggested that she probably would not live until Christmas—six months away. She could not get excited about anything anymore. Her children and her husband did their best to interest her in people, activities, and social functions. None of her former pastimes seemed to spark any interest. What was the point of it all?

Paula was repulsed by the idea of deteriorating and losing control in front of her family and friends. She had always been independent and in control, and she wasn't going to let her loved ones' last memories of her be those of increasing dependence, pain, and disability. That was why she carried that Michigan doctor's address in her wallet. Some people may say bad things about that man, but knowing that his help was available gave her great solace. When her family was all out of the house Paula jumped at the chance and gave him a call to make the arrangements. Next month, before the pain became too intense, he agreed he could come and see her. Now she just had to convince her family.

Paula sat across the desk from Dr. Dan Smyth. "What I need to hear from you is that you will honor my wishes," she said. "I refuse to die slowly and painfully like my cousin Sally did. When the nausea and weakness become too great I want to know that you will be in my corner and will help me depart this life without a hitch. Can I count on you?" Dr. Smyth looked down at his hands. *What were things coming to?* This was the third patient this month to approach him with a similar request. *Was it really such a big deal?* After all, they were all terminal patients anyway. *What did a few months one way or another matter?*

Recommended Resources
Joni and Friends International Disability Center

To learn more about these and other resources, visit www.joniandfriends.org

Books

Available for purchase in the Joni and Friends website store

A Place of Healing: Wrestling with the Mysteries of Suffering, Pain and God's Sovereignty by Joni Eareckson Tada—Joni draws on lifetime wisdom & intense struggles with pain in a powerful understanding that leads to eternal purpose and God's place of rest.

A Lifetime of Wisdom: Embracing the Way God Heals You by Joni Eareckson Tada—Joni shares the rubies of God's wisdom and mercy for living victoriously.

A Never-Give-Up Heart by Beverly Linder—shows parents how God does not give a 'stone' in place of 'bread' to his beloved with guidelines and resources for developing designed potential.

Be Still, My Soul: 25 Classic & Contemporary Readings on the Problem of Pain by 25 authors [including St. Augustine, John Calvin, Martin Luther, R.C. Sproul, John Piper, Tim Keller, Corrie ten Boom and Joni Eareckson Tada] edited by Nancy Guthrie—Classic and contemporary theologians and Bible teachers explore Scripture for the causes and purposes of suffering.

Finding Your Child's Way on the Autism Spectrum: Discovering Unique Strengths, Mastering Behavior Challenges by Dr. Laura Hendrickson—A biblical counselor, former psychiatrist, and the mother of an adult son recovered from autism, Dr. Laura Hendrickson imparts deep understanding with practical ways to work with a child according to his developmental differences.

How to Be a Christian in a Brave New World by Dr. Nigel M. De S. Cameron and Joni Eareckson Tada—Joni uses cutting-edge information and life experience in joining with a foremost bioethics expert to equip Christians for discerning the ethical and moral issues of biotechnology.

Life in the Balance by Joni Eareckson Tada and Friends –This study, for presentation or the individual, tackles our culture's biggest ethical and social dilemmas—including hot topics such as street violence, abortion, autism, genocide and stem cell research.

Same Lake, Different Boat by Stephanie O. Hubach—First-hand, hands-on, and heartfelt advice in a scriptural framework that calls us to transform the church.

The Life and Death Dilemma by Joni Eareckson Tada—Written for families facing agonizing moral or medical choices, Joni tackles what makes life worth living and how to make health care choices with dignity, wisdom, and compassion.

When God Weeps: Why Our Sufferings Matter to the Almighty by Joni Eareckson Tada and Steve Estes—Joni and Steve Estes tackle tough questions about why God allows horrors and hardships.

The Unexpected Gift by Michelle Schreder—A mother of two boys who live on the autism spectrum answers tough questions with hope and practical advice for parents of children with special needs.

Including People with Disabilities in Faith Communities by Erik W. Carter—addresses how congregations, families, and service providers can work together to support the full participation of individuals with disabilities in the faith community.

Other Books

Purchase links available on Joni and Friends 'Help & Resources' web pages

If God Is Good: Faith in the Midst of Suffering and Evil by Randy Alcorn—captures the breadth of human suffering to explain biblical insight into God's exceeding goodness.

Suffering and the Sovereignty of God by John Piper and Justin Taylor, Editors—shows how God uses suffering to glorify himself, to mature us in Christ, and to progress the Gospel. Affirms the sovereignty of God and helps us live more consistently in God's grace.

The End of Suffering: Finding Purpose in Pain by Scott Cairns—relates his own afflictions and probes ancient Christian wisdom, challenging us to a supernatural revision of life's meaning.

The Darkness and the Glory: His Cup and the Glory from Gethsemane to the Ascension by Greg Harris—Professor and theologian examines behind-the-scenes spiritual happenings surrounding Calvary that transcend the physical to reveal deeper truths and glories.

The Problem of Pain by C.S. Lewis -In this classic treatise, apologist C.S. Lewis answers the universal question of how an all-loving, all-knowing God would allow suffering.

Joni and Friends TV Series

Episodes available for online viewing

I've Got Questions featuring Nick Vujicic—a model for overcoming a disability to live a fulfilling life.

Holly's Heart featuring Holly Strother—found freedom embracing God's design for her.

*Making Sense of Autism—**Part One** addresses common myths and looks into the lives of families that include a child with autism. **Part Two** addresses what these families need most from the church—as well as the blessings they bring to churches that fully embrace them in fellowship and service.

Not by Sight featuring Brian Bushway—progressive deterioration of eyesight from age fourteen fosters a Christ-inspired desire to serve others.

Lives in the Balance: The Stem Cell Debate featuring Laura Dominguez—Although embryonic stem cells were once touted for their unique ability to morph into other cells, scientists can now induce adult stem cells to become pluripotent.

The Jennifer Barrick Story: Part 1 & Part 2—God's Word, hidden in a young woman's heart, was the beginning of a new life—after the tragedy of severe head trauma.

The Terri Schiavo Story: Part 1 & Part 2—Terri Schiavo was not dying, and her life should have been measured by value, not quality. Every decision must be viewed in the context of eternity.

When Robin Prays featuring Robin Hiser—watch the amazing faith and ministry of this woman with Down syndrome.

Other DVDs by Joni and Friends

The Father's House: *Welcoming and Including People and Families Affected by Disability*—Practical ideas for becoming a disability-friendly church, addressing fears and misunderstandings that are common when beginning disability ministry.

Websites

Information about these and other resources may be found at http://www.joniandfriends.org/help-and-resources/

Disability Ministry

CCFH: www.ccfh.org– seeks to enhance the lives of persons with disabilities

Friendship Ministries: www.friendship.org—provides models for ministry to people with cognitive impairments.

Lift Disability Network: www.ccpd.org—exists to elevate *Life* in the disability family

Mark 2 Ministries: www.mark2ministries.org —equips the church to evangelize, disciple, and integrate individuals with disabilities.

NACSPED: www.nacsped.com—facilitates the integration and participation of people with disabilities into the Christian community.

Disabilities

Autism Research Institute: www.autism.com—ARI researches autism and other severe behavioral disorders of childhood providing information on prevention, diagnoses, and treatment, with resources for educators.

Disability.gov: www.disability.gov—provides quick and easy access to comprehensive information about disability programs, services, laws and benefits.

Hope Out Loud: www.hopeoutloud.com—dedicated to Bible teaching and helping people understand God's amazing grace.

National Organization on Disability (NOD): www.nod.org—promotes the full and equal participation of Americans with disabilities in all aspects of life.

Endurance: www.endurance.org—provides encouragement for those suffering via a ministry of multimedia resources and seminars.

Disability Rights Education Defense Fund (DREDF): www.dredf.org—advances the civil and human rights of people with disabilities through legal advocacy, training, education, and public policy and legislative development.

Videos Available Online

Autistic Basketball Manager's 20 Point Game—http://www.youtube.com/watch?v=p6cOp6EDFlI.
Autistic basketball manager scores 6 three pointers and 1 two point shot in the last 4 minutes of the game.

Butterfly Circus—Video. http://thebutterflycircus.com/
A short film with the hopeful message of transformation in weakness.

Documentary about Kim Peek "The Real Rain Man"—http://www.youtube.com/watch?v=z0lVdxXTANA
It's Okay to Be Different Kim Peek "The Real Rain Man" has memorized over 12,000 books and reads both open pages of a book at the same time with each eye!

Gov't flags Anti-psychotic drugs at nursing homes—GodTube http://www.youtube.com/watch?v=aNCp7D8nVJc

I Know You Believe in Me—GodTube http://www.godtube.com/watch/?v=J0FEEFNU

Overcomes the tragedy of a spinal cord injury to know that God does believe in you.

Doing the Right Thing Ethics Promo Final 2 small.mov—

YouTube: http://www.youtube.com/watch?v=r07Jdnddiyo&feature=player_embedded#at=25

The Chuck Colson Center: http://www.colsoncenter.org/ethics

Study DVD for small groups to understand the role and need for ethics in every arena of society.

Joni Eareckson Tada on Personhood—http://vimeo.com/2969781

Presentation by Joni Eareckson Tada as introduction for Georgia Right to Life

Joni Eareckson Tada: Suffering for the Sake of—YouTube www.youtube.com/watch?v=GIJADzaNj8k

Joni tells why "Hope is the best thing"

Lines that Divide: Science and Ethics Shaping the Stem Cell Debate Today—www.linesthatdivide.com

California Independent Film Festival Official 2010 selection.

Stephen Wiltshire: The Human Camera—YouTube www.youtube.com/watch?v=a8YXZTlwTAU

Savant transcends the imagination with his detailed drawing after one flight over Rome.

Policy Papers and Articles

For the latest Policy Papers on Bioethics/Biotechnology, Ethics and Healthcare issues,
see our Christian Institute on Disability at
http://www.joniandfriends.org/christian-institute-on-disability/

Other Links and Articles

The Council for Biotechnology Policy, How the United States Manufactured Eugenics for the Nazis,
Nigel M. de S. Cameron

Useless Eaters: Disability as Genocidal Marker in Nazi Germany
Full article text by Dr. Mark Mostert
Regent University website video presentation: www.regent.edu/acad/schedu/uselesseaters/

Joni and Friends International Disability Center

www.joniandfriends.org
P.O. Box 3333, Agoura Hills, CA 91376
(818)-707-5664 TTY (818) 707-9707

Contributing Authors

Dr. Mark W. Baker has a Ph.D. in Clinical Psychology and a Masters degree in Theology from Fuller Theological Seminary, and a certificate in Psychodynamic Psychotherapy from the Southern California Psychoanalytic Institute. He is licensed as a Clinical Psychologist as well as a Marriage, Family and Child Therapist. Dr. Baker is the Executive Director of the La Vie Christian Counseling Center that has a staff of twenty-five Christian Therapists with offices in Pasadena and Santa Monica, California. Dr. Baker's book, *Jesus, The Greatest Therapist Who Ever Lived,* has sold nearly one million copies in several countries around the world.

Rev. Michael Beates is the father of seven children, the eldest born with profound disabilities. He earned M.Div. and S.T.M. degrees from Biblical Seminary in Pennsylvania and the Doctor of Ministry from Reformed Theological Seminary Orlando. Mike teaches Bible and History at The Geneva School in Winter Park, Florida. Since 2000, Mike has served on the International Board of Directors at Joni and Friends and, since 2008, on the Board of Reference for the Christian Institute on Disability. He has written magazine articles, editorial columns and contributed chapters to several books, including "God's Sovereignty and Genetic Anomalies" in *Genetic Ethics: Do the Ends Justify the Genes?*

Clay Boatright and his wife Carole have three daughters, including identical twins who both have severe autism and intellectual disabilities. Clay serves as Board President for The Arc of Texas, the state's oldest and largest nonprofit organization serving people with intellectual and developmental disabilities. The Boatrights are also active members of Prestonwood Baptist Church in Plano.

Renée Bondi is a popular speaker and recording artist. She has been featured in magazines such as Today's Christian Woman and Woman's World and on various radio and television shows, including "Hour of Power." Renée has released five inspirational CDs and is the president of Capo Recording and the founder of Bondi Ministries. The Evangelical Christian Publishers Association nominated her book, *The Last Dance but Not the Last Song—My Story,* for the Gold Medallion Award. Among her many awards and honors is Woman of the Year from the California State Senate and recognition for Outstanding Service to the Community from the U.S. House of Representatives. Renée has a BA in Music Education.

Steve Bundy is the Vice President of Joni and Friends overseeing the Christian Institute on Disability and International Outreach. He was a contributing author to *Life in the Balance: Biblical Answers for the Issues of Our Day,* and co-executive producer with Joni Eareckson Tada of the Telly-Award winning television episodes, *Making Sense of Autism: Myths That Hide the Truth* and *Truth for the Church.* Steve has served as adjunct professor at Master's College and has lectured on disability ministry at educational institutions and conferences around the world. He frequently appears on "Joni and Friends" television episodes, national radio and has written articles or been interviewed for Christianity Today, Charisma Magazine, Focus on the Family and others. Steve and his wife Melissa know firsthand the joys and challenges of parenting a child with special needs, as their own son, Caleb, was born with a chromosome deletion which resulted in global delay and a secondary diagnosis of autism. Steve holds a B.A. in Theology and Missions, a Certificate in Christian Apologetics and an M.A. in Organizational Leadership. He is a licensed minister and has served as a pastor and missionary.

Nigel M. de S. Cameron, Ph.D., President and CEO of the Center for Policy on Emerging Technologies, has been a Research Professor and Associate Dean at the Illinois Institute of Technology where until 2008 he was Director of the Center on Nanotechnology and Society. In 2003, he co-founded the Institute on Biotechnology and the Human Future. He recently edited *Nanoscale: Issues and Perspectives for the Nano Century*. Cameron has served on numerous advisory boards and represented the U.S. on delegations to the UN General Assembly and UNESCO, and been a participant in the U.S./EU dialogue Perspectives on the Future of Science and Technology. He is a member of the Executive Committee of the U.S. National Commission for UNESCO, and has testified before both houses of Congress, the European Parliament and the European Commission's Group on Ethics in Science and New Technologies. In 2008, he was the U.S. Government's nominee to the UN Human Rights Council as Special Rapporteur for the Right to Health. A naturalized citizen of the U.S., he is a native of the UK where he studied at Cambridge and Edinburgh Universities and the Edinburgh Business School.

Chuck Colson (1931-2012) was a popular and widely known author, speaker, and radio commentator. A former presidential aide to Richard Nixon and founder of Prison Fellowship, BreakPoint, and the Chuck Colson Center for Christian Worldview, he has written many books, including *Born Again, Loving God, How Now Shall We Live?, The Good Life* and *The Faith Given Once, for All*—that have shaped Christian thinking on a variety of subjects. His weekday radio broadcast, BreakPoint, airs to two million listeners. In 1993, Chuck was awarded the prestigious Templeton Prize for Progress in Religion; the one million dollar prize was donated to the ministry, as were all of his speaking fees and book royalties. In 2008, President Bush conferred on him the second highest civilian award of the U.S. government, the Presidential Citizen Medal for his humanitarian work with Prison Fellowship. He is a graduate of Brown University and George Washington Law School, receiving his *juris doctor* with honors. He served in the United States Marine Corps, attaining the rank of Captain.

Dave Deuel, M.A., Ph.D. (Cornell University and The University of Liverpool) is the Director of International Academic Studies for Joni and Friends as well as the Academic Director of The Master's Academy International, a consortium of ministry training schools worldwide. Dave served as Regional Director for Joni and Friends in the San Fernando Valley, CA and in board positions for The North Los Angeles Regional Center, All Children's Hospital (Los Angeles), Direct Link for the Disabled and a Governor's Advisory committee for Disability (Sacramento). He is Chairman for the Old Testament and Ancient Near Eastern consultation of the Evangelical Theological Society. Dave focuses his ministry interests on assisting others in starting and developing ministries, primarily on the foreign field. He also ministers with and to persons with disabilities through Joni and Friends' Christian Institute on Disability.

Jon Ebersole has 25 years experience working with people affected by disabilities. He and his wife have three children, two with cerebral palsy, making his experience with disability very personal. He has served with Joni and Friends since 1999, and currently oversees the 23 local field ministry offices around the country. Jon serves the leaders of Joni and Friends across the country with training, guidance and encouragement to lead their local outreach. Jon earned a Masters in Social Work from the University of Illinois and completed a Seminary Certificate of Biblical Studies at what is now Trinity International University.

Chuck Edwards is an author, researcher, and speaker for Summit Ministries, an educational organization whose primary purpose is to prepare students for the intellectual and spiritual challenges of college and beyond (www.summit.org). He is the co-author of the biblical worldview Bible studies, *Thinking Like A Christian,* and *Countering Culture* and a contributing writer/editor for *Understanding the Times, 2nd Edition.*

William (Bill) C. Gaventa, M.Div., serves as Director of Community and Congregational Supports at the Elizabeth M. Boggs Center on Developmental Disabilities, and as Associate Professor, Robert Wood Johnson Medical School, University of Medicine and Dentistry of New Jersey. In his role at The Boggs Center, Bill works on community supports, training for community services staff, spiritual supports, training of seminarians and clergy, aging and end of life/grief issues, and cultural competence. He has been a frequent speaker, trainer, and workshop leader in these areas. As a writer and editor, he has edited newsletters and several books and written articles and chapters. He served as the Editor of the Journal of Religion, Disability and Health for 14 years, now as an Associate Editor. Bill has a wife, Beverly Roberts Gaventa, a Professor of New Testament at Princeton Theological Seminary, and a son and daughter-in-law.

Dr. Laura Hendrickson, trained as a medical doctor and board-certified as a psychiatrist, left her practice 18 years ago to work full-time at home with her son, Eric, who had just been diagnosed with severe autism. She trained as a biblical counselor and currently ministers at the Institute for Biblical Counseling and Discipleship in San Diego, CA. She is the author of *Finding Your Child's Way on the Autism Spectrum: Discovering Unique Strengths, Mastering Behavior Challenges.* Eric has, by God's grace, advanced along the autism spectrum, and today is an honor student at a top California university.

Stephanie Hubach serves as Mission to North America's Special Needs Ministries Director. Mission to North America is an agency of the Presbyterian Church in America. She also currently serves on the Lancaster Christian Council on Disability and the Faith Community Leadership Advisory Board. Steph is the author of *Same Lake, Different Boat: Coming Alongside People Touched by Disability* and *All Things Possible: Calling Your Church Leadership to Disability Ministry.* She has been published in byFaith magazine, Focus on the Family magazine, and Breakpoint online magazine. Steph and her husband, Fred, have been married for 27 years. They have two deeply loved sons: Fred and Tim, the younger of whom has Down syndrome.

Connie Hutchinson is the Director of Disabilities Ministry at the First Evangelical Free Church of Fullerton. She has spoken at conferences and colleges nationwide as an advocate for people with disabilities. Connie traveled in Ghana with a Wheels For The World team, and is currently on the Children to Love Board to help reach orphaned and abandoned children in Romania. She has traveled to Romania, China, and Northern Africa to speak to parents, educators, church leaders and government officials on the value of all people—with or without disabilities.

Julie Keith received a BA degree in Associate Ministry with an emphasis in Disability Ministry, a MA degree in Marriage Family Child Counseling from Pacific Christian College and a Doctor of Ministry degree from Southwest Theological Seminary. Julie has served as Disabilities Minister at several churches, and currently serves as the Special Needs Pastor of In His Image Ministry at First Church of the Nazarene in Pasadena, CA, where she has been since March of 2007. Julie has also worked in social services with individuals who have developmental disabilities and conducted training and education for staff in this field.

Dr. Rick Langer is an Associate Professor in the Biblical Studies and Theology Department at Talbot School of Theology (Biola University), and also Director of the Office for Faith and Learning. He has also spoken and published in the areas of bioethics, theology, and Christian political thought. Prior to coming to Biola, he served for over twenty years as a pastor at Trinity Evangelical Free Church in Redlands, California. He has also taught philosophy and theology at the college and university level for many years. Rick earned his Ph. D. in Philosophy from the University of California, Riverside, and his Masters of Divinity from Talbot Seminary.

Lori Lucore has had a heart for serving with correspondence for Joni and Friends since 2007, specializing in CID issues like bioethics, and currently overseeing resources. She studied International Relations and earned her B.A.in Business Administration. Above all, she enjoys being a mom—to Violet and her brothers and sisters.

David Lyons is an international vice president of The Navigators. He oversees international initiatives, communications, and networking of their five thousand staff in more than one hundred countries. David loves photography and hiking in the mountains of Colorado. David and Renee are the parents of seven children. David's personal experience with Internet ministry led him to envision helping others to grow through their pain through this book and through www.dontwastethepain.com.

Dr. John MacArthur is pastor-teacher of Grace Community Church in Sun Valley, California, as well as a best-selling author, conference speaker, president of The Master's College and Seminary, and president and featured teacher with the Grace to You radio and television ministries. Since completing his first best-selling book *The Gospel According to Jesus* in 1988, John has written many books such as: *The MacArthur Study Bible, Our Sufficiency in Christ, The Gospel According to the Apostles, The MacArthur New Testament Commentary* series and the bestseller *Twelve Ordinary Men*. John and his wife, Patricia, live in Southern California and have four grown children

Dan'l C. Markham served at Joni and Friends from 2001 to 2010, first as Director of U.S. Field Services and more recently as Managing Director of Field Services. He currently serves as a consultant to Joni and Friends. Dan'l has devoted most of his professional life to developing nonprofit organizations, including Christian ministries. He has a bachelor's degree in biblical studies and is an ordained Baptist minister. Markham's background includes being a newspaper reporter and editor, executive director of a regional and national nonprofit organization, serving as a county commissioner, a director at an international Christian relief organization, church planter and senior pastor. He has authored numerous newspaper and journal articles, recently as a contributor for *Disability Advocacy Among Religious Organizations—Histories and Reflections*.

Doug Mazza, President and Chief Operating Officer of Joni and Friends, has overseen an explosive era of growth in ministry and program expansion since coming to Joni and Friends in 1999. Applying his award-winning expertise and skills in corporate leadership, after serving as senior American executive for American Suzuki Motor Corporation and Hyundai Motor America, Doug has taken the vision of Joni Eareckson Tada and helped create all that Joni and Friends is today—the authoritative voice on Christian outreach to the world's 660 million people with disabilities and their families. Ministering to his severely disabled son, Ryan, for more than 30 years, Doug Mazza brings a warm and personal perspective to the development of every program at Joni and Friends.

Jeff and Kathi McNair are career special educators, and professors of special education. They have been involved in ministry to adults with intellectual disabilities for over 30 years. Kathi's area of expertise is students with learning disabilities. Jeff is the Director of the Public Policy Center for Joni and Friends, and also directs the Disability Studies Program at California Baptist University, one of the few graduate programs in disability ministry. He also directs the university's program in severe disabilities.

Dr. Kathy McReynolds is the Director of Academic Studies for the Joni and Friends Christian Institute on Disability. Kathy has a B.A. in Christian Education from Biola University, a M.A. in Systematic Theology from Talbot School of Theology and a Ph.D. in Ethics from the University of Southern California. She has taught in the Biblical Studies Department at Biola University and served on ethics committees for hospitals and universities. Kathy has received numerous prestigious awards, including the Leading Health Care Professional of the World by the International Biographical Center in 2009.

Jackie Mills-Fernald is the director of Access Ministry at McLean Bible Church in Washington, D.C. Her relationship with Access Ministry began in 1999 as a volunteer. Jackie joined the ministry staff that same year and in 2000 became the Assistant Director of Staff and Volunteer Development with a focus on recruitment, training, and overall program development. Since December of 2003, Jackie has served as the Director of Access Ministry and also oversees the Signs of Life deaf ministry.

Dr. Jim Pierson has been meeting the spiritual needs of people with disabilities for more than four decades. His education in speech pathology and special education, his work with a children's rehabilitation center and with adults in residential programs, and authorship of five books about disability ministry establish his reputation. Jim was the 2003 recipient of the Henri Nouwen Award presented by the Religious and Spirituality Division of the American Association on Persons with Intellectual Disabilities. He is the president emeritus of CCFH Ministries.

D. Christopher Ralston is a freelance writer/editor and a doctoral candidate at Rice University in Houston, Texas. He has served as an Assistant Managing Editor of the Journal of Medicine and Philosophy and as Managing Editor of the journal Christian Bioethics. Chris is the co-editor of *Philosophical Reflections on Disability*. He is a member of the Board of Reference for the Public Policy Center of the Christian Institute on Disability at Joni and Friends. Chris is a graduate of Biola University (B.A., Communications; M.A., Philosophy of Religion and Ethics) and Trinity International University (M.A., Bioethics).

Judith Redlich has 32 years of experience in various aspects of the media industry. For twenty years, Judy produced and hosted a television interview show, for twelve years she produced and hosted a weekly radio talk show. As Manager of Joni and Friends Gateway she is responsible for administrating and implementing all of the programs in St. Louis, Mo. Judy completed her Bachelor of Science in Journalism and Psychology from Missouri Valley College. In 2009, The National Association of Professional and Executive Women named Judy "Woman of the Year" in Media Relations, and she received the 2006 Bronze Telly Award.

James Rene has been on staff with Joni and Friends for the last 9 years. For the past three years he has served as the Director of Cause 4 Life Global Missions and Internships for the Christian Institute on Disability. James has been instrumental in developing several Joni and Friends national and international ministries, disability training programs, and ministry resources. He is a frequent speaker at churches, universities, seminaries, and conferences around the world. James serves as the Joni and Friends country liaison to Uganda to build strategic relationships and partnerships and facilitate our vision, mission, and country strategy. In addition to his role at Joni and Friends, he serves as a staff pastor at his home church—Higher Vision Church in Castaic, California. He is a graduate of Living Faith Bible College and Wagner Leadership Institute.

Linda Lyons Richardson is a former merchandise-display artist and garden gift shop owner. She graduated from Montgomery College, University of MD, and studied at Corcoran School of Art. Surviving ten years of ovarian cancer, she now writes and spends time in her greenhouse. She and her husband Steve have two children.

Michael J. Sleasman, Ph.D., is the Managing Director and Research Scholar for The Center for Bioethics & Human Dignity. He has served as an adjunct instructor and online course tutor at the college and graduate level of a number of institutions, including Trinity International University and Wheaton College. Michael received his doctorate in theological studies from Trinity Evangelical Divinity School. He has co-edited and contributed several essays to the volume *Everyday Theology: How to Read Cultural Texts and Interpret Trends.* In addition, he has written a number of book reviews and articles. Michael has been interviewed on a range of bioethical issues by ABC News Radio, Atlanta Magazine, CNS News, Family News in Focus, Medill News, Northwestern College Media, and SRN News.

Linda Smith is the Program Manager of Joni and Friends Greater Boston. She is working to equip churches, support families affected by disability and direct Family Retreats in New England. Shortly after graduating from Houghton College, she became involved in disability ministry and has served in that field for over 30 years. Linda is the author of *Beyond Limits,* a one-year Bible curriculum designed for teens and adults with cognitive disabilities. She also serves as legal guardian for a young adult with physical and cognitive disabilities.

Joni Eareckson Tada is the founder of Joni and Friends International Disability Center, a nonprofit ministry with a global outreach. A diving accident in 1967 left Joni, then 17, a quadriplegic in a wheelchair. Since then, Joni's wisdom and influence have been shared with the world through bestselling books, radio programs, television programs and frequent speaking. Her radio program is carried by over 1,000 broadcast outlets and heard by over a million listeners. Joni is also an accomplished artist and singer. She has served on the National Council on Disability and the Disability Advisory Committee to the U.S. State Department.

Ken Tada taught Government and US History at John Burroughs High School in Burbank, California, until he retired in 2003. He serves on the Board of Directors for the Joni and Friends International Disability Center and he and his wife, Joni, lead teams of disability ministry workers across the country providing practical services and spiritual help to people with disabilities and their families. Ken and Joni have been married since 1982 and reside in Calabasas, California.

Pat Verbal is the Manager of Curriculum Development at the Christian Institute on Disability at Joni and Friends. She is a well-published author of numerous books and articles on Christian education and special needs ministry and has been a featured speaker, sharing from 25 years of experience as an associate pastor and school administrator. She has been interviewed on Pastor to Pastor from Focus on the Family, Trinity Broadcast Network and taught at the Billy Graham School of Evangelism. Pat is a graduate of Azusa Pacific University and holds a M.A. in Pastoral Studies from the C. P. Haggard School of Theology.

Dr. Larry Waters is presently Associate Professor of Bible Exposition at Dallas Seminary and also teaches for their World Missions and Intercultural Studies department. He served as a missionary in the Philippines from 1973 to 1999. His worldwide ministry continues, primarily in the Philippines. He is the author of Bible and Missions curriculum for the Internet Biblical Seminary connected with BEE World, and a New Testament Survey for a large missionary organization. Larry also serves as a Member of the Bibliotheca Sacra Editorial Advisory Committee.

The Christian Institute on Disability

Courses for a Cause that Impact the Culture for Christ

Whether you are interested in pursuing an advanced course of study in disability ministry, or gaining a Christian perspective on complex bioethical issues, or simply wanting to practice "Christianity with its sleeves rolled up" among people with disabilities, you'll find plenty of guidance, support, and training at the Christian Institute on Disability (CID). Our vice president and managing director, Steve Bundy, and his staff stand ready to serve you.

Disability ministry is a growing movement. A Christ-centered education would not be complete without a theology of suffering and disability. A biblical worldview that is shaped by a theology of suffering and disability is one that keeps us in touch with the God who lifts up the most vulnerable. This is a human issue. It is a global issue. It is a Gospel issue. It is an issue that is essential to any Christian institution of higher education that claims theology as its governing discipline. It is relevant to every major discipline offered in higher education. At the Christian Institute on Disability, a student will learn and experience some of the most important aspects of the Christian life through our many programs and internship opportunities.

Courses: Our courses are rich and diverse. The CID provides learning opportunities on a wide range of subjects related to a theology of suffering and disability. The content is nothing short of life changing, appropriate for any serious follower of Christ.

Cause: Our cause is to draw attention to the needs of those who are most vulnerable around the world. Many live with disability. And very few have access to the care they desperately need, especially those who live in developing countries. Worldwide, people with disabilities are much more likely to face poverty, social isolation, slavery, sex trafficking, and discrimination of every kind. Our cause is for their lives—to meet their physical and spiritual needs in the name of our Savior.

Cultural Change: Our ultimate goal is to bring about cultural transformation for Christ. Whether on college campuses, in churches or in the wider culture, our aim is to transform hearts and minds by giving students life-giving truth.

What the CID offers universities and seminaries . . . The Christian Institute on Disability is the academic arm of the Joni and Friends International Disability Center. The CID comes alongside educational institutions in course development in theology, ministry, missions and advocacy as it relates to suffering and disability. The CID currently works with faculty in the departments of theology, education, social work, law, nursing, engineering and other disciplines.

What the CID offers students . . . Students receive a biblical view on suffering and disability while gaining hands-on ministry experience. Courses are offered through collaboration with universities, seminaries or at the International Disability Center. Courses are taught on campuses and online. In working with educational institutions, the CID integrates its three departments of knowledge and experience: Education and Training, Public Policy, and Global Missions & Internships.

Education and Training

The CID Education and Training department prepares disability leaders and ministers in the church, parachurch and educational institutions to evangelize, include and empower those affected by disability. The CID partners with Christian universities and seminaries around the world to offer programs and course work designed to equip new generations of leaders for effective disability ministry.

Public Policy Center

Human life can now be copied and replicated, altered and aborted, cloned and euthanized, patented and redefined. The CID Public Policy Center brings together theologians, ethicists, educators, doctors and attorneys to address hotly debated disability-related issues such as physician-assisted suicide, euthanasia and stem cell research. The goal is to draw on the expertise of many Christian professionals to present a clear, reasonable and biblically-based perspective on these issues. The Christian Institute on Disability is currently accomplishing this through the media, the Church and other public and Christian institutions.

Board of Reference:	Advisory Council:
Mike Beates, D.Min	Franklin Graham
Jerry Borton, M.A.	Christopher Hook, M.D.
Hugh Bryant, Ph.D.	C. Everett Koop, M.D., Sc.D
Christopher Hook, M.D.	David Stevens, M.D.
Jennifer Lahl, M.A.	
Mark Pickup, J.D.	
Chris Ralston, ABD	
William Saunders, J.D.	
Michael J. Sleasman, Ph.D.	
Wesley Smith, J.D.	
Erik Thoennes, Ph.D.	
Greg Trapp, J.D.	
Greg Wood, J.D.	
Wendy Wright	

Cause 4 Life Global Missions and Internships
Experiential learning through hands-on ministry equips the next generation through the Cause 4 Life Global Missions and Internships. Our internships provide a structured learning experience whereby interns receive education and training in disability ministry while serving and witnessing to those who are marginalized and forgotten. Students put into practice the very things they have learned in the classroom, solidifying the educational experience and bringing transformation of heart and mind.

Speak up and judge fairly;
defend the rights of the poor and needy.
Proverbs 31:9

For more information visit the
Christian Institute on Disability at
http://www.joniandfriends.org/christian-
institute-on-disability/

Endnotes

FOREWORD

1. Margaret Chan, 1 Billion People Are Living With Disabilities http://tinyurl.com/3usx3eg

LESSON ONE

1. Michael Yaconelli, *Dangerous Wonder*, (Colorado Springs, CO 2003, NavPress), pg. 143.
2. "You're Not Normal" from *More Precious Than Silver*. © 1998 by Joni Eareckson Tada. Used by permission. Zondervan, Grand Rapids, MI 1998
3. Stephanie Hubach, *Same Lake, Different Boat: Coming Alongside People Touched by Disability*, (P&R Publishers: Phillipsburg, NJ 2006), pg. 27.

LESSON TWO

1. http://www.washingtonpost.com/national/report-15-percent-of-world-population-is-disabled/2011/06/09/AGZcqBNH_story.html
2. U.S. Census Bureau, Report December 19, 2008. http://www.census.gov/newsroom/releases/archives/income_wealth/cb08-185.html
3. The Americans with Disability Act of 1990, Title 42, Chapter 126, Sec. 12102, Definitions.
4. Centers for Disease Control and Prevention, Department of Health and Human Services, http://www.cdc.gov/ncbddd/dd/.
5. "Disability label with change." Dallas Morning News, Friday, September 24, 2010. 14A
6. Lon Solomon, *Brokenness: How God Redeems Pain and Suffering*. (Potomac, MD: Red Door Press, 2006), p. xv-xviii.

LESSON THREE

1. *Hearts in Motion*, (Agoura Hills, CA, Joni and Friends) p. 8.
2. "200 Years: The Life and Legend of Louis Braille," The American Foundation for the Blind, http://www.afb.org/louisbraillemuseum/braillegallery.asp?galleryid=46
3. The book *Louis Braille: A Touch of Genius* by C. Michael Mellor gives an excellent and interesting history of the education of those who are blind.
4. "A Brief History of the American Asylum, At Hartford, For The Education And Instruction Of The Deaf And Dumb," The Disability Museum, http://www.disabilitymuseum.org/dhm/lib/detail.html?id=1371.
5. http://en.wikipedia.org/wiki/Edouard_Seguin
6. From "The Historical Background of Special Education" by Dr. Jeff McNair (www.jeffmcnair.com)
7. Davies, Stanley Powell, *Social Control of the Mentally Deficient*, Columbia University Press, 1930, Reprint Edition 1976, p.37.
8. BUCK v. BELL, 274 U.S. 200 (1927), Superintendent of State Colony Epileptics and Feeble Minded. No. 292., http://caselaw.lp.findlaw.com/cgi-bin/getcase.pl?court=us&vol=274&invol=200
9. Disability Social History Project, http://www.disabilityhistory.org/people.html
10. U.S. Department of Health and Human Services Administration for Children and Families http://www.acf.hhs.gov/programs/aidd/programs/pcpid
11. New York Times, September 20, 2001, http://www.nytimes.com/2001/09/20/us/gunnar-dybwad-92-dies-early-advocate-for-the-disabled.html
12. http://en.academic.ru/dic.nsf/enwiki/2329614
13. http://en.wikipedia.org/wiki/Individuals_with_Disabilities_Education_Act
14. Joni Eareckson Tada and Nigel M. De S. Cameron, *How to be a Christian in a Brave New World*. (Grand Rapids, MI: Zondervan, 2006), p. 82.
15. *Ibid*.

LESSON FOUR

1. The term "developing countries" may also be referred to as "least developed countries," "Global South," "Third World countries," and/or "majority world countries."
2. UN Development Programme, United Nations Enable, http://www.un.org/disabilities/documents/toolaction/pwdfs.pdf
3. http://www.washingtonpost.com/national/report-15-percent-of-world-population-is-disabled/2011/06/09/AGZcqBNH_story.html
4. Statement by the UN High Commissioner for Human Rights, December 2009: http://www.un.org/disabilities/documents/events/idpd09_unhchr.pdf
5. Ibid.
6. Amnesty International Report 2008: http://www.amnesty.org/en/news-and-updates/sixty-years-human-rights-failure-governments-must-apologize-and-act-now-200805
7. http://www.ushmm.org/museum/exhibit/focus/ihrd/comment_post.php
8. http://www.un.org/disabilities/default.asp?navid=12&pid=25#3
9. For more information on educational opportunities visit www.TheCID.org.
10. For more information about L'Arche see http://larche.org/.

LESSON FIVE

1. From the Lausanne Position Paper on Disability, "Hidden and Forgotten People—Ministry among People with Disabilities" (Lausanne Committee on World Evangelization, 2004).
2. "Spiritual Formation: What it is, and How it is Done" by Dallas Willard http://www.dwillard.org/articles/artview.asp?artID=58
3. John Piper and Justin Taylor, *Suffering and Sovereignty of God*, (Wheaton, IL: Crossway Books, 2006), pp. 17, 19.
4. Gene Newman and Joni Eareckson Tada, *All God's Children: Ministry with Disabled Persons*, (Grand Rapids, MI, Zondervan Publishing House, 1993), pp. 18-19.
5. John MacArthur, *Power of Suffering: Strengthening Your Faith in the Refiner's Fire* (Colorado Springs, CO: Chariot Victor Publishing, 1995), pp. 11-12, 22-23.
6. It is beyond the scope of this lesson to delve deeper into these mysteriously wonderful truths. We encourage students to study these issues in John Feinberg's magnificent work, *No One Like Him: The Doctrine of God* (Wheaton, IL: Crossway Books, 2001). This work was consulted for this paragraph.
7. Lon Solomon, *Brokenness: How God Redeems Pain and Suffering* (Potomac, MD: Red Door Press, 2006), pp. 13-14.

LESSON SIX

1. Revelation 20
2. Recommended for further study on theodicy—*Reaching Out and Bringing In: The Role of the Church in Ministry to and with Persons with Disabilities* by Dr. David Anderson (Roseville, NM: Crossing Bridges, Inc. 2008).
3. Ibid., p. 62.
4. Chuck Edwards paper, "Worldview Analysis of Suffering and Disability" published in *Beyond Suffering*.
5. Other relevant passages include 1 Kings 22:22, I Samuel 16:14, Matthew 4:10-11; 8:31-32 and Luke 22:31.
6. Joni Eareckson Tada and Steve Estes, *When God Weeps: Why Our Suffering Matters to God Leader's Guide*. (Grand Rapids, MI: Zondervan, 2002), p. 118.
7. Joni Eareckson Tada and Steve Jensen, *Through the Roof*, rev.ed. (Agoura Hills, CA: Joni and Friends, 2006), pp.195,198-199.
8. Lon Solomon, *Brokenness: How God Redeems Pain and Suffering* (Potomac, MD: Red Door Press, 2006), p. 105.
9. Lausanne Committee for World Evangelism, "Hidden and Forgotten People—Including Those Who Are Disabled." Lausanne Occasional Paper No. 35B, 2004a. http://www.lausanne.org/documents/2004forum/LOP35A_IG6A.pdf
10. John Piper and Justin Taylor, *Suffering and the Sovereignty of God*. (Wheaton, IL: Crossway Books, 2006), p. 18.

LESSON SEVEN

1. Break the Barriers, www.breakthebarriers.org
2. Luke 4:40-41; Matthew 8:16-17; Mark 1:32-34
3. In God's response to Moses, we see his sovereign hand at work in certain persons being born with disabilities. John 9:1-5; Exodus 4:11
4. Richard J. Foster, *Prayer: Finding the Heart's True Home*. (San Francisco: Harper Collins Publisher, 1992), p. 203.
5. Luke 13:16; Acts 10:38; 1 John 3:8
6. Hebrews 13:8
7. 1 Peter 2:24; James 5:15; 1 John 5:14-15
8. Joni Eareckson Tada and Steve Estes, *A Step Further*. (Grand Rapids, MI: Zondervan, 2001), pp. 124-126.
9. John Piper and Justin Taylor, *Suffering and the Sovereignty of God*. (Wheaton, IL: Crossway Books, 2006). pp. 207-208.
10. David Lyons and Linda Richardson, *Don't Waste the Pain: Learning to Grow through Suffering*. (Colorado Springs, CO: NavPress. 2010), p. 144.
11. As quoted in Bengt R. Hoffman, *Luther and the Mystics* (Minneapolis, MN: Augsburg, 1976), p. 196.
12. Joni Eareckson Tada and Dave and Jan Dravecky, eds, *Encouragemant Bible New International Version*. (Grand Rapids, MI: Zondervan Publishing House, 2001), p. 623.

LESSON EIGHT

1. Henrietta C. Mears, *What the Bible is All About*. (Ventura, CA: Gospel Light, 2007), p. 250.
2. Dorothy Kelley Patterson & Rhonda Harrington Kelley, eds. *Women's Evangelical Commentary: New Testament* (Nashville: Broadman & Holman, 2006), p. 129-137.
3. John 3:17, 1 John 2:8, John 1:18
4. Luke 1:1-4:20; 24:44-49
5. Luke 9:51-18:34
6. See Luke 3:1-7:35; 4:16-22.
7. Craig L. Bloomberg. *Jesus and the Gospels*. (Nashville, TN: Broadman & Holman, 1997)
8. Luke 4:14-9:50
9. Luke 10:38, 13:22-17:11
10. Grace Community Fellowship. Retrieved from http://www.gcfweb.org/institute/gospels/luke-intro.html.
11. This is similar to the personal application Jesus stresses in Luke 14:5 regarding the man's son or ox in a well.
12. John Piper, "Whom Shall We Invite to Thanksgiving Dinner?" (Sermon, Bethlehem Baptist Church, Nov. 9, 1980)
13. William Hendriksen, *New Testament Commentary: Exposition of the Gospel According to Luke*. (Grand Rapids, MI: Baker House, 1978), p. 725.
14. John Nolland, *Word Biblical Commentary* (Vol. 35B). (Nashville, TN: Thomas Nelson, 1993) p. 734, 736.
15. Luke 14:15.
16. Luke14:18, literal translation; see G. R. Berry, *Today's Parallel Greek English New Testament*. (Richmond, VA: Foreign Missions Journal, SBC, 1976.)
17. Alfred Plummer, *A Critical and Exegetical Commentary on the Gospel According to St. Luke*. (Edinburgh, UK: Morrison and Gibb Limited, 1989), p. 361.
18. Hendriksen, p. 732.
19. Joni and Friends, "Outreach: Breaking Bread at a Luke 14 Banquet", *Special Needs Smart Pages*. (Ventura, CA: Gospel Light, 2009), p. 142.
20. Paraphrase of 1 Corinthians 11:1

LESSON NINE

1. Millard J. Erickson, *Christian Theology*, 7th printing. (Grand Rapids, MI: Baker Book House, 1989), pp. 1028-1030.
2. Matthew 16:18, 18:17
3. John 21
4. Ephesians 1:22; Colossians 1:18
5. James Strong, *Strong's Exhaustive Concordance of the Bible*. (Peabody, MA: Hendrickson Publishers.)
6. Erik W. Carter, *Including People with Disabilities in Faith Communities*. (Baltimore, MD: Paul H. Brookes Publishing Co., 2007), p. 27.
7. Ibid., pp. 6-7
8. Ephesians 4:16; Romans 12:6-8; I Corinthians 12

LESSON TEN

1. Gene Newman and Joni Eareckson Tada, *All God's Children: Ministry with Disabled Persons*. (Grand Rapids, MI: Zondervan Publishing House, 1993), p. 9.
2. James 2:14-17
3. Commerce Department's Census Bureau on March 16, 2001. U.S. Census Bureau, http://usgovinfo.about.com/library/weekly/aa031701a.htm
4. Pat Verbal, "The Special Needs Ministry Launch Countdown Checklist," *Special Needs Special Ministry*. (Loveland, CO: Group Publishing, 2004), pp. 34-35. Action tool adapted from one by Dr. Scott Daniels and Dr. Steve Green.
5. Pat Verbal, "Getting the Word Out About Your Special Needs Ministry," *Special Needs Special Ministry*. (Loveland, CO: Group Publishing, 2004), pp. 66-67.

LESSON ELEVEN

1. "Awareness: Children with Disabilities Are Valuable to God," *Special Needs Smart Pages* by Joni and Friends. (Ventura, CA: Gospel Light, 2009), p. 14.
2. Pat Verbal, *Give Them Jesus*, (Agoura Hills, CA: Joni and Friends, 2007), p. 7-8.
3. 2 Cor. 1:3-4
4. Colossians 3:17
5. Doug Fields, "My Youth Group and Special Needs," http://www.youthministry.com/?q=node/4996
6. Sizwe David Mabowe, "I Just Needed a Chance," *Special Needs Smart Pages* by Joni and Friends. (Ventura, CA: Gospel Light, 2009), p. 264.
7. Diane Monreal, *On A Role for Jesus! Mission: Unstoppable.* (Agoura Hills, CA: Joni and Friends, 2007), p. 43.

LESSON TWELVE

1. Adapted from Turnbull, A. & Turnbull, R. (2006). The family life cycle and significant intellectual disability [On-line]. Available: http://ici.umn.edu/products/impact/192/over4.html. Originally published in V. Gaylord, J. Agosta, J. Barclay, K. Melda, & P. Stenhjem (Eds.), Impact: Feature Issue on Parenting Teens and Young Adults with Disabilities, 19(2).
2. Dr. Jim Pierson, *Exceptional Teaching*. (Cincinnati, OH: Standard Publishing, 2002), p. 198.
3. Paul Dickens, Jane Young, Sheena Baird, *So My House Will be Full: A Guide to Including People with Disabilities in the Church*, (Agoura Hills, CA: Joni and Friends, 2008). www.joniandfriends.org/store.
4. Disability Statistic Center, www.dsc.ucsf.edu.
5. www.gocasa.org

LESSON THIRTEEN

1. Joni Eareckson Tada, *Pearls of Great Price* (Grand Rapids, MI: Zondervan, 2006), April 27th entry.
2. Dan'l Markham, Discovery of the Lost Mandate: Turning Weaknesses and Religious Attitudes on Their Heads. Unpublished manuscript, 2007b, pp. 40-41.
3. Timothy George, *The Complete Evangelism Guidebook* (Grand Rapids, Michigan: Baker Books, 2006) pp 26-28.
4. Ronald C. Vredeveld, *Expressing Faith in Jesus: Church Membership for People with Intellectual Disabilities* (Grand Rapids, MI: Faith Alive Christian Resources, 2005), p. 12. Available at http://www.faithaliveresources.org/.
5. Ray Pritchard, *He's God and We're Not* (Nashville, TN: B&H Publishing Group, 2003).
6. Ronald C. Vredeveld, Expressing Faith in Jesus: Church Membership for People with Intellectual Disabilities (Grand Rapids, MI: Faith Alive Christian Resources, 2005).
7. Jim Pierson, *Exceptional Teaching: A Comprehensive Guide for Including Students with Disabilities* (Cincinnati, OH: Standard Publishing, 2002).
8. Joni Eareckson Tada, "Kingdom Matters in Disability" (Agoura Hills, CA: Joni and Friends, 2011).

LESSON FOURTEEN

1. http://www.goodreads.com/author/quotes/838305.Mother_Teresa
2. John 20:21
3. Pat Verbal, "How to Partner with Community Agencies," in *Special Needs Special Ministry* (Loveland, CO: Group Publishing, 2004) p.117.
4. Rev. William Gaventa, "Networking with Disability Ministries and Organizations: The Power and Witness of Seeking, Consulting, and Collaborating."
5. Pat Verbal, "How to Partner with Community Agencies," *Special Needs Special Ministry* (Loveland, CO: Group Publishing, 2004) p.113.
6. Woodland Park Baptist Church, Chattanooga, TN. http://woodlandpark.org.
7. Bob and Mary Horning, and John Knight, "A Vision for Disability Ministry at Bethlehem." Accessed at http://www.hopeingod.org/document/vision-disability-ministry-bethlehem.
8. Even a simple blog or Facebook page is sufficient in most cases.
9. Erik Carter, "Launching Communitywide Efforts," *Including People with Disabilities in Faith Communities*. (Baltimore, MD: Paul H. Brookes Publishing Co., 2007), pp. 175-177.
10. To see a short video of this ministry, see http://www.willowcreek.org/disabilities.

LESSON FIFTEEN

1. Joni Eareckson Tada and Nigel M. De S. Cameron, *How to be a Christian in a Brave New World*. (Grand Rapids, MI: Zondervan, 2006), p. 9.
2. Proverbs 2:6
3. Immanuel Kant, *Metaphysics of Morals*, Cambridge Texts in the History of Philosophy, Mary J. Gregor, ed. (Cambridge: Cambridge University Press, 1996).
4. John Stuart Mill, *Utilitarianism*, Thrift Edition (London: Dover Publications, 2007).
5. Peter Singer, *Practical Ethics*, 2nd Edition (Cambridge: Cambridge University Press, 1999).
6. Tom Beauchamp & James Childress, *Principles of Biomedical Ethics*, fifth ed. (Oxford: Oxford University Press, 2001).

LESSON SIXTEEN

1. For a complete and accurate overview of the facts of Roe v. Wade and Doe v. Bolton, please refer to www.encyclopedia.com/topic/Roe_v_Wade.
2. To better understand the many encyclicals on life produced by the Roman Catholic Church over the years, see www.papalencyclicals.net.
3. Peter J. Kreeft, *A Shorter Summa: The Essential Philosophical Passages of St. Thomas Aquinas' Summa Theologica* (London: Ignatius Press, 1993).
4. For a more in-depth discussion on the Human Genome Project, see www.genome.gov/25019879
5. Christopher Ralston, "Dignity, Disability, and Bioethics," White Paper, 2010, page 1.
6. William F. May, *Testing the Medical Covenant* (New York: Wipf & Stock, 2004).
7. Scott B. Rae, *Moral Choices: An Introduction to Ethics* (Grand Rapids: Zondervan, 2009).

Course Study Notes